Praise for Wh

I once heard someone say that many White Christians are two or three good questions away from confessing a White supremacist view. *White Lies* is the book I would give to every White Christian to make sure their understanding of racism and White supremacy could withstand the burden of reality. Daniel Hill exposes the lies that prevent progress in racial justice and brings the truth spoken in love to help readers gain more competence in the fight against racism. Aside from the meticulous research and copious real-world examples, what makes *White Lies* so compelling is that its author speaks with integrity. Hill is doing the work of confronting the temptation to believe "White lies" in his own life and in his ministry as the pastor of a justice-oriented, racially diverse church. If you're ready to take the next step in the journey of racial justice, then you must read *White Lies*.

Jemar Tisby, *New York Times* bestselling author, *The Color of Compromise*

The soul of the White church is at stake! There is an enduring stain on its collective conscience because of the sinful complicity it has with White supremacy and racial injustice. In this book, Daniel Hill bravely pulls back the curtain, exposes the lies, and tells the truth about what it will take to break free from the evil hierarchy of racial difference. This groundbreaking book is for all Christians who want to restore the credibility of the church by embodying the truth and power of the gospel to bring hope and healing to a broken and divided world. I highly recommend it!

Brenda Salter McNeil, author, *Becoming Brave*

This book has given me biblical language and spiritual strategy for the dismantling of White supremacy in my life and also in the world around me. As a Christian, I walked away from this book full of hope that heaven is in this with us and we have been given enough grace through Jesus Christ to engage, learn, and listen. Daniel Hill has written a book that reminds me at every turn of the page that what feels impossible for us to overcome is possible with God.

Kristene DiMarco, worship leader and
Christian recording artist

White Lies is the perfect book for this moment. As more of us awaken to the racial injustices in our country, we continue to ask, "How can I make a difference and participate in confronting racial injustice?" Start here, as Daniel Hill walks us down the path from awakening to becoming an active participant in confronting the evil that is White supremacy. Embracing a spirit of love, empathy, and truth, Daniel embodies this path here and carefully unpacks the White lies that have deceived us.

Kyle Korver, National Basketball Association veteran

Daniel Hill has done it again. In *White Lies*, he offers perceptive analysis, a pastoral heart, and an ability to mark a path forward for many who are stuck in the mire of White supremacy and racial injustice. I believe this book will serve as an important catalyst to reframe the work of justice and reconciliation and to move us to be the kind of people God calls us to be in the world.

Rich Villodas, lead pastor, New Life Fellowship,
and author of *The Deeply Formed Life*

As the White evangelical church slowly awakens to the rootedness of White supremacy in society and the church, the hard work of discipleship will be not only in identifying White supremacy but in doing the slow work of actually dismantling it. At a time when the world seems to be leading the church in responding to racial injustice through protests and movements, this book is a critical tool to help the church engage both in internal self-reflection and correction and in outward ministry and activism, grounded in spiritual disciplines that point the world to the radical, loving, subversive nature of Christ. The church needs many messengers with multiple messages to pursue racial justice and equity, and Daniel Hill is the leader we need now whose own vulnerability and humility have allowed the church to take a hard look at itself and grow into greater likeness of Christ that can impact the world.

Jenny Yang, vice president of advocacy and policy, World Relief

This is a historic moment in America. We are living through a racial awakening, and many White folks are leaning in, listening, marching, and searching for ways to participate in the movement for justice and liberation. In addition to listening to Black and Brown voices and reading books by people of color, we also need to do some of our own work as White folks. This book is a massive contribution to the conversation around faith and race in America.

Shane Claiborne, author, speaker, activist

white
lies

white
lies

white
lies

Nine Ways to Expose and Resist the Racial Systems That Divide Us

daniel hill

ZONDERVAN BOOKS

ZONDERVAN BOOKS

White Lies
Copyright © 2020 by Daniel Hill

Published in Grand Rapids, Michigan, by Zondervan. Zondervan is a registered trademark of The Zondervan Corporation, L.L.C., a wholly owned subsidiary of HarperCollins Christian Publishing, Inc.

Requests for information should be addressed to customercare@harpercollins.com.

Zondervan titles may be purchased in bulk for educational, business, fundraising, or sales promotional use. For information, please email SpecialMarkets@Zondervan.com.

ISBN 978-0-310-17415-8 (softcover)
ISBN 978-0-310-35853-4 (audio)

Library of Congress Cataloging-in-Publication Data

Names: Hill, Daniel, 1973- author.
Title: White lies : nine ways to expose and resist the racial systems that divide us / Daniel Hill.
Description: Grand Rapids : Zondervan, 2020. | Includes bibliographical references.
Identifiers: LCCN 2020015425 (print) | LCCN 2020015426 (ebook) | ISBN 9780310358510 (hardcover) | ISBN 9780310358527 (ebook)
Subjects: LCSH: Race relations—Religious aspects—Christianity. | Social movements.
Classification: LCC BT734.2 .H52 2020 (print) | LCC BT734.2 (ebook) | DDC 277.3/083089—dc23
LC record available at https://lccn.loc.gov/2020015425
LC ebook record available at https://lccn.loc.gov/2020015426

Published in association with the literary agency of Mark Sweeney & Associates, Chicago, Illinois 60611.

Cover design: Micah Kandros
Cover photo: Mikhail H / Shutterstock
Interior design: Kait Lamphere

To my beloved community at River City.
I wouldn't be who I am without you all.
I'm forever grateful for a place
where I can love and be loved,
and where we can work out the full dimension
of following Jesus together
in a transformational manner.

Contents

introduction

The Parasite of
White Supremacy

It's not likely you meditate on the idea of parasites often—really, why would you? But when it comes to the core message of this book, it's the perfect place to start.

Let's begin with some important facts that may be helpful to know about parasites. For instance, did you know:

- A parasite is an organism that lives within another organism, typically referred to as the host.
- Without a host, a parasite is unable to live, grow, and/or multiply. For a parasite to survive, the host must survive as well.
- Parasites are *never* beneficial for the host. They thrive by stealing the resources of the host.
- Parasites are incredibly difficult to detect. For example, 70 percent of parasites are not visible to the human eye.
- A parasite and its host evolve together. The parasite adapts to its environment by living in and using the host in ways that sustain the parasite's existence while continuing to harm that of the host.

1

Now that we have become pseudo-experts on parasites, what does it all mean?

Let's jump over to Dr. Willie Jennings, who is considered to be one of the premier public theologians in America, particularly with regard to race and Christianity, and who has written a number of seminal books on the subject. When Dr. Jennings speaks about White supremacy, I am quick to listen.

When describing the nature of White supremacy, here's the shorthand image he uses: *it is a parasite.*[1]

That's provocative enough, but it also elicits an immediate follow-up question: If White supremacy is a parasite, what is the host it has embedded itself in? Dr. Jennings's claim? *Christianity.*

Wow, what a picture! To help us gain an immediate and visceral image for understanding the historical reality of White supremacy, he suggests we think of White supremacy as the parasite and Christianity as the host it has embedded itself in for protection and survival.

With that in mind, look again through the list of key facts that describe parasites. Instead of reading them in a general way, consider the detailed application of White supremacy as a parasite and of Christianity as the host it is embedded in. It's a terrifying exercise.

We will explore the full meaning of this parasitic relationship throughout the book, as well as the White lies that sustain this relationship, but allow me to immediately highlight one serious and urgent facet of this unholy alliance. One of the greatest threats facing American Christianity is the severe divide along racial lines that continues to grow more severe with each passing year. The 2016 and 2020 elections served to bring the divide to the forefront, but these are only one of a dozen indicators that highlight the same reality.

I would contend there is no factor that plays a bigger role in this divide than the inability of White Christians to meaningfully process this parasitic relationship between White supremacy and Christianity. Similar to the growing polarization we see on many fronts, White Christians tend to move toward one of two opposite poles when they are exposed to this parasitic relationship.

At one end of the extreme are those of us who have been conditioned in such a way that we either cannot or will not honestly acknowledge that White supremacy has found a way to parasitically embed itself in Christianity. Those of us in this group have never learned to carefully parse the one from the other, and as such, we lack the critical thinking skills that are necessary to decouple White supremacy from White Christianity. Therefore, when we hear someone attack White supremacy, we often interpret it as an attack on our faith itself. The tragic result of this failure is that we end up defending not only the Christianity we love but also the White supremacy we should despise.

At the other end of the extreme are those of us who have learned to identify the parasite of White supremacy, as well as its fusion with Christianity, but who have used that insight as a basis for outrightly rejecting Christianity. Rather than doing the hard work of analyzing the sinister manner in which it has embedded itself to Christianity and evaluating what Christianity says about an evil ideology like White supremacy, this group often chooses to settle for an oversimplified caricature of the Christian faith. In this way, the group's inability to decouple the one from the other repeats the same failing result as those representing the first pole.

The fallout from these intensifying poles is catastrophic. It divides the church, compromises our collective witness, and renders us useless in the fight against White supremacy.

This is why the message of this book feels so urgent. The only reason this parasitic relationship has lasted so long is that it is shrouded in a cloud of lies. As White Christians, we have lost our ability to tell the truth about the parasitic presence of White supremacy within the faith we love, and as a result, we don't know how to move forward, even when we believe we are ready to.

Therefore, the purpose of this book is to grow in our ability to tell and apply the truth of Christ and his kingdom to the problem of White supremacy. It is to expose the lies that allow this parasitic presence to survive generation after generation. It is to resist the racial systems that continue to divide us. It is to position us as active participants in the work of the risen Christ, who is bringing the good news of God's kingdom—a kingdom that will ultimately dismantle the kingdom of White supremacy.

Before we jump all the way in, let's look at five important introductory statements.

1. This Book Builds on *White Awake*

When I started River City Community Church in January 2003, I promised God I would not publish anything regarding race. I didn't think the world needed another White guy talking to people about issues that most affected non-White people. I sincerely intended to keep that promise, but over the years, God began to speak in a new way. The mentors of color who had provided such critical guidance and direction for the ministerial work I did began to more directly invite me to participate in their work. They were established veterans in exposing, illuminating, and confronting White supremacy, and they appreciated that I happily submitted to their lead in this work.

But even as they were regularly investing in the growth process of White people, their conviction grew that for many, there was a struggle to grasp the full depths of White supremacy without interacting with the story of other White folks who had gone on this journey. Therefore, these mentors began to challenge me to become more vocal about my own racial awakening process and to actively contribute to their work by sharing some of my own discovery process as to the far-reaching nature of White supremacy.

That invitation eventually culminated in the writing of *White Awake: An Honest Look at What It Means to Be White*. It is there that I talk about the unique challenges we as White people face—White Christians specifically—when we attempt to awaken to and understand White supremacy through a faith lens. I spend a lot of time addressing the internal defenses that are bound to go up when this journey is taken seriously, and I chart out a path for developing a resilient spirit that steadfastly moves toward truth, justice, and equity.

In *White Lies*, I build on the platform of *White Awake* and move much deeper into the conversation of how White Christians can position ourselves to actively participate in the resistance and confrontation of White supremacy. While I invite you, the reader, to step into this conversation from wherever you are, it also seems important to mention this intended sequence. It can be challenging to position yourself as a potential participant when you have not yet dealt with the many internal defenses that come with a racial awakening process. So starting with *White Awake* is always an option to consider.[2]

2. This Book Uses the Language of Spiritual Practices

I hope the ideas I propose in *White Lies* will find resonance beyond just the walls of Christian organizations. I have presented this material in settings ranging from banks to law firms and civic leadership hubs, and I am confident that it translates to secular settings as well as religious.

With that being said, I want to fully acknowledge that I

come to this subject matter in a distinctly Christian manner. And even more specifically, I approach these ideas from the lens of a pastor. For instance, when I talk of the seriousness of the parasitic relationship between White supremacy and White Christianity, there is nothing theoretical about that for me. Instead, I begin to immediately picture real people—people whose spiritual lives feel like they are in the balance. It is the person who senses the impact that White supremacy has had on the development of her Christian identity, but who feels a sense of terror that if she starts pulling the thread, the whole thing might come apart. It is the person who has become mortified by the way he sees White supremacy operate in religious spaces in plain sight and who is now in a full-fledged wrestling match with doubt, wondering if Jesus can still be who he really says he is, even in the midst of such a seemingly broken religious system.

With this as my starting point, I have framed each big idea in this book around the language of spiritual practices. A spiritual practice is an action that we can take that can help deepen our connection to the power of the divine, and this is a critical component of resisting and confronting White supremacy. I am convinced that any and all efforts we make, when not first established in the supernatural, everlasting power of God, will end up falling flat. So each chapter is a practice for following Jesus . . . and for rising up against the forces of White supremacy in his name.

3. This Book Talks about White Supremacy . . . a Lot

White supremacy is a term that can feel very charged for many White people. I am aware of that. But that doesn't change the importance of using it a lot.

One of the unfortunate reasons for this discomfort is that its popular usage is often exclusively reserved to describe the most extreme, violent, and inflammatory expressions of White supremacy (i.e., images of tiki torches and combat boots in a White nationalist rally in Charlottesville, Virginia, or instances like Dylann Roof's killing spree in a Charleston, South Carolina, church in the name of White supremacy).

White supremacy is first and foremost an ideology, which means that its tentacles reach infinitely farther than those extreme expressions. It is operating everywhere, all the time. When we fall for the trap of avoiding the term until its ugliest manifestations show up, we disempower ourselves and others from being able to resist and confront it in its multitude of everyday forms. This is arguably the much more important front to fight it on, so it's important that we learn how to think and talk about White supremacy differently.

I will provide a much more in-depth analysis of White supremacy in practice three and would advise you to consider all four words in that chapter (see p. 61) as part of a comprehensive description of White supremacy. But I believe there is also value in having a faster, more concise definition, so I will point to the very helpful work of Dr. Chanequa Walker-Barnes to provide a foundation to stand on as we prepare to dive deeply into it:

> White supremacy: The systemic evil that denies and distorts the image of God inherent in all human beings based upon the heretical belief that white aesthetics, values, and cultural norms bear the fullest representation of the *imago Dei*. White supremacy thus maintains that white people are superior to all other peoples, and it orders creation, identities, and social structures in ways that support this distortion and denial.[3]

4. This Book Refers to Non-White People Groups as BIPOC

In the above definition of White supremacy, Dr. Walker-Barnes highlights the way this ideology maintains that White people are superior to all other people groups. Therefore, in race conversations, there has always been a need to differentiate the experience of White people as they interact with the superiority messages of White supremacy from the experience of non-White people as they interact with the inferiority messages of White supremacy, as well as a need to point out the tendency of White supremacy to erase the identities of non-White people in relation to Whiteness. For some time now, the term "person of color" (often abbreviated POC) has been the most common way to make this differentiation.

For as helpful as the term POC has been, many thought leaders around race have begun to move away from it. While they recognize the importance of making a delineation between the White experience and the non-White experience, they also rightfully point out that the term POC is not nearly robust enough to effectively hold space for such a wide range of racial experiences.

The term gaining the most traction in its place right now is BIPOC, which stands for Black, Indigenous, and People of Color. This term attempts to acknowledge and honor the significant differences that accompany the journey represented by the three distinct racial histories in America.

- First, there is the Native history, which is the story of Indigenous communities that were dispossessed and forcibly removed from their homeland.
- Second, there is the African history, where millions of Black people were forcibly stolen—kidnapped from their home country—and then brought to America as slaves without consent.

- Third, there is the immigrant history, where communities of people have moved to America with the intention of staying and living here. While there has always been a variety of reasons for immigrating, the two most common causes have traditionally been employment opportunities and the need to escape a violent conflict in their home country.

The differences among these racial histories are very significant, and the ways in which White supremacy has harmed each racial group are distinct. Therefore, the term BIPOC is less about comparing the experiences and histories of each group to each other, and more about recognizing the importance of addressing the uniqueness of each in a thoughtful and comprehensive manner.

It feels important to mention this here, not only to introduce the term, but also to recognize that it won't be the final evolution. The term BIPOC will not last forever, nor should it. The reason that terms like this are important is not so that we can create a permanent identity marker or demonstrate a capacity for being politically correct in our terminology. They are important because White supremacy is evil, and it harms people. And worse, it evolves. While its attack on the personhood and livelihood of communities of color remains consistent, its tactics don't. Therefore, the ways we think about, talk about, respond to, and organize against it must also evolve.

5. This Book Is Built on the Brilliance of the Team I Am Blessed to Work With

I am the one authoring this book, but this project is in every way a collaborative effort. God has given me the gift of a lifetime by allowing me to work with an incredibly smart and culturally diverse team of leaders who love Jesus with all their hearts, who seek the kingdom of God with all their lives, and who understand the multiple facets of White supremacy better than anyone I've ever encountered. I'm so thankful for the way this team provides leadership for River City Community Church,[4] and for the ways they disciple Christ-followers of every background into a way of life in Jesus that empowers them to resist and confront White supremacy on a daily basis.

I will introduce some of them later in the book, but one name I specifically want to draw out in the introduction is Shumeca Pickett. Shumeca is a key leader at River City, and as such, we get to partner on race-related efforts in very meaningful ways there. In addition, Shumeca founded and leads one of the most well-respected social impact consultancies in the city of Chicago called Alfred Dewitt Ard.

Through her firm, she and I have had regular opportunities to speak together, to test ideas, and to implement organizational efforts designed to resist and confront White supremacy. I will refer to many of these stories throughout the book and wanted to introduce her to you up front as one of my most valued thought partners and friends in this work. And I can't encourage you enough to visit her website and learn more about her work at www.alfreddewittard.com.

With these five introductory statements in place, let's jump in.

Stop Being Woke

I was invited to lead a staff training day at a well-known nonprofit organization in the Midwest. This nonprofit had a strong reputation for work that focused on compassion and justice for the marginalized. But their lack of emphasis on racial justice concerned many of their advocates. In particular, the organization was often criticized for having an all-White staff, especially since most of the work they did was in communities populated primarily by ethnic minorities.

Their leadership took the criticism to heart and began to wrestle with how best to respond. They decided to put a number of protocols into place to address their hiring practices, and within two years, they had increased the diversity of their workforce to the point that 20 percent of their employees came from non-White backgrounds. The organization was very proud of this accomplishment and began to publicly celebrate their progress. In a sense, they celebrated being "woke."

The feeling of triumph didn't last long though. As the workforce became increasingly diverse, the internal conversations became increasingly intense. This nonprofit had a strong organizational culture, and they took pride in passing on these principles to incoming employees as part of the orientation process.

But to their surprise, the employees of color were not nearly as enthusiastic about these principles as the White employees typically were. In fact, some of the new employees shared with the leadership the personal difficulty they experienced when it came to the navigation of the culturally White ethos. When asked to describe some of the cultural norms that felt White in their orientation, they identified three in particular:

- *Organizational efficiency.* Incoming employees were quick to acknowledge that the organization's reputation for being highly productive was rightly deserved. However, it also became apparent that this productivity came at a high cultural cost. A constant commitment to efficiency and productivity left nearly every initiative feeling urgent, and as a result, the stated commitment to include diverse voices almost never materialized. The value of getting things done fast continuously trumped the value of hearing the important ideas and perspectives of those outside of the majority culture.
- *Decision-making protocols.* While it was clear that the number of ethnically non-White employees was increasing, it did not appear that this new influx had much impact on the organization's overall decision-making process. The pervasive feeling was that upper management either already assumed they understood what these employees needed or, worse, didn't care. The fact that overtures by these new employees fell on seemingly deaf ears only further increased the suspicion that the power held by the White stakeholders was largely unnamed and uninterrogated.
- *Overvaluing of harmony and undervaluing of conflict.* One of the consistent traits externally touted about this organization was the high degree of harmony shared by employees across the board. However, from the inside, it appeared this

harmony often came at the cost of the transformation that is often possible only through conflict. One of the primary manifestations was the regular use of the label *troublemaker* to describe those who were brave enough to name racial offenses and/or microaggressions. Even when the tone was kind and conciliatory, it was the person bringing attention to the issue who would inevitably become the focus—not the issue that was creating discomfort in the first place.

In response to the contrasting realities that White employees and BIPOC[1] employees were experiencing, a number of potential responses were explored. Eventually the leadership team decided to organize a D&I committee (diversity and inclusion) that would explore the organizational culture together. The group was made up of a combination of established White leaders and newer BIPOC employees, and the hope was that some common agreements would form and that concrete suggestions would be proposed to the leadership team.

The intentions were good, but the experiment didn't end well. Each committee meeting would end in frustration, and the gulf in perspectives only widened. The group eventually hit a breaking point, with the employees of color informing their White counterparts that they no longer felt safe engaging in these conversations together. As an alternative, the BIPOC employees suggested that the White employees do some of their own work on these conversations. More specifically, the suggestion was to create some White-only learning spaces in the organization where these pressing concerns could be discussed in a culturally homogenous space. This created some hurt feelings, but ultimately the White staff took them up on the suggestion.

As a result, the White staff compiled some suggested resources and ended up reading my book *White Awake* together. The book resonated with the staff. They asked if I would spend a day with them talking through the principles in the book, with the hope of finding some new ideas they could apply to the conflict they were facing with their non-White counterparts.

I was honored by the request and agreed to do so. In advance of the session, I met with their director of training, and we discussed the needs of the participants—their level of comfort with race conversations, current level of cultural competency, responses to previous conversations on the topic—and then considered how to best contextualize the time together. The agenda was agreed upon, and the outline was sent in advance to the staff.

When the training day came, we spent the first thirty minutes doing introductions and sharing stories about how and when we had first been introduced to the reality of race. I was then asked to take some time to review what I believed to be foundational principles for White engagement around race. I got about five minutes into the training when I was suddenly interrupted.

"Um, excuse me, Dr. Hill, can you please pause for a moment?"

I looked out in the audience to locate the source of the interruption and was surprised to discover that it was the executive director of the nonprofit. I was initially pleased when told he would be in attendance, as it seemed to model a posture of curiosity for the other White employees who were there. But suddenly I wasn't so sure.

He continued, "I'm sure this material you are sharing is helpful for beginners, but that's not who you are talking to right now. *You are actually speaking to an extremely woke group*—we know all about the history of race, and we understand that it's a really big deal. We only have one day together, so I'm hoping you can maybe speed this up and get to some of the deeper stuff?"

I was dumbfounded by both the interruption and the challenge to the material. What I was covering was an extension of the curriculum that my team had collaboratively developed, and it had been vetted many times prior to this training.

I had no idea what to do next, so I just awkwardly stood there. The executive director took advantage of the silence and asked if he could suggest an alternative approach to our time together. I handed him the microphone, and he shared his vision with the group. He said, "I know you all care deeply about the issue of race, and I'm proud of how woke we are as a group. I think we should capitalize on our time together and leverage that collective concern to address this problem head-on. I say let's roll up our sleeves and spend our time working today. How does that sound?"

The group seemed to be in alignment with his vision, and the verbal affirmations were all he needed to continue down this redirected course. He pulled out a flip chart and asked them to name the top three race-based problems currently facing the organization. They identified what they saw as three big problems, and from there he divided them into work groups to analyze, formulate a proposal, and then report back to the larger group.

I stayed for the remainder of the day as a passive participant, but it was all a fog from that point forward. I was lost in my thoughts and feelings and trying to make sense of what had happened that morning. Part of me was feeling shocked, embarrassed, and even angry that I had been publicly challenged.

But another part of me was second-guessing myself. Interruption aside, maybe the executive director had been right to redirect the conversation. *Did I underestimate the cultural competency of this group?* I wondered. Maybe I had moved too slowly. Maybe his instinct was right—perhaps a collaborative work session was the right starting point.

I had a chance to sit down with one of my mentors the following week. She had worked in the corporate sector for close to thirty years, and over the last decade she had been focused almost exclusively on diversity and inclusion initiatives in the marketplace. She was the one who had coached me on how to approach this particular assignment, and she had followed that up by proactively scheduling a follow-up meeting so we could debrief. I was hopeful she could provide clarity about my experience.

I wasted no time replaying the details of the whole experience. I told her the whole thing had me second-guessing myself and begged for help in interpreting the day. I also assured her that I wanted to learn and grow from this and reminded her that she had full license to say whatever she needed. If she was seeing something I wasn't, I was genuinely ready to hear whatever constructive critique she had.

But instead of sharing a critique, she just gave me a sweet smile—one of those smiles that comes from decades of experience with similar types of encounters. "I'm sorry that happened to you," she said, "but there is a silver lining in it. You just got to see firsthand why *woke* is such a dangerous word."

That was not exactly the response I was expecting from her. Though I had replayed every detail of the experience in my head many times, it had never once occurred to me to consider the use of the word *woke* as a key to interpreting the whole thing. And going beyond that, it occurred to me that I had never once associated the word *woke* with dangerous. Overused, perhaps. But dangerous?

She continued. "The word *woke* is problematic at two different levels. The first is very specific to the word; the second is more about the motivation behind the word."

To illustrate the first point, she put it into question form: "Did you know that *woke* is a term that was invented in the Black community? [It was gracious of her to ask, but I'm pretty sure she already knew my answer was no.] *Woke* was developed in the sixties as a shorthand version of *stay woke*, and that was an important phrase in my community. It was a collective reminder that we need to remain conscious of the Black struggle against the very real presence of White supremacy. When someone would say, "Stay woke," to me, I knew exactly what they were saying—that they saw me, that they saw what I was up against, that they saw how real the struggle was. So that is the first reason the word *woke* is dangerous, particularly when it is used by White people. They are using a word that has a rich history they're often oblivious to, and they risk co-opting it for their own purposes."

She then transitioned to the second danger. "Just as important as the problem with the word is the motivation behind the word. While I want to trust that most White people who use it mean well, I suspect they don't realize how revealing it actually is." She paused and put it into question form again. She asked me, "When a White person says they are woke, what do you think they are trying to communicate?"

I hadn't thought much about this, so my answer was simply reflexive. "I don't know. I guess they—we—are hoping to prove to other people—probably people of color in particular—that we see race and that we understand it and that we are trying to do our part."

"Yes," she said. "That is what I hear when I hear a White person use the word *woke*. And I can understand why a White person longs to reach this fixed state of enlightenment. I can see why they long to prove to me that they are allies in the work. But that is such a dangerous idea."

I was tracking with her logic, though the actual danger of the word was still escaping me. I asked her if she'd be willing to make it abundantly clear for me.

"Well, you actually got to see firsthand why it is dangerous. So let's use that experience to illustrate. This training you just did—you said the need arose because a cross-cultural committee was started to explore racial dynamics together, right? But it quickly dissolved because the employees of color didn't want to have any more conversations with the White leaders.

Now, I don't know them, but I can guess what happened in those meetings—I'd be willing to bet that what these employees of color ran into was the brick wall we call *woke*. Once White folks deem themselves as woke, they come in assuming they have the same baseline of knowledge as BIPOC. While they may now possess a greater knowledge of the history of race in America, they do not have lived experience as a BIPOC who endures White supremacy daily. So the starting point for BIPOC and White people in conversations about race is always different.

"Now, I'm not saying we don't want our White counterparts to move forward in an awakening journey. It goes without saying that we want them to stay teachable and curious—to want to understand race better. But do we want them to be woke? No, at least not in how the word has come to be understood. Once they convince themselves they are woke, they will think they have arrived. They won't see the need to be challenged anymore or to have blind spots revealed. And *that* is why *woke* is so dangerous."

By this point I'm guessing there is little mystery left as to the overall point of this chapter. And yet I don't want to just jump to the end and declare, "Stop being woke!" As in most arenas of life, the transformation we so badly need cannot be found solely through behavior modification. While it would make the journey far simpler to just extricate the word from our vocabulary, to do so would not lead us into the depths of change we're searching for. What we need to do is dig even deeper and explore why it is that this word has become so popularized in the first place. What is it about this word that draws in so many of us?

Why Is the Word *Woke* So Popular?

Allow me to come at this first practice from another angle. In developing this practice for my own journey, I have found a helpful analogy in the way the Bible instructs us to deal with fear. Fear is one of the most powerful emotions we experience as human beings, and it has the potential to completely paralyze us when we fail to deal with it. Therefore, it seems both significant and expected that the Bible addresses the subject matter so frequently. Did you know that "fear not" is the most frequently repeated command in the Bible?

During my early twenties I was dealing with a lot of fear, and I decided to study each of the instances of "fear not." I assumed I would find stories akin to mine—anxiety-ridden men and women who should know better but who continually gave in to fear. But that's not what I found at all. In most cases, the men and women who were commanded to "fear not" actually had really good reasons to be afraid. In fact, it went even further. It was often God who created the situation of fear as an opportunity to test and stretch their faith. Consider just a few examples:

- Abraham was told to "fear not" in a vision that would completely uproot his and his family's life (Genesis 15:1). Who wouldn't be terrified if they were told to leave everything they had ever known and head toward a destination not yet revealed?
- The people of Israel were told to "fear not" after they temporarily escaped Egyptian slavery but were now barricaded in by the Red Sea (Exodus 14:13). Who wouldn't be terrified when on their right was an immovable body of water, and on their left was a swarm of angry soldiers coming at them?
- Joshua was told to "fear not" while mourning the loss of his mentor Moses and being summoned to lead the people into the Promised Land (Joshua 1:9). Who wouldn't be terrified at the prospect of leading an entire nation on a dangerous mission, especially when his predecessor had been unable to fulfill the assignment?

- Mary was told to "fear not" by the angel Gabriel, who had come to deliver the news of the coming incarnation of God (Luke 1:30). Who wouldn't be terrified by the prospect of telling her husband-to-be that God was about to divinely conceive the Son of God into her womb?

This was a critical discovery for me. These were not fear-filled people who just needed to "buck up" and stop being afraid. They were facing incredible situations that were genuinely terrifying, and they wouldn't have been human if they looked at those opportunities without feeling fear. So when God told them to "fear not," was God asking them to just flip a switch and change their behavior?

I don't think so. I think it's actually the opposite. By commanding them to "fear not," God was inviting them into a deep, introspective relationship with the fear that was already present—fear that was vying for control of their actions. So if they were going to learn to "fear not," they would first need to come to grips with the fact that they were afraid. By acknowledging the presence of fear and by coming to understand its power, they could then develop a vision for transformation that would lead them to new heights of courage.

This theological discovery helped me develop a concrete practice for dealing with fear. In order to "fear not," I needed to diligently follow these three steps:

1. Acknowledge the presence of fear.
2. Come to a deeper understanding of the power of my fear.
3. Develop a God-inspired vision for moving from fear to courage.

White Christians need to confront the motivations that fuel the desire to be woke in the same way we can confront fear.

We can't get rid of fear without acknowledging and understanding it, and the same is true for the subject matter at hand.

So using those same three steps of the practice for confronting fear, we can humbly confront our pride in being woke and move to real transformation.

1. Acknowledge that the desire to be seen as woke lives deep inside of White people. I was invited to speak at a seminary recently to a group of White pastors who were about to finish their Master of Divinity program. This seminary does a good job of integrating race into their theological education, and the director of this program assured me that this was a group of pastors who were very conscientious about the subject matter. Therefore I spent the morning session covering the material of this chapter (probably unsurprising!). We talked together about the popularity in White circles of being deemed as woke, and I passed on the lessons instilled in me about the dangers of its unchecked motivations. I shared how I've come to see this desire as an act of pride and talked about the need for those of us who are White to commit to an ongoing posture of listening, learning, and surfacing blind spots.

When the first session was over, I connected with the director of the program to see how he thought it was going. He looked at me with a semi-defeated look and said, "Unfortunately, not as well as I'd hoped. I personally thought the content was great, but as I'm talking to the pastors in attendance, they are telling me that they don't fully see the relevance of this conversation. While they can see how it might be helpful for some White people, they say it's not particularly applicable to them."

Now, is it possible that this just happened to be the one group of emerging White leaders unaffected by the deeper desires represented by the word *woke*? I suppose that's theoretically possible, but I highly doubt it. A far more likely explanation is self-awareness—or the lack of it. I don't believe it's malicious, and I don't think they (or we) shrug off the need for introspection around the idea of being woke as an overt act of pride, but I nonetheless find this to be a constant reality. White folks who want to be engaged in the work of confronting race tend to be chronically unaware of how badly they want and need recognition of having reached this enlightened status.

Let me tell you another story. I was once invited by another director of D&I to do a one-day training with a large company in Chicago. I met with her beforehand to learn more and asked her to expound on the problems she faces as she tries to transform the organization's culture. Her response was as piercing as it was insightful:

> I used to think the biggest challenge at this organization was represented by the White folks who didn't care about racial disparities. That is still a problem, of course. But I'm realizing now that, functionally, my far bigger problem is all the woke White people who have key leadership positions here. They started their journey by doing the work to educate themselves on the basics of race, of which I'm glad. But that same posture of learning that was demonstrated early in the journey seemed to suddenly transform into something else. In short order they moved from student mode to teacher mode. They're no longer trying to understand race as much as they're trying to dictate solutions for fixing it. They confuse intellectual knowledge with experiential understanding and no longer wholeheartedly seek critical feedback on their perspectives or ideas. As a result, our efforts completely stall. The holdup no longer feels like White folks who refuse to engage with race. Instead, it's White folks who are certain they understand it. You'll see it when you get here—it's a circle of decision-makers who are all White—and all supposedly woke.

If I was only allowed to share one anecdote with a White person who is enthusiastically setting out on this path, it would be this story. I don't think that most of us who are White see how big of a problem this assumption of being woke is, which is why we don't spend the necessary time engaging in introspection and self-reflection.

2. Come to more deeply understand why this motivation is so powerful. Why do we want to be woke? What is the allure of being crowned with this status? These are questions I ask of myself constantly. I've asked them to dozens of self-aware White folks engaged in work like this as well. What is it about this label that makes it so attractive?

I was tempted to write an entire chapter just on the answers to this question, but for the sake of brevity, I'll confine my remarks to the top three reasons I hear. I don't think this list is exhaustive, but hopefully it will spark deeper levels of self-reflection for those who are genuinely willing to probe our unidentified yet very powerful motivations.

The label woke *is powerful because we do not want to be associated with "those" White people.* It's hard to ignore the fact that a large percentage of the White population in America still lives in a state of denial when it comes to the impact of race on every facet of our society. Whether it shows up in the annual celebration of Columbus's "discovering" of America or in the blaming of African Americans for "Black-on-Black" crime or in political ideologies that harm marginalized non-White citizens while hiding behind phrases such as "make America great again," we see the multitude of ways that the obvious realities of White supremacy are somehow filtered, minimized, and ultimately ignored. Given this dangerous landscape, it becomes somewhat inevitable that those of us who are White and waking up to race will want to immediately and definitively distance ourselves from any kind of association with this slice of the White population.

I see the motivation to be seen as woke almost always beginning there. At the most basic level, we want the world to know we don't operate like that—we hunger to be recognized as having a qualitatively different relationship with race than those who intentionally choose to ignore it. Or said another way, to be woke is to mean we are not like "them"!

It is regarding this first motivation that I believe the message of Christianity provides a unique pathway to freedom. At the core of an authentic reception of the gospel message is a shift in how we come to understand our identity. Said a different way, to be saved by Jesus is to come to a new knowledge of who we are (and who we are not) through God. Though we used to, we no longer identify ourselves by what we do for work or how we dress or who we hang out with or how much money we earn. And of particular relevance to this point, we no longer find identity based on how we measure up against others.

It was actually this very tendency that led to some of the most rebuking words from Jesus to the Pharisees (read his parable in Luke 18:9–14, as he talks about a Pharisee who gained his identity by comparing himself to others he felt superior to). So while it is understandable that we would look to establish a sense of identity by comparing ourselves to those we perceive as less enlightened, it is nonetheless dangerous to ourselves, to others, and to the larger goal of confronting and dismantling White supremacy.

The label* woke *is powerful because we dream of eventually reaching a permanent state of enlightenment. I think most of us carry this fantasy that if we take the racial awakening journey seriously enough—if we read the right articles, study the right history books, listen to the right podcasts—we will eventually land at an arrival point where we can exhale and join the ranks of other woke White allies. It's a fantastical place where all major lessons have already been learned. It's a place where all blind spots have already been exposed. It's a place where I am on equal footing in my knowledge of the issue with those who represent the margins. It's a place where my credibility is solid enough that I can tell jokes about race without repercussions. It's a place where I no longer have to be sensitive to the multitude of cultural vantage points on an issue, because my own sense of instinct is so well developed. It is a place where I no longer have to worry about being corrected, because I never make mistakes anymore. It is a place where I no longer say anything stupid or say the wrong thing at the wrong time.

Do you see the threads of this fantasy inside yourself? I sure see it in myself. I think there are many reasons this fantasy is so common in White folks who deeply desire to be active participants, but to explore them here would take me farther down this path than I want to go in this chapter. For the purposes of dealing with this second motivation, I believe we have to do the same with this fantasy as we do with every other fantasy: we must find our way back to reality.

When I begin to slip into a mode of fantasizing about graduating to some type of fixed state of enlightenment, here are a couple of truths I remind myself of. *First, my whole life has been socialized by, through, and inside a system of White supremacy.* While I was growing up completely oblivious to the system—or worse, internalizing messages of superiority—most of my BIPOC friends were growing up *having* to learn it in order to survive. The gap in understanding between these two realities is almost immeasurable. *Second, I remind myself that even as I slowly close the necessary knowledge gap involving the system of White supremacy, this is not the same thing as lived experience.* My intellectual understanding of race does not compare to being the lone minority presence in any given space. Nor does it compare to fearing for my life as I get pulled over by the police. I've also never had to figure out how to have "the talk" with my children. I've never had to worry about being dragged out of my home by an ICE agent.

Though the fantasy of reaching some type of fixed, enlightened point is understandable, I need only to remind myself of these truths to remember that it is indeed just that—a fantasy. The reality is that I am on an ongoing journey of discovery.

The label woke *is powerful because we long to be independent agents of change.* I met recently with a White leader who is a respected veteran in this work. She is respected for her humble attitude as she partners in cross-cultural settings. I was grateful to glean life lessons from her. One of the first lessons she passed on was a caution about what *woke* represented for White folks. It was affirming to hear how central this idea had been in her journey. I asked her to elaborate on how she had learned to be cautious about this term. She responded, "I have had to come to grips with the fact that a big reason I want to be thought of as woke is directly tied to my pride."

This is a pattern I notice in myself as well, so I asked her if she could elaborate on what that specific connection to pride looks like for her. "Here's one clear example I've come to identify," she replied. "Once I began to realize how serious the problem of race is, I felt like I needed to do something to improve the problem. Perhaps that is not pride, but the desire to make change on my own terms certainly was. Despite the fact that there were all kinds of opportunities to serve under seasoned and credible leaders who were working within their own communities, I felt the need to prove that I could bring about change on my own. I wanted to establish myself as an independent agent of change."

Choosing to pursue change outside of the guidance of seasoned leaders made immediate sense as a form of pride. I asked her if there were additional ways she saw this phenomenon of seeking to be an independent agent of change play out. She explained that a lot of White folks begin their journey with a clear admission that the system of race is something they typically haven't thought about and still don't understand well. But she notices something that happens along the way, specifically for White leaders who are actively searching for ways to participate in solutions to race-based problems. Whereas they used to center voices of people of color in their initial process, they start to shift toward a centering of their own thoughts and ideas. And whereas they used to demonstrate a healthy dependence on people of color to tutor them from lived experience, they start to long for an independence that no longer requires this ongoing mentorship. She sees this desire as a direct symptom of wokeness. The more woke that White leaders deem themselves to be, the more likely they are to see themselves as fit to lead efforts directed toward race in an independent fashion, disconnected from critical feedback on their approaches or theories of change.

This insight was incredibly helpful. She put words to another dimension of wokeness that I had not yet named for myself.

I asked her how she had learned to combat this dangerous motivation in herself, and I loved the clarity and depth of her answer. She said that when it came to her desire to actively participate in combating race, she had adopted Romans 12:3 as her life verse: "For by the grace given me I say to every one of you: Do not think of yourself more highly than you ought, but rather think of yourself with sober judgment, in accordance with the faith God has distributed to each of you." This, she said, was how she could quickly gain a pulse on whether she was demonstrating healthy dependence or unhealthy independence. When she was giving in to pride, she could see how she was thinking more highly of herself than she ought. When she was living from more of a Spirit-filled, humble place, she was able to authentically evaluate her journey through a prism of sober judgment.

3. Develop a God-inspired vision for moving from pride to humility. Behavior modification regarding the words you use has a place, but behavior modification will not help change your heart. I believe the only way we can truly move toward the transformation we so badly need is by clearly acknowledging that the desire within us to be deemed as woke is real, and that it is fueled by pride. Once we get in touch with this reality, it becomes much easier to see why it is so dangerous, as pride always is.

From there, we can develop a vision for ourselves that keeps us moving, by the Spirit of God, from pride to humility. We can examine ways we have moved from pride to humility in other arenas in our lives and apply our findings to this journey. From overconfidence in self to reliance on others. From autonomy and independence to collaboration and dependence. From a position of security to a position of vulnerability. From seeking to establish ourselves as experts to seeking a permanent posture of learning.

The problem addressed in this chapter goes far deeper than the word *woke*. Though this word will eventually go out of style, as all co-opted, pop culture phrases do, what it represents for the White person seeking to actively participate in race-based work will not. So the practice of this chapter—stop being woke—remains the starting point of this journey, regardless of which word is currently used to describe it.

This will always need to be the first practice because it represents the most fundamental battle within the human soul: pride versus humility. Is it an overstatement to say that the whole of the Christian message comes down to this? I don't think so. Warnings of the insidious nature of pride are found from the beginning of the Bible to the end. James, the half brother of Jesus, summarizes the warning like this: "That is why Scripture says: 'God opposes the proud but shows favor to the humble'" (James 4:6).

practice two

Beware of Diversity

I was twenty-four years old when I experienced my first meaningful awakening to the system of race. This is an embarrassing admission, since it should have happened much sooner than
it did. But embarrassment aside, I still reflect on this awakening
often, because it represents the definitive starting point for my
journey. It was at this moment that I began to specifically ask
the question that drives this book: *Once a White person becomes
convicted about the realities of racial injustice, what is the best way to
become an active participant in confronting them?*

This question burned deep inside me and sent me on a search
for someone or somewhere that could help me process it. At
this point in my life, I was working full-time at Willow Creek
Community Church, a predominantly White megachurch. I was
not situated within a network where these types of questions
were being asked on a regular basis. But I was hopeful they were
being asked somewhere.

After a lot of digging around, I was glad to discover some
churches and Christian organizations that seemed to be meaningfully engaging racial justice. I was eager to learn from them,
so I began to read everything they published and eventually
visited as many of them in person as I could. When I arrived,

I inundated their leaders with endless questions and copiously recorded their answers in my growing journal dedicated to this work.

Though the organizations I studied represented a fairly wide range of traditions, I quickly took note of the fact that their approach to race was strikingly similar. When they described the problem as they saw it, almost every one of them began their rationale with some version of this oft-referred-to quote from Dr. Martin Luther King Jr.: "11:00 on Sunday morning is the most segregated hour in this nation."[1]

The ongoing reference to this quote represented an idea that many of these organizations referred to as their *theory of change*. A theory of change is a concept that organizations use when discussing how they want to pursue transformation in a particular area of society and essentially summarizes one's approach through three questions: (1) What is the problem that the organization is looking to address? (2) What is the proposed solution to that problem? (3) How will the organization take steps toward that proposed solution?

So when it came to strategies for engaging with race, most organizations I interacted with built their theory of change on this perceived need to move from segregation to diversity. Using the same three questions from above, it typically went like this:

1. What is the problem? Segregation.
2. What is the proposed solution? Diversity.
3. How will the organization take steps toward that proposed solution? Make diversity a priority across the board.

Once it became clear to me that the prevailing theory of change within the White Christian world was built on the pursuit of diversity, I put my head down and went to work. The logic of moving from segregation to diversity matched my level of understanding at the time, so I dedicated the next four years of my life to this cause. Some of this pursuit happened through collaborative efforts within the confines of Willow Creek Community Church, where I was working. Much of it happened through a satellite community that a team of us launched through Willow Creek in a North Side neighborhood of Chicago. My leadership of this new community was certainly an imperfect component of the story,[2] but I still think it's fair to say we were genuine and very serious about building a culturally diverse community.

Over time, we began to experience a modicum of success with this vision, at least based on the standard used in churches at that time. In *People of the Dream: Multiracial Congregations in the United States*, sociologist Michael Emerson developed a popular definition of a multiracial congregation as one where no single racial or ethnic group accounts for 80 percent or more of the membership.[3] Our relentless push toward diversity helped us easily clear that mark, and yet I couldn't shake the feeling that something still didn't feel right. The whole reason we had pursued diversity in the first place was in response to the problem of race, but an honest appraisal left me wondering if our changing demographics had really made an impact. Worship was a centerpiece of our weekly service, for instance, yet outside of a more diverse set of musicians, it didn't feel qualitatively different than when we were an all-White community. Preaching was also a centerpiece, yet that too felt largely the same, even as our attendees appreciated the introduction of some new and fresh voices into the rotation.

At a visceral level, there was one thing that felt more similar than ever: difficulty in talking about race. By this point I had grown familiar with the challenge of addressing race in all-White settings, but I had just presumed that this difficulty would dissipate as the cultural diversity percentage correspondingly rose. But now I realized that my assumption was wrong.

Trying to get folks to wrestle with terms like *White supremacy* was just as hard (maybe harder!) in the diverse setting I was now in as it had been in the all-White spaces I previously occupied. And conversations around topics that affected marginalized groups, like police brutality or immigration reform, were just as charged and polarizing as they had been in all-White spaces.

It was in the midst of this season of struggling with diversity that I had the chance to attend a weekend conference on racial justice—and of particular importance, one that was led by BIPOC. That was an incidental detail at the time, but with the benefit of hindsight, it would end up explaining a lot. When talking about race, this conference had a different tone than I was accustomed to. The speakers were plainspoken about the history of White supremacy and consistently named the way this ideology communicated a set of lies about human value and dignity. The conference explored the social, political, and economic realities of White supremacy in a way that was grounded in love but unflinching in its analysis.

Just as notably, especially given my starting point, the conference stood out for what it did not talk about: diversity. I was borderline startled that there were no conversations on the importance of having friends of different ethnic backgrounds. Equally surprising was the lack of conversations about the importance of multiethnic church congregations, even though it was a Christian conference. While I didn't sense any direct antagonism toward diversity-related efforts, it was nonetheless clear that diversity was a low priority. Instead, the focus of these conversations was the critical task of confronting and dismantling White supremacy.

What happened next came more through a series of small steps than in one giant moment, but it was nonetheless apparent that a big shift was happening in me. I was poised for another critical jump forward in my blindness-to-sight journey and was ready to see something I had not been able to see before. When it finally settled, the message had become clear: I had spent the last four years of ministry working from an incomplete, and possibly even flawed, theory of change. I had operated under the false premise that the primary problem of race was largely segregation, and that the primary solution to race was therefore oriented toward overcoming segregation with intentional efforts to promote diversity.

But now, suddenly, I could see the immense problem in that approach. Was segregation real? Of course. But was that the root of the problem of race? Of course not.

Segregation was a symptom of a much larger issue. The deeper problem of race was the ideology of White supremacy—an ideology that had created extremely powerful and durable structures that continued to systematically target those deemed as less than. As such, I was going to need to completely shift how I thought about diversity.

I tell this story through the lens of my own discovery process, but this phenomenon goes far beyond my own experience. In fact, one of the most striking patterns I've observed in more than two decades of studying Christian approaches to combating racial injustice is that the commitment to this diversity-centric theory of change only grows stronger with time. In the White Christian world, for instance, the call to diversity has grown exponentially over the past two decades. When I was a young minister, more than twenty years ago, I would regularly attend church growth conferences. Of the dozens I attended, I can only recall diversity coming up one time. And when it did, it was treated as a unique call that certain ministers might be drawn to, not a normative expectation for all ministers. Fast-forward to its modern incarnation, and you can no longer go to a dominant-culture church growth conference without hearing a relentless message on the importance of diversity.

It's not only in the White Christian world that this is true. The emphasis on diversity has become the normalized approach in the business world as well. I didn't have enough experience to realize this early in my journey, but I've now come to see that the corporate sector has bought into this theory of change just as strongly as (if not more than) the White Christian world. The corporate world in America, whose racial history is no different from the rest of the society, is marked by a brutal relationship with White supremacy. As such, every major industry is characterized by its typical symptoms: a history of closed leadership circles populated by White people (typically men), hiring practices that give significant preference to White applicants over BIPOC applicants, and ongoing struggles to recruit and retain BIPOC employees.[4]

As the overall consciousness of these industry disparities grows, businesses are being called out publicly to account for this history, and demands are made for a proactive response. When that happens, you can guess what the response is, right? The company starts a diversity program.

In the introduction, I mentioned Shumeca Pickett, who is on the leadership board of our church and is a valued thought partner. Shumeca founded Alfred Dewitt Ard, a social impact consultancy in Chicago. It has been telling to watch how her organization has shifted in response to the consistent commitment to a diversity-centric theory of change. Most of her clients come out of the business world, and this approach is so pervasive that in response she has changed her consulting approach.

Now, when a company pursues her services, she will inform them up front that a large part of her work is to move organizations away from a diversity-centric theory of change. Instead, she suggests an alternative approach and offers her services in collaboratively developing a multidimensional strategy that acknowledges the value of diversity yet focuses on more directly confronting White supremacy within the organization.

This illustrates how far-reaching the diversity-centric theory of change is, as well as the need to be better equipped to deal with it. Those of us who are White and who desire to participate in efforts to combat racial injustice in White-centric institutions must learn how to "practice" diversity better.

But my purpose here is not to dismiss the power of diversity, nor to minimize the role that diversity can play in confronting White supremacy. I'm actually convinced of the opposite. Diversity becomes a very powerful tool when used properly. But addressing diversity without confronting White supremacy does not achieve the desired result.

To better practice diversity, I suggest we think of this practice as being split into two halves. We need to deepen our capacity on two different fronts:

- We must deepen our capacity to clearly describe how diversity becomes dangerous.
- We must deepen our capacity to clearly describe how diversity becomes beneficial.

When Diversity Becomes Dangerous

Diversity becomes dangerous when we treat it as an *end* goal and not as a *means* to the end goal. What does it look like when the priorities of an end and a means are reversed in an unhealthy way?

An African American woman was hired at a large White church. The leadership of the church had experienced a racial awakening, and in response they developed this position for her. The story she shared with me (recorded anonymously, so as not to jeopardize her job) highlights the dangers when diversity becomes an end instead of a means to an end:

I was excited about the awakening that this church had about race, and I believed they were very sincere in this newly formed desire to become a diverse church. My confidence was further bolstered when they followed up their stated commitment by creating a staff position to provide leadership for this new initiative. And I was beyond honored when they offered that position to me.

I've been in this role for two years now, and we have definitely made strides in the arena of diversity. When I came on staff, it was still unusual to see any BIPOC in the congregation. But now, according to the results of our latest survey, 25 percent of the Sunday attenders identify as being BIPOC. So clearly, we've made a lot of progress on that front.

But if I'm honest, I admit that I lacked the foresight to see how problematic it would end up being that we built our entire strategy around diversity. One of the clearest signs of this problem comes in the form of ongoing silence from our church leadership about current events that reveal ongoing racial problems in our country. There are all these new BIPOC folks who are now part of our congregation, and they have all of these important questions about how our church leadership is planning to address the problem of White supremacy—both in our city and in our church. But each time the questions are asked, leadership dodges them and instead responds by excitedly pointing to the statistical growth of diversity in our overall population. It's as if the presence of diversity gets translated as a free pass from needing to collectively confront the actual problems caused by race.

So what I now see happening is a gap forming between the White folks in our church and the BIPOC people in our church, and it scares me. When the White folks talk about race relations, they speak in almost exclusively optimistic terms. For them, the progress our community has made around diversity trumps all other concerns. They feel proud of our church for tackling the problem head-on, and they see the work as being mostly done now.

When the BIPOC folks talk about race relations, it has an opposite tone. They came to this church because they perceived it to be a community that was willing to courageously enter into conversations about the ongoing problem of race. They were eager to participate in cross-cultural coalitions that were longing to do something about it. But that initial hope is quickly fading into pessimism. They sense the ongoing reticence in our church to talk honestly about White supremacy, and they suspect it is largely fueled by the fear of offending the White stakeholders. So even though we have become so much more diverse in the last two years, I'm not sure we have actually made any progress. And since I'm the one who meets one-on-one with all of these disillusioned BIPOC members, I fear we have actually contributed to making things worse for them.[5]

The content of this story, as well as the rawness with which it is shared, is a gift to those of us who want to learn. It brings clarity to a set of dynamics that is consistent in every type of organization I have worked with—be it a church, a nonprofit, or a business. Treating diversity as an end instead of a means to an end typically creates a significant chasm between the experience and attitude of the White stakeholders and the experience and attitude of the BIPOC stakeholders in that organization.

For White stakeholders, increased levels of diversity almost always translate into a feeling of surging optimism. As a whole, the White community has been conditioned to see segregation as the problem and diversity as the answer. Therefore when those of us who are White see a once-segregated organization begin to change in its composition, our instinctive response is to celebrate that and showcase the progress. And with each successive increase in diversity, that optimistic sense of being "successful" only increases.

Feelings are different for racially conscious BIPOC within White organizations that experience increased levels of diversity. I often think of a quote from legendary activist Angela Davis, who when discussing diversity-centric theories of change bluntly summarized the problem like this: "It makes no sense to be included in an institution or a society that hasn't changed . . . It makes no sense for racially marginalized communities to be included in a society that remains as racist as it was before they were included."[6] When BIPOC folks experience an organization that talks a lot about diversity but demonstrates little interest in seeking either institutional or societal change, they tend to become increasingly pessimistic and disillusioned.

As depressing as this may sound, there are plenty of reasons for hope too. Let's start with the African American woman who shared the above story. Remember, she was initially optimistic about the direction of her church. She was ready to roll up her sleeves and help them in their efforts to pursue greater diversity. I meet BIPOC leaders like her in every organization I work with. Their very presence serves as a consistent reminder to me of the grace of God. Why does someone like her want to help a church like that? Why does someone like her want to help a church like mine? Why is it that, despite experiencing an endless stream of racial offenses throughout the course of her life, she still has the hope and stamina to try again? Only the grace of God can explain something like that, and it provides a template of hope for the potential transformation that can still happen.

Her presence there and the potential she saw in the organization at the point of their initial racial awakening also set the stage for the second half of this practice: *deepening our capacity to clearly describe how diversity becomes beneficial.* Let's imagine that the leadership of this church realized they were actually using diversity in a dangerous way and treating it as an end goal instead of a means to the end. What would that look like?

When Diversity Becomes Beneficial

Before getting into the content of the second half of the practice, I want to share a couple of important foundational principles behind the way I'm approaching this. First, as I describe how diversity can become beneficial, I am only describing it *in terms of how it can become beneficial to those of us who are White.* For BIPOC people, diversity tends to be a complicated subject matter. While there are times some may deem it as helpful, more often than not, it creates a greater burden for them. (As an aside, if you have trusted relationships with BIPOC friends and mentors, you should ask them how they feel about initiatives in White organizations to increase diversity. There will undoubtedly be a range of answers, but each could present you with a wonderful opportunity for ongoing awakening.)

That leads to the second underlying principle: In talking about the cultural identity journey for a White person, my baseline conviction is that *our most desperate need*—whether we realize it or not—*is to move from blindness to sight.* I'm convinced we will remain ineffective in the battle against White supremacy if we don't internalize this need deeply.

Why is this so important to remember? There are a lot of reasons, but I'll pick just one for now. One of the most salient privileges that comes with being White in America is that we don't ever *need* to learn about White supremacy. We've had a host of reasons to remain oblivious, even as White supremacy emanated all around us growing up. Human nature is what it is. Without some type of drive that eclipses self-interest, White folks in this country have always been, and always will be, unmotivated to recognize White supremacy.

Of course, this is the exact opposite experience of many BIPOC, particularly those who were raised in America. From early on, the threats that came with White supremacy became obvious:

- labels that categorized them as "different" from the White norm
- messages that they were fundamentally inferior, which became internalized
- treatment that differed from that experienced by their White peers
- direct warnings of what might happen if they interrupted the White way of life

This list could go on and on, but the larger point is acknowledging that a BIPOC sees and experiences White supremacy from an early age, while a White person may never have to see it.

You may have BIPOC friends who have spent their entire lives learning to see and navigate it. You may know White adults—or you may be one yourself—who have experienced a lightbulb moment of awakening. From that awakening comes a desire to join in the important work of confronting White supremacy. One group has spent their entire lives looking at this problem, and the other group is just being introduced to it.

It is important that we don't confuse the moment when the lightbulb of awareness first turns on with actually being able to comprehensively see White supremacy. Said another way, the lightbulb moment is important, but it's just the beginning of a long journey of moving from blindness to sight. We will always be dependent on those with the lived experience to aid us in our journey of seeing what we cannot see. This is true at the individual level, and it's true at the organizational level as well.

That leads to the thread that will hold these next three points together. How can diversity be helpful, particularly to White individuals and White organizations? *It will help us see.* That is why we badly need diversity. When diversity helps us see better, it works powerfully. When we skip over or minimize the need to see better, diversity actually becomes one more tool used to perpetuate White supremacy.

So how do we learn to see, aided by diversity? How do we help others see? Here are three areas where diversity, when utilized correctly, can become extremely beneficial in the transformational process of moving from blindness to sight:

- seeing God more clearly
- seeing ourselves more clearly
- seeing the world more clearly as it is

Seeing God More Clearly

One of the passages that has most profoundly shaped both my understanding of Jesus and my call as a Christian is Colossians 1:15–20:

> The Son is the image of the invisible God, the first-born over all creation. For in him all things were created: things in heaven and on earth, visible and invisible, whether thrones or powers or rulers or authorities; all things have been created through him and for him. He is before all things, and in him all things hold together. And he is the head of the body, the church; he is the beginning and the firstborn from among the dead, so that in everything he might have the supremacy. For God was pleased to have

all his fullness dwell in him, and through him to reconcile to himself all things, whether things on earth or things in heaven, by making peace through his blood, shed on the cross.

While there is much truth to draw from this passage, two things stand out in relation to this chapter. First, the apostle Paul reminds us that the ministry of reconciliation is not one that begins with human beings or that even belongs to them. The ministry of reconciliation comes from and belongs to *Jesus alone*. Jesus is the ultimate reconciler, so this is his work! Second, Paul gives us all of these names of Jesus (image of the invisible God, firstborn over all creation, source of all created things, head of the church) to help clarify his ultimate intention—"so that in everything he might have the supremacy."

That phrase in particular helps me to remember that race-related work is rooted in a deeply spiritual struggle. While the system of race has created all kinds of savage inequalities at the social level, neither its origins nor its sustaining powers are ultimately social in nature. This is a spiritual battle. The intention of Jesus Christ is to reign supreme over the entire created order, and in the words of Paul, anything that vies for supremacy—be it visible or invisible—represents an idolatrous throne, power, ruler, or authority that competes with Jesus. That's one of the many reasons I think it's important that we continue to use the term *White supremacy*. Speaking of it like that keeps the spiritual nature of this battle in focus and makes it more difficult for followers of Jesus to dismiss race as some type of secondary social problem.

Which leads us back to diversity. One of the primary dangers of worshiping in an all-White space is that it becomes exceedingly difficult to see, name, and respond to the spiritual contest happening between White supremacy and Christ supremacy.

Even if a White congregation wanted to see this more clearly—which they too rarely do—there are few credible resources within White Christian circles that can help with this. Historic voices within Christian circles, particularly those of the conservative persuasion, were either silent on this issue or, worse, outrightly complicit with White supremacy.[7] And it barely improves when we fast-forward to modern times. One needs to do only a basic survey of the preaching catalog of America's most popular Bible teachers to see how scarcely this spiritual contest is named and taught. And even when race does find its way into the discourse, the conversation rarely goes beyond a true but superficial reminder that acts of racism are bad and that we should instead treat all people equally.

I hope I don't come across as judgmental or self-righteous when I make these observations. My motivation is simply to engage in honest dialogue about our need to grow spiritually and the corresponding lack of resources available to us for this journey. I am neither above nor removed from this struggle myself. Like all White people, I pay a dear price when I remain trapped in a White echo chamber for too long.

What is the role of healthy diversity in this first area of seeing God more clearly? At a bare minimum, diversity reminds us that Jesus designed the church to function as a body with diverse parts and that we need each other if the body is going to work correctly and function in a healthy way. The fact that most of the American church is so badly fractured around race has a tremendous impact on our ability to have the image of Christ formed fully in us. What we need is to hear and learn from all parts of the body. A long history of invalidating certain voices and overvalidating others has created a church milieu in which very few White Christians ever get meaningfully exposed to good Bible teaching outside of White, educated, middle-class males (of which I am one). That inevitably leads to spiritual anemia and erects a barrier in our path to seeing God fully and being formed in the image of Christ.

The need for diversity in the quest to see God more fully goes even further than that. Throughout the Bible we see that one of the best pathways to knowing and loving God comes through the naming and confronting of idols that stand in the way of our devotion to him. Therefore, prophets were raised up by God within each generation to speak against idolatrous worship and to call people to repent and return to the covenantal love of God. The need in our modern world is no different from what the ancient world needed. We need God to send us prophets who can clearly name these competing idols and call us to meaningful repentance.

I believe that White supremacy represents one of the most powerful idols in America's history. The White church will have difficulty finding freedom from its grip without a resurgence of this same type of biblical, prophetic witness. Because it is so challenging for White people to see White supremacy clearly, it goes without saying that the prophets we need will come from outside of the White community. When diversity works right, this happens regularly, and the church is different because of it.

But unfortunately, we once again run into the powerful reality of White supremacy. A conversation I had recently with an African American pastor illustrates how quickly the prophetic stream gets undercut by White supremacy. This pastor and I have known each other for a long time, and his story has long served as a source of inspiration to me. His life has been marked by deep episodes of pain, and many of the scars he carries came from the hands of White people. Yet instead of choosing the human instinct to hate, he has experienced a profound call from God to forgive and to seek the ministry of reconciliation. He believes God has called him to be a loving voice for transformation in White communities, and he does it with tremendous grace and kindness.

Sadly, there was a big setback in his reconciliation work. He asked if we could meet and if he could have the freedom to vent in an unfiltered way. He had recently fulfilled the final steps of his ordination process within a large historically White denomination. Both he and the leaders of this denomination repeatedly affirmed his call to be a reconciling voice within their community. In that spirit, they invited him to speak at their national denominational gathering, and he took them at their word. He preached about the dangers of White supremacy and urged each church represented in attendance to take that caution seriously.

I listened to his talk afterward. It was wonderful. It was biblically sound, filled with grace, and very helpful for moving this denomination forward on its journey. Unfortunately, that's not how most in attendance felt. Many of them were offended, believing he was insinuating that they were all racists. As a result they flooded the inbox of the denominational leadership with letters and emails. The leadership had initially affirmed the content of his talk, but after the steady flow of complaints, they reversed their position. They responded with an article in the denominational newsletter modifying much of what he said and committing to being more cautious in how they addressed race in the future.

This pastor was devastated. As he processed the pain of having the leadership reverse course based on public pressure, he said something unforgettable: "I want to believe that reconciliation is possible. I want to believe that a White denomination I have embraced can also embrace me in return. I want to believe that in the same way this denomination embraces the words of White prophetic voices, so too can they embrace the words of Black prophetic voices. But after an experience like this, I wonder if it's actually possible. Maybe I didn't hear God right. Maybe the ministry of reconciliation can't happen when it comes to White supremacy."

This story illustrates what could happen through diversity, even if it feels just beyond reach. What might have happened had that denomination truly listened and responded to the words of this prophetic voice? The possibility was there to see God in a more robust way, to see sin in a more piercing way, and to respond with meaningful action and bear clearer witness to Christ and his kingdom. When that opportunity fizzled away, it resulted in a loss for everyone. The denomination lost. The pastor lost. The communities in which these churches are located lost.

This is why the practice of diversity is so important, as long as it's carried out in the right way. I pray you never lose sight of your own need for diverse prophetic voices in your life. I also pray you will be used by God in White spaces, that the people you lead will see the same thing. We must seek out new revelation as to why our communities need this, what they lose if they don't have it, and what type of infrastructure must be put in place to assure that prophetic voices can be heard.

Seeing Ourselves More Clearly

In 2016, a documentary film on James Baldwin was released titled *I Am Not Your Negro*. Raoul Peck based the film on thirty pages of notes that Baldwin had started in 1979, but not finished, on three friends who had been murdered—Medgar Evers, Martin Luther King Jr., and Malcolm X. The film shares some of Baldwin's most poignant quotes on White supremacy, and one of them feels of particular importance:

> You cannot lynch me and keep me in ghettos without becoming something monstrous yourselves. And furthermore, you give me a terrifying advantage: you never had to look at me. I had to look at you. I know more about you than you know about me. Not everything that is faced can be changed; but nothing can be changed until it is faced.[8]

James Baldwin had such a way with words, and the beginning of this quote paints a real but terrifying picture. It's a picture that matches the way I understand the biblical teaching of sin. At some level, I think something monstrous lives inside of all of us, and without the grace of God we are all capable of very dangerous and dark things. So when Baldwin says that lynching people and keeping people in ghettos led to our becoming something monstrous ourselves, I wince in pain while also saying amen to the truth being told.

When I share this quote in person, I often hear a White rebuttal that goes something like this: "But I wasn't there when lynchings happened [or slavery or Jim Crow or conquest of America or you fill in the blank], so that doesn't apply to me. It's not fair to say I have taken something of the nature of that monster onto myself."

But even that rebuttal does little to diminish the point Baldwin is trying to make. Even if we as modern White people were not the ones to actually lynch another precious human being, or even if we were not the ones to join a Sunday crowd that gathered as spectators to watch a lynching, we've still been raised in the same culture of White supremacy that allowed for those lynchings in the first place. The culture of White supremacy that enabled those evils is just as operative now as it was then, and we are still breathing in that same air and are complicit in new atrocities against African American people.

Let me continue the point by switching over to Dr. Diane Langberg, a leading Christian psychologist with expertise in trauma recovery and a clinical faculty member at Missio Seminary. She says it like this: "Culture is like oxygen—it is the air you breathe. And like breathing we often never stop to think about what we are inhaling unless the air is so nasty we are forced to. It is amazingly easy to be both anesthetized to the surrounding culture and blinded by it."[9]

I think this is what Baldwin was getting at when he referenced the "terrifying advantage" he held as a Black man, compared to the experience of the typical White person. White folks are handicapped on the path of transformation. In his words, "You never had to look at me. I had to look at you. I know more about you than you know about me."

I realize I'm talking here in primarily negative terms, and I admit that I have to fight against cynicism at times. I believe there is an opportunity for White folks to experience our own version of liberation from White supremacy. But we have to believe we are damaged to experience that liberation. Currently only a minority of White folks actually believe this.

My first hope and prayer for you begins with your own journey of awakening and transformation. I hope and pray that the deeper you get into this journey, the more sensitive you become to the impact of White supremacy on yourself. I hope this leads to a growing sense of the need for diverse community. I pray you'll come to see diversity not as an end in and of itself, but as a means to greater freedom and healing.

My second hope is that you will be able to help reframe the vision of diversity in whatever spaces God grants you favor within. I hope you can especially help the White folks in these spaces to see the need for sight and for healing. I pray we can change the things we measure in communities that hope for diversity—that we will stop tracking the percentage of diverse attendees and instead start tracking the degree of personal liberation that the White folks in the community are experiencing due to the gift of diversity they are partaking in.

Seeing the World More Clearly as It Is

One of my deepest convictions is that the Bible portrays spiritual blindness as one of the most dangerous states people can find themselves stuck in.[10] As the Spirit of God reveals to us the dangers of blindness, as well as the freedom that can come through healed sight, I believe we should literally become desperate to find the liberation that comes through healed eyes. This theme is resonant throughout the Bible, but the passage that has most shaped my view—particularly the way desperation should define our longings—comes from a parable of Jesus in Luke 16:19–31. Jesus uses an interesting rhetorical device on his way to the point, as he describes the contrast in the experiences of two different men. Making the parable even more distinct, Jesus gives only one of them a proper name while describing the other based solely on his earthly possessions.

Character One is introduced to us simply as "a rich man," and he serves as the primary subject. He is a man of extravagant wealth, as evidenced by a wardrobe of purple and fine linen (the finest fashion money could buy) and a lifestyle of "luxury every day." Character Two lives on the other end of the economic spectrum and is socially disenfranchised on almost every level. His name is Lazarus (which means "God has helped"), and he is a beggar, covered with sores and so hungry that he camps out at the edge of the rich man's table, hoping that a scrap of food might fall from his table.

The juxtaposition of these characters begs us to take note of the high cost that this rich man paid to achieve the worldly dream of status. By building the foundation of his identity exclusively on wealth, he forfeited the opportunity to discover who he was in God. As such, Jesus leaves him nameless, remembered only for the riches he had amassed in his short time on earth. As important as that is, it is what happens next that really shaped my understanding of the desperate need to see.

As Jesus tells the parable, the rich man dies and ends up in Hades, which some take to represent hell. I realize this backdrop of hell is not an insignificant detail, and I've studied a wide range of commentators in the hope of gaining greater understanding of its meaning. There are two different interpretations of what the inclusion of Hades could mean. One group of commentators believes that by placing the story in Hades, Jesus is intentionally teaching on the afterlife through this parable. Another group believes that the unique way Jesus tells this parable points to Hades as being more of a metaphor to describe just how detached from reality this man is. I can see the wisdom in both interpretations and sense it's important to acknowledge the presence of both. With that being said, it's what happens next that feels so important, and both groups of commentators agree that Jesus is making a strong statement about blindness-to-sight through what the rich man does next.

While in a state of torment in Hades, the rich man looks up and is somehow able to see the beggar Lazarus, who is by Abraham's side. The rich man cries out to Abraham and says, "Have pity on me and send Lazarus to dip the tip of his finger in water and cool my tongue, because I am in agony in this fire" (Luke 16:24). What a shocking response! One would assume that being plunged into Hades would have turned this rich man into a person who was sorrowful and repentant. One would also assume that, if given the chance to make things right with Lazarus, the rich man would jump at the opportunity.

But that's not what happens. Instead, we learn that the spiritual eyesight of this rich man was just as damaged in Hades as it had been on earth. Before the rich man's death, his concerns focused exclusively on the things of this earth. He paid attention to money, status, and power—all things Lazarus was in short supply of. So if the rich man even noticed Lazarus at all, it was likely nothing more than a stare of contempt.

Had a trip to Hades changed any of that? Was he seeing differently now that his senses had been completely shocked? No! When he spots Lazarus, he looks at him through the same blinded state. Lazarus remains an inferior figure to him, notable more for his ability to serve the needs of the rich man than for anything else. And this we see, through the storytelling genius of Jesus, was the ultimate tragedy of this man's life: he never saw himself as blind and therefore never sought the opportunity to find liberation in Jesus. He was blind on earth and remained so in Hades. Perhaps that is even one of the reasons Hades is so central to the parable. Perhaps being mired in spiritual blindness is its own form of hell on earth.

There's a lot more I could say about that passage and what it has meant to my journey, but what does it have to do with the need for diversity? Let's put it in good preacher language and look at the passage as revealing both a problem and solution. On the problem side, let's assume for the sake of this point that Jesus indeed was using this parable largely to reveal the predicament this rich man faced—namely, that as his life became increasingly defined by wealth, comfort, privilege, and power, his ability to see clearly decreased commensurately. This wouldn't be the only time Jesus described the problem of an inverse relationship between sight and wealth. In the Sermon on the Mount, when talking about the dangers of money, Jesus says, "The eye is the lamp of the body. If your eyes are healthy, your whole body will be full of light. But if your eyes are unhealthy, your whole body will be full of darkness" (Matthew 6:22–23).

If disconnection from reality and increasing blindness are the risks that come with increasing power, privilege, and wealth, then what's the solution? How do we combat the very real and scary threat of blindness? The right answer in church is always *Jesus*, and I'm not suggesting the answer is anything less than that. But as I reflected particularly on this parable of the rich man and Lazarus, I wondered what the specific invitation is from Jesus. Is there a solution that might have changed the outcome of this rich man? Was there a way he could have functionally moved from blindness to sight?

As I meditated on those questions, the answer became obvious. The path to liberation had always been right in front of him. God sent the rich man a gift in the form of Lazarus. If the rich man had become disconnected from seeing the world the way it was, then what better opportunity could there have been than to be led into transformational sight by the Holy Spirit, through the lived experience of someone like Lazarus?

That is how I have come to see the need for diversity in my own life. While I would not classify myself as a rich person based on how much money I have in my bank account, I would nonetheless classify Whiteness as a distinct and powerful form of capital in this society. Not everyone will agree with me on this point, but I believe that the structured economic reality that has formed around the belief in White superiority is as potent a currency as anything in our society. Anyone who is White—particularly if you add in social components such as education, social mobility, gender, and so forth—is automatically rich in the things of this world. With Whiteness comes the constant risk of disconnection from what's really happening in the world.

That is where diversity carries the promise of transformation. When we allow ourselves to be taught by those who see the world as it really is, we can be healed, becoming healthy and whole human beings.

practice three

Clearly Define Race

I f you want to confess your own racism, feel free. But don't
you dare accuse me of being a racist. I've had friends of color
since high school, and I care deeply for them. And . . . I live in
the most diverse neighborhood in my city. And . . . I have never
once mistreated a person of color. I am not a racist! And I don't
appreciate any insinuation that would imply otherwise."

These were the surprising words from a man who had
attended a talk I had just completed on race at an almost all-
White Christian college that was collectively grappling with this
reality. The administration asked if I would share my ongoing
journey of blindness-to-sight. They advertised it to their local
community and named it "Christian Conversations: How the
Bible Talks about White Supremacy." I was honest about my
own shortcomings in the journey and did my best to talk through
the biblical importance of every Christian confronting White
supremacy, but especially White Christians.

I ended the lecture with a closing prayer, and when I opened
my eyes, this man was already at the front of the line, waiting for
me to come down from the stage. I had talked in the first person
through the entire address, and I couldn't recall saying anything
that directly communicated that I thought he (or anyone else

for that matter) was an overt racist. But that didn't change the certainty of what he thought he heard. He restated his argument a few different ways, with the message remaining consistent: he was not a racist, and he was upset that there was even a hint of a possibility that I was grouping him with those who were.

While the heightened emotion that came with this man's plea was a clear clue that something deeper was going on with him specifically, his response also highlighted one of the primary challenges to gaining momentum in the work of confronting White supremacy: *a majority of White folks have bought into a definition of race that, while not completely wrong, is woefully deficient.*

A deficient definition of racism is not limited to this man. The prevailing definition of race in nearly every White-centric environment I have worked in has been deficient. We need to define race more precisely. We also need to learn how to differentiate our new definition from the currently established definition. I would like to start by asking two questions: (1) What is the prevailing definition of race? (2) Why is this prevailing definition so dangerous?

The Prevailing Definition of Race

This man's rebuttal illustrates how the mainstream definition functions. Though I never mentioned who is racist or not racist in my talk, that didn't stop him from being offended. Why? Because he had mapped his definition of race onto mine.

The prevailing definition of racism is wrapped around the idea of individuals who commit bad or good behaviors. Said negatively, racists are bad people who engage in bad behaviors, motivated by their bad prejudices. There are lighter versions of bad, such as using inappropriate words or telling crude jokes. Then there are the more extreme versions of bad, such as engaging in outright discrimination or affiliating with an overtly White supremacist organization.

The meaning of antiracism, then, is simply the inverse. According to the spirit of this definition, the opposite of racists (bad people who do bad things) are good people who engage in good behaviors, motivated by their notions of goodness. There is a rudimentary form of good, which only means you don't do any of the bad things listed above. Then there are the exceptionally good people—people who work for a nonprofit or relocate to a poor community or become a schoolteacher in an under-resourced neighborhood. But again, the meaning remains the same—antiracism is defined in terms of individual people doing individual acts of kindness, largely for the purpose of counteracting the bad people out there doing bad things.

There really are bad people who do bad things. I am not suggesting otherwise. Individuals who act out of a prejudiced motivation are legitimate threats to those they scorn. There are also good people who do good things to alleviate the problems created by racism. This is significant. We need more of that. But this definition of racism, built on a foundation of good or bad deeds by individuals, is deeply flawed and deficient.

Why Is This Prevailing Definition So Dangerous?

I want to refer to the work of Ijeoma Oluo to spotlight the deficiency of the mainstream definition, built on good or bad behaviors. Oluo wrote a *New York Times* bestseller called *So You Want to Talk about Race*, and in it she repeatedly warns the reader to beware of defining racism through the lens of individuals with racial prejudice who then act out of that prejudice.

To demonstrate the dangers of this approach, Oluo draws an analogy to a cancer patient looking for a holistic prognosis on what she or he is facing:

> How we define racism also determines how we battle it. If we have cancer and it makes us vomit, we can commit to battling nausea and say we're fighting for our lives, even though the tumor will likely still kill us. When we look at racism simply as "any racial prejudice," we are entered into a battle to win over the hearts and minds of everyone we encounter—fighting only the symptoms of the cancerous system, not the cancer itself. This is not only an impossible task, it's a pretty useless one.
>
> Getting my neighbor to love people of color might make it easier to hang around him, but it won't do anything to combat police brutality, racial income inequality, food deserts, or the prison industrial complex.[1]

I often reflect on this quote, and the analogy of a cancerous system was the first thing that came to mind when the man in the opening story angrily confronted me about the insinuation that he was racist. While I had no reason to doubt his intentions, I couldn't help but reflect on the insufficient definition he was building his defense upon. As he told me about the friendships he had developed, and the community he lived in, and the many other good things I'm sure he was doing, all I could hear was his attempt to battle cancer by treating nausea. His love of his friends might make him easier to hang around with, but ultimately those good deeds do nothing to battle racial income inequality, food deserts, or any of the other problems Oluo mentioned.

Oluo isn't done yet. She returns to the danger of building the foundation of our antiracism work on a definition of individual prejudice and says this:

When we use only the . . . definition of racism, as any prejudice against someone based on race, we inaccurately reduce issues of race in America to a battle for the hearts and minds of individual racists—instead of seeing racists, racist behaviors, and racial oppression as part of a larger system . . .

What is important is that the impotent hatred of the virulent racist was built and nurtured by a system that has much more insidiously woven a quieter, yet no less violent, version of those same oppressive beliefs into the fabric of our society. The truth is, you don't even have to "be racist" to be a part of the racist system.

The dude shouting about "black-on-black crime" is reinforced by elected officials coding "problem neighborhoods" and promising to "clean up the streets" that surprisingly always seem to have a lot of brown and black people on them—and end with a lot of black and brown people in handcuffs. Your aunt yelling about "thugs" is echoed in our politicians talking about "super-predators" while building our school-to-prison pipelines that help ensure that the widest path available to black and brown children ends in a jail cell. But a lot of the people voting for stop-and-frisk crime bills or increased security in schools would never dream of blaming racial inequity on "black-on-black crime" or calling a young black man a "thug."[2]

I think Oluo is spot-on with how she summarizes the way that this individualized view of racism ultimately handicaps our ability to truly battle race. When we reduce issues of race in America to a battle for the hearts and minds of individual racists, we have moved away from the core of the problem. That's not to suggest, of course, that we shouldn't be concerned for the hearts and minds of people. Instead, it's emphasizing that the hope of individual conversion is not enough when it comes to doing battle with the system of race. Therefore, how we define race must address the larger system—a system that has woven racist beliefs into the very fabric of our society. If the way we define race does anything less than that, we handicap our ability to frame the true nature of the battle that lies before us.

Defining Race Clearly

It's an intimidating task for everyday folks to attempt to define race in a holistic manner. Whenever I attempt to define race clearly, I face a primary challenge. It is likely the same challenge you will face when engaging in this pursuit. There is real tension that comes with defining race, because race is complex, with many layers and dimensions to it. Most of us should sign up at a top university for a rigorous semester studying the history of race to get an adequate understanding. Even then, we'd barely scratch the surface.

That being said, there is also a significant risk that comes when the complexity of the task stops us from working toward defining race in an accessible way. We all live, work, and serve in White spaces that are built on this mainstream yet flawed definition of race. We need to recognize there is much to learn about race and avoid giving overly simplistic definitions that neglect the deeper dimensions. We also must find ways to develop accessible pathways to understanding race in a more holistic manner, so that those who are genuinely open to learning can keep progressing on their learning journey. Our definition must embrace both sides of this tension.

When opportunities to present a holistic definition of race arise, I believe it's important to take advantage of them. We can't carry around a PowerPoint presentation in our pocket or always tell the inquiring person that they should go to a week-long antiracist workshop. Yet by committing these four words to memory—*construct*, *narrative*, *systems*, and *evil*—I've been able to use them in all kinds of situations, and I believe you can too.[3]

Word One: Race Is a Social *Construct*

This is the foundation on which the other three dimensions rest. Since the idea of race as a construct is one that tends to be uniquely confusing for White people—especially White Christians—I will share a bit of my own journey with this concept.

When my racial awakening journey began, I lived and worked in an all-White setting. I quickly realized this would be a less-than-ideal environment for going deeper into my learning journey, so I set off on a quest for mentors who would consider investing in my journey. It took time, but I eventually developed relationships with a pair of mentors who agreed to tutor me on the deeper meaning of race. Both started the process in the same place. These mentors told me that if I ever hoped to gain a deeper understanding, I would need to fully wrap my head around this very concept, namely, that race is a social construct.

This confused me on many levels. I kept getting stuck on how the notion of race as a social construct seemed to conflict with my theological convictions. My starting point was a deep belief that God was the author of life and that the creation of human beings was an inherently divine function. So I resisted the notion, assuming we had a difference of opinion as to where the human experience began.

But it turned out I was completely wrong. Neither of them was challenging my theological conviction, and neither saw my conviction as something that should distract me from facing the reality that race is a human-made construct. To help get me moving in the right direction, they gave me an exercise that proved to be enormously helpful. They showed me that one of the ways to most clearly get to the meaning of race as a social construct is to create a mental delineation between two words: *ethnicity* and *race*. This was groundbreaking for me. For most of the White folks I've worked with, this distinction has been helpful as well.

Ethnicity

People identify with each other based on commonalities such as language, history, ancestry, nationality, customs, cuisine, and art. This identification indicates one's ethnicity. In her wonderful book titled *Beyond Colorblind*, Sarah Shin writes, "White Americans have often thought of themselves as not having an ethnicity, as if *ethnic* is a politically correct term replacing *people of color*. But the Greek word *ethnos* means the nations, and we each are descendants of *ethnos* . . . None are excluded from the invitation to recognize their ethnicity and invite Jesus in."[4]

As opposed to the construct of race, which we'll discuss below, *ethnicity is a reflection of God's design*. In Acts 17, for instance, Paul spoke to the people of Athens about the sovereign nature of the way God created the world and finished his thought by saying, "From one man he made all the nations [*ethnos*], that they should inhabit the whole earth; and he marked out their appointed times in history and the boundaries of their lands" (Acts 17:26).

From this verse, and from passages like it, we see that our ethnic heritage is a reflection of Jesus' very self, and that the ethnic heritage we were born into reflects God's sovereign hand in human history. It's important to remember that while the cultures that emerge from these collective commonalities will always be imperfect (because human nature is such), ethnicity is nonetheless a reflection of God's sovereign design. Moreover, it's clear from biblical wisdom that ethnic differences are not just something we experience on earth—they remain part of our resurrected and redeemed experience in eternity. In Revelation 7:9, when describing the nature of humankind in the resurrected state, the author writes, "After this I looked, and there before me was a great multitude that no one could count, from every nation [*ethnos*], tribe, people and language, standing before the throne and before the Lamb." Professor and theologian Dr. Walter Strickland writes, "Ethnicity will come with us to heaven—race will not."⁵

Race

It often surprises people to learn that race is a relatively young human construct. One of my favorite books on race, *The Color of Compromise*, presents a historical overview of the construct, as well as the ways that Christians supported the development of this construct. When addressing how historically young the construct of race is, Dr. Jemar Tisby explains:

> Race has been so inscribed into American society that nowadays it is hard to imagine another reality. But in the early decades of European contact with North America, the racial caste system had not yet been developed. Race is a social construct. There is no biological basis for the superiority or inferiority of any human being based on the amount of melanin in her or his skin. The development of the idea of race required the intentional actions of people in the social, political, and religious spheres to decide that skin color determined who would be enslaved and who would be free. Over time Europeans, including Christians, wrote the laws and formed the habits that concentrated power in the hands of those they considered "white" while withholding equality from those they considered "black."⁶

Dr. Tiffany Potter is a professor of eighteenth-century studies at the University of British Columbia. When teaching on race, she too emphasizes the relative newness of this construct.

Not every race scholar pinpoints the origin of race to this exact date, but most certainly agree that this is the essential time period when the construct began to solidify:

> The term "race," as we know it, did not exist before approximately 1749, when French scientist Georges Le Clerc, Comte de Buffon, used it to describe what already existed as notations of cultural difference in studies such as that of Swedish naturalist Carl von Linné. Linné removed the quality of reason from the definition of the human species and divided the species "Homo" into Europaeus, Americanus, Asiaticus, and Africanus (just as all other species might be divided). As Nicholas Hudson and Roxanne Wheeler have documented, it was not until the 1770s that "complexion emerged as the most powerful testament to the new value accorded to visible racialized differences."[7]

Besides its newness, the other big idea from the summary above is the clarity that human beings are the ones who created race—not God! And to make it even worse, we designed it for purely evil reasons: to justify the barbaric realities of both settler conquest and transatlantic slavery.[8]

Let's look to the words of some of the prominent activists, intellectuals, and theologians writing on race to develop this point. Dr. Michelle Alexander is a renowned writer, civil rights advocate, visiting professor at Union Theological Seminary, and author of the seminal book *The New Jim Crow*. She talks unflinchingly when describing the evil motivations behind the creation of this construct:

> The concept of race is a relatively recent development. Only in the past few centuries, owing largely to European imperialism, have the world's people been classified along

racial lines. Here, in America, the idea of race emerged as a means of reconciling chattel slavery—as well as the extermination of American Indians—with the ideals of freedom preached by whites in the new colonies.[9]

She adds some commentary to this description of the construct of race, and I appreciate both her candor and her depth. She writes, "It may be impossible to overstate the significance of race in defining the basic structure of American society. The structure and content of the original Constitution was based largely on the effort to preserve a racial caste system—slavery—while at the same time affording political and economic rights to whites, especially propertied whites."[10]

Dr. Audrey Smedley, a professor of anthropology at Virginia Commonwealth University, writes about the motivations behind the design of the construct of race:

> Race and its ideology about human differences arose out of the context of African slavery . . .
>
> In the latter part of the 17th century the demand for labor grew enormously. It had become clear that neither Irishmen nor Indians made good slaves. More than that, the real threats to social order were the poor freed whites who demanded lands and privileges that the upper class colonial governments refused. Some colonial leaders argued that turning to African labor provided a buffer against the masses of poor whites.[11]

One of America's foremost public theologians, Dr. Cornel West, offers important commentary on this subject as well. In his seminal book *Race Matters*, Dr. West describes the construct of race, built on Black oppression and degradation, as the linchpin of American democracy:

White Lies

Yet the enslavement of Africans—over 20 percent of the population—served as the linchpin of American democracy; that is, the much-heralded stability and continuity of American democracy was predicated upon black oppression and degradation. Without the presence of black people in America, European-Americans would not be "white"— they would be only Irish, Italians, Poles, Welsh, and others engaged in class, ethnic, and gender struggles over resources and identity. What made America distinctly American for them was not simply the presence of unprecedented opportunities, but the struggle for seizing these opportunities in a new land in which black slavery and racial caste served as the floor upon which white class, ethnic, and gender struggles could be diffused and diverted. In other words, white poverty could be ignored and whites' paranoia of each other could be overlooked primarily owing to the distinctive American feature: the basic racial divide of black and white peoples. From 1776 to 1964 . . . this racial divide would serve as a basic presupposition for the expansive functioning of American democracy, even as the concentration of wealth and power remained in the hands of a few well-to-do white men.[12]

The social construct of race is the foundation on which the other dimensions of race rest. Unlike ethnicity, which is a reflection of God's creation, the construct of race was created by human beings.

Seeing race as a construct that was created with expressly evil intentions helps us keep the terminology clear when talking about race. For instance, I regularly hear well-meaning White Christians say, "God did not create multiple races. There is just one race—the human race." While I understand the sentiment behind this, I also do my best to gently remind people that talking like this contributes to the problem of mix-matching distinct terms

64

like *ethnicity* and *race*. It's important to see that God deplores the creation of the construct of race, because it represents a direct assault on God's beloved image bearers. *Race is a by-product of human depravity, not the creation of a good and gracious God.*

The distinction between ethnicity and race is also a critical building block for understanding White supremacy. Typically, when White supremacy gets critiqued, those of us who are White become instantly defensive. One of the primary reasons we feel this way is the lack of distinction between ethnicity and race. A sign that a White Christian is maturing in their understanding of White supremacy is when they can simultaneously embrace the fact that they are fearfully and wonderfully made (Psalm 139:14)—which includes their appointed time in history (Acts 17:26)—*and* that White supremacy is a horrible social convention that must be confronted and dismantled. Those ideas are not in conflict with each other.

It's of the utmost importance for White people to learn to see this fundamental contrast between ethnicity and race. Here's a summary of these contrasting realities:

- Ethnicity has been around for as long as humans have; race is relatively new.
- Ethnicity is a reflection of God's design; race is a reflection of humanity's design.
- Ethnicity is a reflection of a good God; race is a reflection of the most depraved and wicked parts of humanity.
- Ethnicity is something that can be redeemed and celebrated; race cannot be redeemed and must be dismantled.

Word Two: Race Operates by a *Narrative* of Racial Hierarchy

What gives the construct of race so much staying power is the *narrative of racial hierarchy*. This phrase has a long history, but it has become more recently popularized by Bryan Stevenson, the founder of the Equal Justice Initiative (we'll examine his work more closely in the next chapter). The narrative of racial hierarchy is the functional operating system of White supremacy, so it is a critically important phrase to understand. To bring greater clarity, let's break the phrase into two parts.

First, *narrative*. The dictionary defines *narrative* as "a way of presenting or understanding a situation or series of events that reflects and promotes *a particular point of view or set of values*."[13] The construct of race wouldn't survive without an organized and dedicated campaign to promote a certain story of why the construct was needed in the first place. There was a particular point of view that the narrative was designed to promote.

Second, *hierarchy*. What was the point of view that the narrative was designed to propagate? In a word, the story of race has always been one of hierarchy. When explaining race in his book *How to Be an Antiracist*, Dr. Ibram Kendi says it fundamentally rests on two ideas: "that the races are meaningfully different in their biology and that these differences create a *hierarchy of value*."[14] In order for White supremacy to survive, the construct of race needed a believable set of lies that presented the situation of human value as one determined by where human beings were placed by God in this racial hierarchy.

We will explore the narrative of racial hierarchy over the next two chapters, but for the purposes of defining race well, I simply propose this question: Why was this set of lies so badly needed? Why were those in power so dependent on the narrative to spread their point of view?

It would be hard to find a clearer answer than *greed*. In 1 Timothy 6:10, the apostle Paul warns that "the love of money is a root of all kinds of evil. Some people, eager for money, have wandered from the faith and pierced themselves with many griefs." That warning feels incredibly applicable to the construct of race, since race has always been tied to economics, as well as to the desire to possess more material resources. It is no coincidence that the two most significant forms of oppression our country has ever seen are also the two most profitable: conquest and slavery. We could not have become the economic superpower we are today without the conquest of the Native people and the enslavement of Black people.

Though greed and self-interest would have been the more honest way to describe the rise of America into its position as a global power,[15] that narrative did not mesh well with the emerging story of manifest destiny.[16] So an alternative narrative was created, based on the construct of race, that tried to develop a logic for the utter domination and subjugation European settlers imposed on Native and Black people in America. The only way these horrors could be portrayed in a morally palatable manner was to relentlessly describe Native people as intrinsically savage and Black people as inherently inferior.

Let's consider a snapshot of each people group and the way the narrative was used to create a form of propaganda that justified their treatment.

The narrative and Native people (conquest). The initial draw to America was the promise that Europeans could acquire free land from "sea to shining sea."[17] This was an inevitable recipe for a bloody conflict, since this "free" land was already inhabited by millions of Native people. And of course that's exactly what happened. The colonial era unleashed a reign of terror, and Native people endured an onslaught of massacres, military occupations, removal from ancestral territories, sexual abuse, forced removal of their children to boarding schools, and disease. The atrocities decimated the population. Historian Donald Fixico writes, "By the close of the Indian Wars in the late 19th century, fewer than 238,000 indigenous people remained, a sharp decline from the estimated 5 million to 15 million living in North America when Columbus arrived in 1492."[18]

If you were a European immigrant during that era and saw what was happening to Native people, surely your moral compass must have screamed out for justice, right? But whatever outrage was present was eventually drowned out by the narrative of racial hierarchy. The propaganda behind this narrative was incredibly vigorous, and a nonstop message was communicated that pitted the superiority of White European people against the looming danger that Native people represented to their (our) way of life. One of the most common depictions of Natives was as *savages*, a word typically reserved for animals that were fierce, violent, and uncontrolled.[19]

The Declaration of Independence also reveals the centrality of the narrative, as it was aimed at Native people. One of the most celebrated lines in the document that established our nation is its articulation of the following fundamental ideas: "We hold these Truths to be self-evident, that all Men are created equal, that they are endowed by their Creator with certain unalienable Rights, that among these are Life, Liberty, and the Pursuit of Happiness."[20]

But the same document later states this: "[The present King of Great-Britain] . . . has endeavoured to bring on the Inhabitants of our Frontiers, *the merciless Indian Savages*, whose known Rule of Warfare, is an undistinguished Destruction, of all Ages, Sexes and Conditions" (emphasis added).[21]

Dr. Michelle Alexander accurately points out the power of this narrative: "Eliminating 'savages' is less of a moral problem than eliminating human beings."[22] This is the exact narrative used in the Declaration of Independence. Not only were Native people excluded from unalienable rights, but they were depicted as "merciless Indian Savages." In contrast, White people were called "Inhabitants of our Frontiers," which portrayed them as the more deserving, superior group of people who needed to defend the land against the merciless savages. That is a powerful and diabolical story line.

The narrative and Black people (slavery). The conquest of the American frontier was not the only instance in which the social construct of race was leveraged to justify and validate behaviors that would otherwise be considered barbaric. The American economic project didn't just require free land; it needed an unpaid labor force. The insatiable appetite for free labor fueled the rapid ascension of the transatlantic slave trade.

Over a three-hundred-year period the transatlantic slave trade transported an estimated 11 million Africans to the Americas in one of the most astonishing forced human migrations in history. Everything about the process was terrifying. It would begin with enslavers marching their captives hundreds of miles to the western coast of Africa, the slaves tied together with wooden yokes around their necks. Then slave traders would rip families apart and sell them separately to slave ships heading to the Americas. Slaves endured a nightmarish two- to three-month journey across the Atlantic, often shackled together and in life-threatening conditions—all so that the American economy (as well as other countries' economies) could maintain rapid growth.

Just as a narrative was needed in order to justify the conquest of Native people, so too a narrative was needed in order to justify the enslavement of Black people.[23] A narrative was developed and broadcast about the inherent superiority of White people and the inherent inferiority of Native and Black people.[24]

The survival of the construct of race depended on the social propaganda that came from the narrative of racial hierarchy. This narrative was initially created to justify the horrendous conditions that led to our national rise as an economic superpower, and the narrative has become only more entrenched and ingrained into the fiber of our country since then. As time has gone on, the narrative has expanded beyond Native peoples and Africans to also evaluate the human worth of other groups of color, based on their proximity to White superiority or Black inferiority. This narrative is what made the system of race so deadly in our early history, and it is what allows race to remain deadly in our modern society.

Word Three: Race Inflicts Its Damage through *Systems*

Let's return to the man who was offended by my presentation on race. His response went beyond just personal defensiveness; it provided an illuminating example of what happens when someone operates off of the mainstream definition of *racism*. As we examine systemic racism, we'll see that the deficits of the mainstream definition become even more obvious. While individual actions matter, focusing too much on them serves to distract us from the far more serious threat. Ultimately, the biggest problems facing our society around race are not individuals doing bad things, but the profound inequities that are perpetuated and advanced by systemic racism.

Let's start with a definition of systemic racism so we're all on the same page. Dr. Joe Feagin is a professor at Texas A&M University, author of more than sixty books, and a well-respected sociologist. His definition is regularly referenced within the social sciences and humanities, and in his book *Racist America*, he defines it like this:

> Systemic racism includes the complex array of antiblack practices, the unjustly gained political-economic power of whites, the continuing economic and other resource inequalities along racial lines, and the white racist ideologies and attitudes created to maintain and rationalize white privilege and power. *Systemic* here means that the core racist realities are manifested in each of society's major parts . . . Like a hologram, each major part of U.S. society—the economy, politics, education, religion, the family—reflects the fundamental reality of systemic racism.[25]

Feagin's definition highlights a couple of important features of systemic racism. First, he reinforces this important idea that *systemic racism, by definition, represents something very different from individual racism.* While individual racism is real, it is different from the categories listed here, including the economy, politics, education, family, and, yes, even religion! So when we talk about race, we should always assume an emphasis on *systems thinking* over some type of accounting process of individual behaviors.

Second, he reminds us that *when we think of racism through a systems lens,* we come to realize that *there is nowhere in this country we can go without being absolutely surrounded by this reality.* Feagin notes that when we are talking about the "systemic" aspect of race, we are talking about "the core racist realities . . . manifested in each of society's major parts." He then says something the gravity of which would be easy to miss if we don't slow down to reflect on its depth: *systemic racism is infused into each major part of United States society.* Do you see how far-reaching this definition is? Every single part of American society is shaped by a systemic racist reality. This is why we must define race in a holistic way. This is why we must think in systems.

Systemic racism is a broad topic that when thought about correctly should take us down a path that touches on almost every critical sector in society. When talking about systemic racism, for instance, we should be mindful of both the historical and present inequalities represented in the education system, the health care system, the housing system, the policing system, the legal system, the judicial system, the incarceration system, and the banking system, just to name a few. Addressing the specific challenges facing each of these systems, however, goes beyond the scope of this book (not to mention beyond the scope of my personal training), so I won't attempt to guide the discussion down each of those necessary pathways. What I would like to emphasize within this section, though, is the high degree of difficulty that leaders in Christian spaces will face when trying to get White folks to engage with the idea of systemic racism.

One of the classic works describing this high degree of difficulty is *Divided by Faith*, a landmark book (particularly in the evangelical community) written in 2000 by sociologists Michael Emerson and Christian Smith. By means of a nationwide telephone survey and face-to-face interviews, they probed the grassroots of White evangelical America in an attempt to get an accurate reading on where White evangelicals were regarding race. What they found was that many White evangelicals were indeed concerned about race but thought about it in almost exclusively individualistic ways. They had been groomed to think of the problem of racism as a matter of the heart, and therefore they also saw the only solution to racism as the changing of a human heart.[26]

Given what we've covered in this chapter so far, this should not be a huge surprise. The mainstream definition of racism continues to center on individuals who engage in either good or bad deeds, so thinking of racism as strictly a condition of the heart is not that big of a leap for White evangelicals to take. What *Divided by Faith* showed through research, though, was a severe consequence of this individualized view of race: White evangelicals didn't *believe* in systemic racism. The spiritual formation they received in their White churches focused exclusively on the repentance and conversion of the sinful individuals at fault, and as such, the pervasive injustice that perpetuates racial inequality remained unseen and invisible to White congregants.

Any thoughtful consideration of transformation will include the changing of a human heart, so that is not necessarily problematic in and of itself. The problem that *Divided by Faith* so clearly illuminated was that this emphasis on individual heart change came almost fully at the expense of a commensurate focus on systemic transformation. This is extremely problematic on many levels. It not only leaves the White Christian oblivious to the larger systemic problems created and reinforced through the narrative of racial hierarchy but also leaves them feeling that the work of racial justice is done as long as they have repented of any personal sins they can think of.

Unfortunately, the story around this sight gap between individual and systemic only appears to get worse over time. In 2015—fifteen years after *Divided by Faith* had been published—a trio of researchers set out to study the impact that multiracial churches had in closing this gap for White Christians. Writing for the journal *Sociology of Religion*, they reported their discouraging findings.[27] When it came to the blindness-to-sight journey of White Christians, the article revealed that proximity to Christians of color had virtually no impact on how they viewed the reality of systemic racism.

If that weren't bad enough, the three researchers discovered something else troubling. When Christians of color get proximate to White Christians, it is actually the Christians of color who find their views evolving. An article in *Christianity Today* states, "The study found that 72 percent of African Americans in predominantly black churches believe that the reasons for racial inequality are structural, rather than an individual's lack of motivation. But only about half (53 percent) of African Americans in multiracial churches believe the same thing. That percentage closely tracks with whites and Hispanics in multiracial congregations, 54 percent of whom believe racial inequality is structural."[28]

Kevin Dougherty, a Baylor sociology professor and one of the study's authors, is quoted by *Christianity Today* as saying, "The typical African American outside of the multiracial congregation is fairly aware that there are structural issues in place that continue to perpetuate inequality . . . But African Americans within multiracial churches don't report that same level of structural awareness." Dougherty then summarized the findings of the study in a single, haunting sentence: "Instead of the predominantly white majority changing its views, it appears that African Americans start to think more like whites about the origins of inequality."

When I read that quote from Dougherty, I again think of the metaphor from Ijeoma Oluo: "When we look at racism simply as 'any racial prejudice,' we are entered into a battle to win over the hearts and minds of everyone we encounter—fighting only the symptoms of the cancerous system, not the cancer itself. This is not only an impossible task, it's a pretty useless one."[29]

This is the dual challenge facing leaders in White Christian spaces. Not only must we convince White Christians to see the systemic realities of race; we also must work to prevent White-centric views of race from transforming the thinking of those who would see it otherwise. We must define race in a way that illuminates its systemic nature.

Word Four: Race Is Sustained by Supernatural *Evil*

The fourth dimension of race has been hinted at throughout each of the first three points, but it's such a major component that it deserves its own heading within the larger definition. At its most fundamental level, race is *evil*. Failure to acknowledge this dimension of race puts us at risk of skipping right past that which makes this deadly system so powerful.

Though there was nothing akin to White supremacy during biblical times, I feel confident that the apostle Paul would classify this dangerous ideology within the same cosmic structure as that which he located other evil strongholds: "Our struggle is not against flesh and blood, but against the rulers, against the authorities, against the powers of this dark world and against the spiritual forces of evil in the heavenly realms" (Ephesians 6:12).

I'm convinced we cannot understand the true depths of White supremacy if we don't learn to view it through this type of cosmic lens. In the same way that the presence of God points to supernatural good in the world, so the presence of Satan points to supernatural evil in the world. I will develop this idea in a much more robust way in chapter 5. But to conclude this chapter, I urge us to remember that while White supremacy absolutely is an ideology used to create, sustain, and justify oppressive social systems, it is not *just* an ideology. White supremacy also represents a spiritual principality developed, guarded, and protected by supernatural evil.

practice four

Attack the Narrative

It is January 1984 in a small town in rural Georgia. The death penalty has been outlawed for years, but the state of Georgia reinstated it in 1973. It is here that the movie *Just Mercy* opens, and we are immediately introduced to Bryan Stevenson, a role played to near perfection by Michael B. Jordan. The arc of the story is headed toward Stevenson's eventual founding of the Equal Justice Initiative, as well as his rise to becoming a national thought leader on racial justice. But in this moment, Stevenson is still a nervous law student from Harvard. He has recently taken on an internship with the Southern Prisoners Defense Committee (SPDC), and one of their priorities is attending to the reinstated death penalty. They are working tirelessly to respond to the daily calls they're receiving from inmates who have been scheduled for execution.

That's where Stevenson comes in. He was sent by SPDC to locate one of these inmates, a man named Henry, to inform him of his status. SPDC did not yet have the resources to assign a lawyer, but they wanted Henry to know that they were at least able to confirm that his execution would not happen in the next calendar year.

As Bryan Stevenson sits in the car on his long drive to this rural prison, he wonders what the encounter with Henry will be like. He has no idea how Henry will receive him, and as such, he begins to rehearse multiple versions of his introduction speech.

When the time comes for them to finally meet, the filmmaker takes us up close to Stevenson so we can watch the progression of his emotional responses. The first is *surprise*, as Stevenson is taken aback by how young Henry is. He was aware of his age from the file, but seeing this young man in person creates a completely different experience. Henry looks no older than Stevenson himself, and his demeanor reminds Stevenson of many of the friends and family he grew up with.

The second emotional response is one of *sorrow*. The reality of the fate that awaits Henry begins to sink in. Added to that, Stevenson thinks of Henry's ongoing separation from his wife and children, the nonexistent legal representation he has received up until now, and the subpar treatment he is experiencing in the prison. In this state of sadness, all Stevenson seems to be able to muster is a repetitive version of "I'm sorry."

Finally, after much stammering over his words, Stevenson finds the clarity to articulate the single message he was sent to deliver to Henry: *You are not going to die this year.*

To Stevenson's surprise, Henry's response is one of exuberant joy. Henry had recently been avoiding contact with his wife and children due to the possibility of his imminent death, but with this news, a sudden wave of liberation comes rushing in. Henry grabs Stevenson's hand to express his deep relief, and from there they dive into immediate and deep conversation. The chemistry between them is palpable, and they end up talking for more than three hours.

The beauty of the connection comes to a sudden and abrupt end when the prison guard reenters the room. He brusquely shackles Henry's wrists and ankles, to the point that Henry is in obvious pain. Stevenson is dismayed by the excessive use of force and begs the guard to loosen the cuffs. But the guard completely ignores him.

Stevenson continues to search for a way to meaningfully intervene, but Henry assures him the efforts are unnecessary. "It's okay, Bryan," Henry tells him. "Don't worry about this. Just come back and see me again, okay?" Stevenson agrees and watches with amazement as Henry demonstrates grace, strength, and resiliency in the midst of such a seemingly impossible moment.

As the guard drags Henry out of the room, something happens to Stevenson that seals the significance of this moment. Henry begins to sing at the top of his lungs, and the words grab hold of something deep in Stevenson. They are the lyrics to "Higher Ground," a hymn that Stevenson had often heard in his own church upbringing:

> *I'm pressing on the upward way,*
> *New heights I'm gaining every day;*
> *Still praying as I'm onward bound,*
> *Lord, plant my feet on higher ground.*
>
> *Lord, lift me up and let me stand*
> *By faith on Heaven's tableland;*
> *A higher plane than I have found,*
> *Lord, plant my feet on higher ground.*[1]

This encounter serves as the catalyst to confirm Stevenson's call to dedicate his life to a passionate and permanent pursuit of racial justice. From there, *Just Mercy* (both the film and the best-selling memoir it is based on) follows the true story of Stevenson as he eventually graduates from Harvard, turns down a litany of lucrative jobs, and heads to Alabama to defend wrongly condemned prisoners (or those who were not afforded proper representation) on death row. The story focuses on one particular man who was the recipient of a grave miscarriage of justice and who ends up condemned on death row.

The man's name is Walter McMillian, and his character is powerfully portrayed by Jamie Foxx. Despite a mountain of evidence to the contrary, McMillian has been condemned to death for the murder of a young White woman who worked as a clerk in a dry-cleaning store in Monroeville, Alabama. Dozens of alibi witnesses had come forth to verify that McMillian was at a church event eleven miles away at the time of the murder, and yet the nearly all-White jury convicted Mr. McMillian of capital murder and sentenced him to life imprisonment without parole.

The movie continues by charting the multitude of legal and political barriers that Stevenson and the Equal Justice Initiative (EJI) must maneuver as they seek justice for McMillian. Eventually, McMillian is released, but not before surviving six agonizing years on death row for a crime he did not commit. It is a moving story that highlights the formidable obstacles that often stand in the way of justice. It also showcases the power that, in the words of Dr. Martin Luther King Jr., comes from "the vision to see that injustice must be rooted out by strong, persistent, and determined action."[2]

The story that *Just Mercy* tells of Mr. McMillian's false conviction and eventual exoneration brought an important contribution to the larger discourse around race in America, for which I am thankful. Just as importantly, the commercial success of *Just Mercy*, as well as the subsequent interviews with Michael B. Jordan, Jamie Foxx, and Bryan Stevenson, brought a new level of national attention and focus to the subject matter of this chapter—*the narrative of racial hierarchy*.

The scope of the work that Stevenson and EJI have embarked on in their quest for justice is remarkable. Each of their three umbrella categories of social impact—criminal justice reform, racial justice, and public education—is worth exploring and learning more about.[3] Beyond admiration for the whole body of work that defines their impact, what makes Stevenson such a sought-after speaker, teacher, and lecturer is the precision with which he is able to pinpoint the root of all of these social evils. He repetitively points out that it is the narrative of racial hierarchy that allowed these systems to form in the first place, and it's the narrative that continues to fuel their momentum. "I think the North won the Civil War," Stevenson regularly says, "but the South won the narrative war." As such, the narrative remains a set of evil lies that continue to wreak havoc throughout our nation. If we ever hope to actualize any real racial justice and equity in our country, we are going to have to find a way to collectively attack the narrative, dismantle it, and then rebuild on the truthful narratives that come only from God.

"Why Do We Need to Keep Talking about Slavery?"

When I speak of the transformation that comes from interacting with Bryan Stevenson's precise thinking around the narrative of racial hierarchy, I do so from firsthand experience. My most vivid encounter with this came in a training Stevenson did with a group of pastors, most of whom were White. As Stevenson talked about this "narrative war," he continually tied the origins of the narrative to the advent of slavery.

After hearing this connection one too many times, one of the pastors in attendance finally asked this question. He had been growing increasingly uncomfortable with what felt like an overemphasis on slavery and asked, "Why do we need to keep talking about slavery? I know slavery was terrible. But it has now been abolished—and largely due to the abolitionist efforts of White Christians, right? And besides, I have never personally owned slaves. In fact, my European great-grandparents have only been in America for two generations, so I don't even come from an ancestral line that owned slaves. I'm trying to find solutions to the problem of race that work here and now. Conversations around slavery just lead to anger, shame, and despair in my congregation. When we keep bringing it up, we just make things worse. I'm hoping we can find ways to move the conversation to the next level."

As the pastor finished his question, I found myself feeling both a bit embarrassed (for reasons that are probably obvious) and a bit relieved, since some version of this same question had often been posed to me by White folks wrestling with race. While I would do my best to respond, I always sensed my answer was dangerously incomplete. I knew slavery was one of the primary scourges on our national record, but I always struggled to describe the current connection in a way that made much sense. As such, I was particularly curious to see how Bryan Stevenson would address it.

Stevenson was clearly ready for this question and knew exactly where he wanted to take the group in response. He asked if we would participate in an imaginary exercise—one that would lead to an even more foundational question he hoped we would wrestle with. He asked each White pastor to imagine being alive during the time of slavery and to imagine what it was like to be pastoring White people during this era. This was obviously uncomfortable, as none of us wanted to be associated with slave owners, but he pushed us to stay with it. He urged us not to disassociate from the White people who lived at that time. They were like us in so many ways—church-attending, Bible-believing, Sunday-schooled Christians who in every other regard were doing their best to live holy lives before God.

And yet the obvious fact is that most White Christians went along with slavery. There was always a remnant that stood against it, but ultimately, slavery could continue to exist only because it received the mainstream support of White Christians. Stevenson reminded us that as part of a self-proclaimed "Christian nation," White Christians possessed a disproportionate amount of influence and power to dictate where the country moved on many social issues, particularly slavery. If at any point a critical mass of resistance would have formed, slavery would have ended much sooner. But the opposite happened. Instead of using the Bible to combat slavery, theologians twisted Scripture to defend it. Whether they pointed to the curse of Ham in Genesis 9 or to Paul's exhortations for slaves to obey their masters in Ephesians 6, White Christians used an endless series of justifications to maintain the status quo. And when that got added to the need to protect economic self-interests, the commitment to race-based slavery (Christian and not) went so deep that we ended up needing to fight a bloody Civil War over it.

This is what set up the deeper question that Stevenson wanted to pose and wanted us to wrestle with: How was it that the majority of good, White Christians—Christians who read their Bible, who went to church every Sunday, and who were generally committed to a lifestyle of holiness—had reconciled the teachings of the Bible with the practice of slavery? How had White human beings who followed Jesus convinced themselves it was okay to own Black human beings?

A deafening silence enveloped the room in answer to this question. As we sat there reflecting, Stevenson shared his hypothesis. The only answer that made sense—the only answer that could explain White Christian support of slavery—was the *narrative of racial hierarchy*.

That was the destination Stevenson had carefully guided us toward, and it didn't take long for us White pastors to get there. As he continued to develop his hypothesis as to why the narrative of racial hierarchy was the ultimate root of the problem, there was a collective awakening in the room. We began to realize that though slavery was a profoundly grotesque *social* system of injustice, what sustained it was ultimately a *dark and powerful spiritual reality*. The narrative of racial hierarchy, created largely to justify slavery, functioned like a rival deity. It had been erected with the specific intention of attacking the very pinnacle of God's creation—human beings fashioned in the likeness and image of God's very self. God had been declaring one story about human worth since the dawn of creation, but this rival god now declared a contrary story. And despite being good, Bible-believing Christians, almost every White person in the United States chose to put their faith in the false story of the narrative over the true story of God's creative essence. Stevenson challenged us to see the full impact of the narrative. He challenged us to honestly consider whether we had really made much, if any, progress in the necessary unveiling and confronting of this exact same narrative in modern times.

It would be hard to overstate what happened to me that day. Like Paul, who saw for the first time when Ananias prayed for the scales to be removed from his eyes, I could suddenly see the stakes of this "narrative battle" that waged before us. I realized it wasn't just the White Christians in the early nineteenth century who were caught in the battle between good and evil. We as White Christians—here and now—are caught in the midst of this same battle.

Examining the Narrative

In the last chapter, we looked at the narrative of racial hierarchy as a carefully constructed set of lies that communicate a story of human value based on the color of one's skin. Based on this set of lies, the superiority of Whiteness is elevated to the top of the hierarchy, and the inferiority of Blackness is relegated to the bottom.

Dr. Chanequa Walker-Barnes, who wrote an insightful book on race titled *I Bring the Voices of My People*, highlights this role that the narrative plays as part of the overall structure of White supremacy:

> An important feature of White supremacy is that it rank-orders the value of humanity based on proximity to whiteness. The closer one is to whiteness, the more value she is believed to have. This rank ordering has taken various forms and rationales over time, evolving to incorporate newly immigrating ethnic groups. One thing that has remained constant in the racial hierarchy has been that Black identity is always on the bottom. This is why the Black-White binary is important in racial reconciliation. While people of color broadly are victimized by racism, the forms and degree of victimization vary based upon where each racial/ethnic group is grafted along the Black-White continuum.[4]

This is the essential idea that Stevenson is getting at when he talks of the "narrative war." In a helpful article titled "What Well-Meaning White People Need to Know about Race," Stevenson describes it like this:

> I genuinely believe that, despite all of that victimization, the worst part of slavery was this narrative that we created about black people—this idea that black people aren't fully human, that they are three-fifths human, that they are not capable, that they are not evolved. That ideology, which set up White supremacy in America, was the most poisonous and destructive consequence of two centuries of slavery. And I do believe that we never addressed it. I think the North won the Civil War, but the South won

the narrative war. The racial-equality principle that is in our Constitution was never extended to formerly enslaved people, and that is why I say slavery didn't end in 1865. It evolved.[5]

Three ideas in this quote are worth examining and will set the stage for the concrete action steps we need to take as we prepare to attack the narrative. The first idea is one that Stevenson also alluded to in the story above—the link between slavery and the narrative. There is an almost unending list of terrible things that came from slavery: rape, molestation, torture, murder, theft, kidnapping, and a host of other evils. Stevenson fully acknowledges all of these evils and has even built a museum to ignite a national conversation around the importance of recognizing this history.[6] But as evil as all of these are, Stevenson continues to provoke our national consciousness around the fact that what held all these destructive evils together was the narrative. Notice the serious language he uses as he introduces this thought: "The *worst part* of slavery was this narrative that we created about Black people—this idea that Black people aren't fully human, that they are three-fifths human, that they are not capable, that they are not evolved."

The second idea is the way the narrative of racial hierarchy "set up" the ideology of White supremacy. While scholars debate how far back the origins of White supremacy go, most would agree with Stevenson that the era of slavery is when the narrative of racial hierarchy became the functional operating system of White supremacy. It was at this point in human history that the narrative was essentially "created," in the words of Stevenson. One of the clear implications is this: If you want to understand the ideology of White supremacy, you must understand the narrative of racial hierarchy. And if you want to understand the narrative of racial hierarchy, you must understand slavery. The two are forever bound in history. And the two are forever linked to the future vision of justice that we move toward.

The third and final idea that is of vital importance is this notion that we should think of this work as a "narrative war." This language introduces a very different paradigm for combating race from some of the more common paradigms we have explored in earlier chapters, such as the pursuit of diversity or the management of the good versus bad behaviors associated with racist/antiracist efforts. While both of these have their place, they remain ineffective when they fail to locate themselves within this narrative battle over human value and dignity.

On one side of this narrative war is God, declaring the glory of the *imago Dei*. Latin for "the image of God," this is the majestic truth that all human beings are created in the image and likeness of God and therefore have infinite value and worth. The narrative of the *imago Dei* begins on the opening page of Scripture, when the creation account tells us that "God created mankind in his own image, in the image of God he created them; male and female he created them" (Genesis 1:27). The narrative of the *imago Dei* is what leads us to a true and transforming experience of loving ourselves and loving our neighbor. The narrative of the *imago Dei* is what caused King David to reflect and say, "What is mankind that you are mindful of them, human beings that you care for them? You have made them a little lower than the angels and crowned them with glory and honor" (Psalm 8:4–5).

On the other side of this narrative war is a rival god who challenges the true humanity of God's image bearers at every step of the journey. Through the narrative of racial hierarchy, this force for evil sneered at the biblical account and redefined human value along the axis of a racial caste system. Rather than seeing all human beings as image bearers created in the likeness of God, this narrative linked human worth to supposed divine positioning on the hierarchy of race. This evil narrative lied to us then, and it lies to us now. It lies to White people, telling us we represent the apex of human value. It lies to Black people, telling them they represent the opposite. It lies to non-Black people of color, telling them their value can only be attained through proximity to Whiteness. The message has always been evil, and it represents a full-fledged and ongoing narrative war.

Attacking the Narrative

What does it look like to attack the narrative? This theme will be repeatedly referenced in the following practices, but I'd like to specifically explore three ways I believe we can and must live out this practice in an immediate fashion:

1. Name the narrative as the sin that is lurking at our door.
2. Identify the narrative as the link between historical injustice and modern incarnations.
3. Link systemic justice to the narrative battle.

Name the Narrative as the Sin Lurking at Our Door

The first time the Bible uses the word *sin* comes as part of a vivid object lesson in Genesis 4. The recipient of the lesson is Cain, who we come to discover is growing increasingly angry with his brother, Abel. We are not told all of the details of what incited this growing rage, but what's clear is that God sees Cain barreling toward the precipice of something foolish as a result. Rather than passively allowing Cain to walk down a path of destruction, however, God decides to actively initiate a loving intervention. God wants Cain to know that God sees Cain's frustration and anger, and that these escalating feelings can and should be brought to God. God also wants Cain to know that the temptation to violently act out his feelings of anger will only lead to harmful consequences and therefore urges Cain to reconsider his plans. The loving intervention climaxes with a warning, and the warning doubles as our introduction to the word *sin*:

> Then the LORD said to Cain, "Why are you angry? Why is your face downcast? If you do what is right, will you not be accepted? But if you do not do what is right, sin is crouching at your door; it desires to have you, but you must rule over it."
>
> *Genesis 4:6–7*

Two features of this description feel deeply significant. These features help us to understand sin in general and also provide a template for theologically categorizing the narrative of racial hierarchy.

Feature 1: Sin functions like a predator. The traditional definition of *sin* often focuses on behaviors and obedient living, and that makes sense. But in the introduction to the word *sin*, we get something that is much more far-reaching than keeping or breaking rules. Here sin is depicted in an almost personal manner, with the analogy suggesting a function similar to a hunter in the wild. The Hebrew word used is the same one that describes a predator slowly stalking its prey before eventually striking. As such, sin here sounds more like something we would witness in the animal kingdom than something we witness when someone breaks a rule—even a big one. This metaphor depicts sin as being powered by a darkness that desires our ultimate destruction, which, unfortunately, is exactly what happened to Cain.

Feature 2: Sin hides. If it's not already scary enough to see sin depicted as a predator, we also see that sin intentionally disguises its threat level in the hope of lulling its prey into a false sense of comfort. Even though God compares sin to a predator on the prowl, it's interesting to see that it's not one that is strutting around in the open, flaunting its strength. Instead, this fearsome hunter is coiled in the corner, just out of sight. He is crouching down, waiting for the opportune time to pounce. This is a significant detail, because it gets to the crux of what went wrong. God warns Cain about the danger represented by this predator, but also reassures Cain that as long as he takes the danger seriously, victory will be his. Failure to rule over it would come only through the choice to be willfully ignorant of its threat. Through this analogy, we see both the positive truth—that we can rule over and defeat sin—and the warning: the only way sin becomes powerful is when we choose to treat it as powerless.

The image of a deadly predator disguising itself as a harmless threat seems like the perfect way to describe the sin represented by the narrative of racial hierarchy. In the same way that Cain's unchecked sin led to the death of his brother Abel, so too has the unchecked sin of the narrative led to the death of our brothers and sisters of color. Cain's murder of Abel led to God saying, "What have you done? Listen! Your brother's blood cries out to me from the ground . . . which opened its mouth to receive your brother's blood from your hand" (Genesis 4:10–11). I believe God would say the same thing to the church in regard to the ways we have passively allowed the sin of the narrative to go historically unchallenged and to create the conditions for so much bloodshed.

During the age of conquest, the sin of the narrative lurked, and hundreds of thousands of Native people were killed. *Their blood cries out to God from the ground.*

During the age of slavery, the sin of the narrative lurked, and hundreds of thousands of African people were raped, molested, tortured, and murdered. *Their blood cries out to God from the ground.*

During the age of lynching, the sin of the narrative lurked, and more than 4,700 people were hanged, drowned, and burned alive.[7] *Their blood cries out to God from the ground.*

And yet, despite the overwhelming evidence before us—despite the witness of hundreds of thousands of brothers and sisters whose blood calls out to us from the ground—it seems we are no closer to collectively calling the narrative of racial hierarchy a sin now than we were back then. I see this over and over. I spend a lot of time in White Christian circles, and I am continuously amazed at how complacent we are about the threat level represented by this sin. Even those of us who can regurgitate the facts of past calamities seem to remain strangely calm when it comes to the ongoing threat level of the narrative of racial hierarchy. If the sin of the narrative hunted us like a predator then, why would it not do the same now? If the sin of the narrative wanted to "have" us then (another chilling aspect to the metaphor in Genesis 4), why would it not want to have us now?

This theme came up in a significant way at a pastors retreat I spoke at recently. The experience was meant to serve as a weekend getaway for this group of pastors and as an uninterrupted space where they could talk honestly and openly about the reality of White supremacy. To this group's credit, most of them came ready to wrestle with this challenging theme, and most of them seemed sincere in their desire to actively confront White supremacy at both a personal and collective level. But as the weekend progressed, it also became obvious that the subject was increasingly overwhelming for some of them.

In our final session, one of the pastors finally confessed that he struggled with all the emphasis on race. He gave an admonishment to the group that he imagined as being necessary to keep us on track: "It's good that we're talking about this important social challenge. But let us also remember that as pastors, our primary task is to fulfill the Great Commission that Christ has put before us. As such, our focus is to call on people to repent of their sins, to place their faith in Christ, and to teach them to become disciples. If we are going to pray for and work for something, let's ensure it's not a social issue. We should pray and work for revival. Only when revival comes will we see these social issues truly be dealt with."

Rather than rebutting his comment with a philosophical argument, I chose instead to focus on our common ground. This pastor and I both shared the view that Scripture is authoritative in the sense that it points to the ultimate authority found in Jesus,[8] and we both shared a conviction that Scripture is a primary means by which God chooses to reveal truth to us. So I invited him to reflect with me on Genesis 4. He was quite familiar with the encounter between God and Cain but had never stopped to consider its relevance to the conversation about White supremacy.

The next hour of discussion was an absolutely holy time together. Through the power of the Spirit of God, he finally began to see things that had eluded him up to that point. He began to realize that the sin of the narrative was defined by traits surprisingly similar to the sin God warned Cain about. He began to realize that the sin that had come to rule over Cain was surprisingly analogous to the sin of White supremacy that had come to rule over our country for centuries. He began to realize that in the same way Cain enabled the power of this sin through his denial, so we as the church had enabled the power of White supremacy through the denial of the narrative of racial hierarchy.

And then he did something that shocked everyone in the room. Nobody was asking for this—I'm not sure they even disagreed with his original statement—and yet he turned to the group and publicly apologized for his ignorance. In a humble spirit of confession, he began to repent of and recant each thing he had said just an hour earlier:

"I repent for talking of the Great Commission as if it doesn't include Christ's reign over White supremacy. I repent for talking of the repentance of sin as if it doesn't include the narrative of racial hierarchy. I repent for talking of discipleship as if it doesn't include teaching followers of Jesus how to recognize the dehumanizing rhetoric of this false god of race. I repent for talking of revival as if it can actually happen outside of a widespread acknowledgment of our complicity with all of these."

That room was one of the most hallowed spaces I have been in. I believe with all my heart that repentance is the key to accessing God's presence, and I believe that one of the primary reasons the larger White church continues to falter is because we are unable or unwilling to repent for our complicity with White supremacy. But wow, when it does happen, it is an incredible experience! As I witnessed the real-time transformation of this pastor, I began to believe that perhaps it could happen within the larger church as well. If he as an individual could learn to see the sin of the narrative of racial hierarchy, then why couldn't we as a collective? If he could learn to link revival to repentance for the sin of White supremacy, couldn't all of us?

Sin is crouching at your door; it desires to have you, but you must rule over it.

These were God's words to Cain. And I believe these are God's words to the White church. The narrative of racial difference is the sin that crouches at our collective door. It desires to have us. But we must learn to rule over it, not the other way around.

Identify the Narrative as the Link between Historical Injustice and Modern Incarnations

One of the most transformative events we do as a church is take our members on a trip to Montgomery, Alabama, where the Equal Justice Initiative has opened two museums, each of distinct and critical importance. The first is the National Memorial for Peace and Justice, "the nation's first memorial dedicated to the legacy of enslaved Black people, people terrorized by lynching, African Americans humiliated by racial segregation and

Jim Crow, and people of color burdened with contemporary presumptions of guilt and police violence."[9]

The EJI's website notes, "The memorial structure on the center of the site is constructed of over 800 Corten steel monuments, one for each county in the United States where a racial terror lynching took place. The names of the lynching victims are engraved on the columns." There is a six-acre park surrounding the memorial that contains identical monuments "waiting to be claimed and installed in the counties they represent." Part of its vision is to "serve as a report on which parts of the country have confronted the truth of this terror and which have not."[10]

Words cannot express what it's like to walk through this museum and take in the breadth and depth of the lives lost to racial terrorism and to process this together as a community.

The second is the Legacy Museum, an 11,000-square-foot facility built on the site of a former warehouse where enslaved Black people were imprisoned. Located midway between a historic slave market and the main river dock and train station where tens of thousands of enslaved people were trafficked during the height of the domestic slave trade, the museum uses interactive media, sculpture, videography, and exhibits to immerse visitors in the sights and sounds of the history of the domestic slave trade.[11] The genius of the museum is twofold: (1) it creates an emotional experience that connects both heart and mind to the racial terrorism of slavery, and (2) it shows how the sin of the narrative of racial hierarchy serves as the unbreakable link between every one of these forms of racial terrorism.

The reason I am sharing in great detail about these two museums is twofold. First, if we are going to have any hope of attacking the narrative in its current forms, we must understand its historical roots. James Baldwin made this astute observation about the ongoing reality of history, and it's applicable to the journey we're on:

History, as nearly no one seems to know, is not merely something to be read. And it does not refer merely, or even principally, to the past. On the contrary, the great force of history comes from the fact that we carry it within us, are unconsciously controlled by it in many ways, and history is literally present in all that we do.[12]

The importance of clearly reckoning with our history cannot be emphasized enough. The transformational journey of moving from blindness to sight requires a deeper understanding of this "great force of history" than most of us who are White currently possess. As such, we need to pursue tangible pathways for reckoning with this history. We need it for our own ongoing learning journey. And we need to facilitate it for those in our spheres of influence who are looking to go on this type of learning journey.

I will never forget when we took our first church trip to visit these two museums. We rented a large bus and brought nearly forty people from our church on a forty-eight-hour round trip from Chicago, Illinois, to Montgomery, Alabama. We left early on a Friday morning and designed the trip to return in time for our Sunday service. On the way down to Alabama, we watched documentaries and engaged in group exercises to prepare people for what they were about to encounter. On the way back to Chicago, we created space for people to share what it was like to be immersed so deeply into this "great force of history." Many grieved, mourned, and lamented about these painful chapters they had never learned about. Others shared the significance of emotionally contending with a history they had intellectually engaged but had never experienced in such a visceral way. It was transformative in a way we had never been able to reproduce through lectures, seminars, and book groups, and we vowed to continue creating these type of experiential learning opportunities for our congregation. I strongly recommend you consider doing the same within whatever learning community you are part of. If at all possible, take a trip to visit these two museums.

The second reason I highlight these two particular museums is directly related to their unique ability to share the story of our collective history through the lens of the narrative of racial hierarchy. Consider the National Memorial for Peace and Justice as an example. Its overall purpose is to expose its guests to the tragic history of lynchings and to pay homage to the precious souls that were lost through these terrorist acts. It certainly accomplishes this purpose. But even as it does, it also accomplishes the additional task of illuminating the ferocity of the narrative. As you walk through this moving exhibit, you find yourself getting one history lesson after another on the link between the narrative and these unlawful executions. By the time you leave, you walk away with an entirely new consciousness about how pervasive the narrative is and how downright evil it is. You realize that something like lynchings could never happen without a widespread agreement with the lies of the narrative first occurring.

The experience of the Legacy Museum is very similar. When someone walks through this gallery, they are virtually assured of developing a more holistic understanding of the historical timeline of slavery. But just as importantly, they discover how that system of slavery could survive only through the power of the narrative. The narrative emerges as the clear link between historical injustices during the era of slavery and the modern incarnations of these same injustices in our present reality.

It feels important to give you a sense of the way the museum makes this connection through the lens of the narrative, so I will conclude with a glimpse into how they do this. Below are sixteen short excerpts from the museum. As a guest walks from one historical photograph to the next, these excerpts help explain how and why the particular atrocity happened. As you read through them, notice how regularly EJI uses the language of the narrative to weave these stories together. Let's pay attention to the way EJI links the multitude of historical injustices through the lens of the narrative, and let's learn together how to locate present injustices in the frame of this "narrative war":

- The enslavement of Black people in the United States lasted for more than two centuries and was justified by an elaborate narrative of racial inferiority. This ideology has endured beyond the formal abolition of American slavery.
- Beginning in the seventeenth century, millions of African people were kidnapped, enslaved, and shipped across the Atlantic to the Americas in cramped vessels under horrific conditions. Nearly 2 million people died at sea during the agonizing journey.
- Over the next two centuries, the enslavement of Black people in the United States created wealth for millions of White Americans. In the Southern economy, slavery primarily centered around cotton and tobacco crops grown on large plantations dependent on the labor of enslaved men, women, and children who toiled in the fields and worked in the plantation owners' homes.
- American slavery began as a form of indentured servitude that could be overcome. However, by the time the United States Congress abolished the international slave trade in 1808, the institution of slavery had developed into a permanent hereditary status essentially tied to race. Black people's lifelong and inescapable enslavement was defended by legal, political, religious, and scientific institutions as justified and necessary and was enforced through violence.
- By the time the international slave trade was abolished in 1808, enslavement had become a permanent status for kidnapped Africans and their descendants.

- The system of American slavery created a permanent racial hierarchy that both grew from and reinforced racial prejudice. Advocates of slavery falsely claimed that science and religion supported the fact that White people were smart, hardworking, and intellectually and morally evolved, whereas Black people were dumb, lazy, childlike, and in need of guidance and supervision.
- This narrative of racial inferiority justified a system where enslaved people were deprived of all legal rights and autonomy. In addition to labor exploitation, African Americans faced the constant threat of violence, abuse, and murder, as slave owners had the power to sell, exploit, attack, rape, and even kill enslaved men, women, and children with impunity.
- The domestic slave trade (1808–1865) permanently separated nearly half of all Black families in the United States. Domestic slave trafficking brought large numbers of Southerners and travelers from the North into contact with the inhumanity of enslavement; scores of people witnessed the trading and separation of Black families at auctions.
- In an attempt to preserve slavery in the face of the abolitionist movement, Southern states seceded from the United States and formed the Confederacy in 1861, sparking the Civil War, the deadliest war in American history, with more than 1 million casualties. The Confederacy ultimately surrendered in 1865, and slave states were immediately forced to emancipate enslaved people in the territory. Later, the Thirteenth Amendment abolished slavery throughout the United States "except as a punishment for crime."
- In the South, where the enslavement of African Americans was widely embraced, resistance to ending slavery persisted for another century following the passage of the Thirteenth Amendment in 1865.

- The legal instruments that led to the formal end of racialized chattel slavery in America did nothing to address the narrative of racial hierarchy that sustained enslavement, nor did they establish a national commitment to the alternative ideology of racial equality. Black people were legally free from involuntary labor, but that did not mean Southern Whites recognized them as fully human or equal. White Southern identity was grounded in a belief that White people were inherently superior to African Americans, and after the Civil War, there was a violent reaction to the call for Black equality.
- The federal government's lackluster commitment to civil rights and security undermined the promise of freedom. Instead of given a chance at economic, social, and political equality, African Americans across the South were forced into sharecropping—working on White-owned land in exchange for food and lodging. Many lived in slave quarters, received insufficient food and no pay, and had no protection.
- The era of "second slavery" was underway. Through convict leasing, African Americans were arrested, branded criminals, charged with false crimes, fined, and then sold to private interests for state profit. Thousands of prisoners were re-enslaved in mines and on farms or plantations, where conditions were horrific, and many died.
- Lynching became a vicious tool of racial control. Between 1880 and 1940, more than four thousand African American men, women and children were killed in "racial terror lynchings," public acts of violence and torture that traumatized Black communities throughout the country.
- Between 1910 and 1940, nearly 6 million refugees fled the South in response to the threat of racial terrorism.
- Millions of Black people—refugees from racial terrorism—fled the South for urban ghettos in the North and West

during the first half of the twentieth century in a massive forced exodus known as the Great Migration. This forever altered the demographic landscape of America.[13]

Link Systemic Justice to the Narrative Battle

One of the first consultations that Shumeca Pickett and I did together was at the request of a distinguished fellowship in the city of Chicago designed to equip and develop emerging business leaders. Thirty applicants from four different industries (law, banking, education, and housing) had been selected, and a cross-disciplinary curriculum was designed for them. They would spend one full Saturday each month focused on a key social reality, in the hope that at the conclusion they would become empowered change agents for the common good of our city.

Racial injustice was part of the curriculum, and Shumeca and I were invited to facilitate the all-day session on this topic. We divided the day into three parts and organized each section around the three interlocking dimensions of race covered in chapter 3. We did one session on race as a social construct, one on the narrative of racial hierarchy, and one on systemic racism. Since it was a secular space, we did not do a fourth session on race as evil, though we did allude to this regularly throughout our training.

When the time came for the final session on systemic racism, we were initially uncertain how to structure the time in the most effective way. It was the first time we had trained business leaders with this level of professional expertise, and we were searching for the right balance. On one hand, we knew we needed to handle the session with humility, since they had far more expertise in law, banking, education, and housing than we did. On the other hand, we also knew that the scholastic tracks that trained professionals in these fields rarely dove deeply into the history of the systemic racism in those particular fields, and we were determined to center the need for that type of exploration.

We decided to use another Bryan Stevenson rhetorical device to help them make the critical connection between the narrative explored in the previous session and the systemic racism we were now exploring. Stevenson often uses the metaphor of gardening to make this point. For instance, when he is illustrating the connection between the history of racial injustice within the system of slavery and the current state of racial injustice within the incarceration system, he will use this metaphor.

To those who are gardeners, he will ask this simple question: "What happens if you pull weeds out of your garden but don't get down to the roots?" The answer is always the same: "The weeds will come right back!" And that is precisely the challenge we face when it comes to the narrative of racial hierarchy. We may have overturned the very real and deadly system of slavery in 1865, but we never got to the roots that allowed for its birth and sustenance. And because we never got to the roots, the same evil that manifested itself as slavery has just evolved into uniquely new and deadly forms of evil.

We shared this metaphor with the thirty business leaders and encouraged them to consider how it might shape the way they approached the exploration of the inevitable history of racial injustice that existed within each of the industries they represented. How had the historical root of the narrative shaped the current reality of their specific industry? We then asked them to cluster with others in the same field as them, to collaboratively identify ways in which the narrative of racial hierarchy had played a role in defining the inequities within their field, and then to report back on ways they could meaningfully attack the narrative.

The results were incredible. Not one person got stuck on the idea of personal racism, as we feared they might (i.e., "Don't accuse me of being racist"). Nor did anyone struggle with seeing the relationship between the historical narrative and the present inequalities within their field. Each of the groups was able to identify very specific ways the narrative had shaped systemic inequalities within their industry, and even more encouragingly, each had specific ideas for how they could concretely attack the narrative.

A school superintendent shared about an epiphany she had about the deficiency in the curriculum in her district when it came to the narrative and vowed to change that immediately. An attorney found himself resonating with Stevenson's language of the "presumption of guilt" that often shapes the biases of both lawyers and judges in the courtroom and developed a strategy for bringing greater awareness and attention to that. One of the investment bankers confessed that he had been cynical throughout the course of the training and had brought that cynicism into this exercise with fellow bankers. However, as he listened to the stories of his colleagues, he discovered that the problem was actually with him. Most of them were quite aware of key moments in the history of banking that had confirmed the narrative, and he realized he had bought into his own version of the narrative. He committed not only to continuing his own personal work but also to taking the institution he worked for on a learning journey that connected their present reality with the larger history of systemic inequality in the banking industry.

It was amazing to see industry leaders make this connection, and it brought comfort to Shumeca and me to know that at least thirty business leaders in our city would go to work that next week expressly intending to attack the narrative within their field.

This experience also painted a compelling picture of how the church can think about discipleship as it relates to attacking the narrative. I've already explored two critical ways we must do that. Most importantly, we begin by recognizing how serious a sin the narrative is. What would it look like if churches across the nation taught people about the sin of the narrative? What if our churches inspired and equipped people to go back into their vocations with practices to attack the narrative that are specific to the profession they were trained in?

Duel with the Devil

I have to admit, we've gotten a lot of pushback on this topic. A number of our staff workers have asked why we're suddenly placing such a significant focus on race. Some have even hinted that we've lost our way as an organization. As a pastor, you must hear this a lot as well. How do you respond? Why has White supremacy become such a significant priority for you?"

This was the question directed to me as part of a larger panel curated to discuss faith and race. The event was hosted by a large Christian organization based in the United States but with a far-reaching presence across the globe as well. They were historically better known for their overseas mission work than their work at home, but that was beginning to change. The organization had gone through its own racial awakening process and was now beginning to use the term *White supremacy* as part of its domestic mission statement.

This new focus created a predictable pushback from a wide range of employees, and the leadership was trying to discern how to press forward with this vision while remaining sensitive to the concerns of some of their stakeholders. This weekend training was an important part of that process. They billed it as an opportunity for staff to be equipped and empowered on critical leadership issues, and they had brought in four practitioners who each led a specific module around race. Now that the four modules had been completed, the president of the organization had asked the four of us to join him for a two-hour panel discussion that would tie together all the themes.

The first two questions he presented had been very conceptual in nature, and each of the practitioners seemed to answer with ease. But when he asked this question about the Christian motivation for addressing White supremacy, I felt the urgency increase. I realized there was nothing conceptual about this one—that it represented the real concerns of staff members throughout the organization. I wished in the moment that he would have directed the question to any one of the practitioners but me. But I also realized he had likely intended for me to answer this one. I was the only White person on the panel, and most people in the crowd were White. He seemed to be hoping I could build a bridge to their ongoing concerns.

I kept trying to think of a more clever way to say it, but every time I considered the question, only one word came to mind. So I finally blurted out my motivation for confronting White supremacy: "Jesus!"

The crowd burst out in laughter. I wasn't trying to be funny, but I suppose this reaction should have been expected. One of the standing jokes for church folks is that it doesn't really matter what the question is—the answer is always "Jesus!" It probably sounded like I was just toeing the party line.

The moderator was really in tune with the moment, though, and he accurately sensed that there was nothing playful about my answer. He could feel the fierceness with which I said it and chose to press in even harder. "Good answer—of course the answer should be *Jesus*! But can you get more specific about that? If we're honest, we have to acknowledge that, technically speaking, the Bible never mentions White supremacy. So how can we be certain that confronting White supremacy is such a high priority to Jesus?"

I appreciated this back-and-forth, and I could see he was doing his best to take this conversation right up to the point of discomfort for his people. It was the right move. So we kept going.

"Let's start with some of what we absolutely know to be true about Jesus," I replied. "We know, for instance, that Jesus is the good shepherd and that he has come to bring life, and bring life abundantly [John 10:10–11]. Based on the clear intention that Jesus uses to describe himself, we can begin to identify some of the clear traits that can be expected as by-products of that abundant life. Forgiveness of sins, identity rooted in love, new purpose in life, and Spirit-led empowerment represent just a handful of the wonderful hopes that come as a result of this vibrant union with Christ."

I paused and then continued. "As wonderful as the promise of abundant life is, we must soberly remember that the promise also comes with a caution attached to it. Jesus warns of a very real threat that looks to attack that abundant life. Jesus repeatedly reminds us that evil is real, is dangerous, and, in this case in John 10, is compared to a thief. Whereas the intention of Jesus is abundant life, the intention of the thief is to steal, kill, and destroy. Based on this clear intention, we need to thoughtfully consider how it is that the thief goes about this process of attacking the life that Jesus longs for us to experience. Or to use the analogous words of Paul in Ephesians 6, we need to prepare ourselves to take our stand against the devil's 'schemes.' This is what leads me to take White supremacy so seriously. If you ask me or the leaders in our church community to list the primary schemes that the evil one uses to attack the purposes of God, we would rank White supremacy at the very top of that list."

The staff in attendance at this training were surprised by this response. They knew and loved John 10:10—particularly the back half: "I have come that they may have life, and have it to the full." Yet at a functional level, most of them admitted they hadn't given serious enough reflection to the fact that this promise was so closely tethered to the threat of personified evil that intentionally looks to sabotage and destroy this fullness of life. To compound matters, most of them had been conditioned to think of White supremacy as a fringe social movement led by racist extremists, not as a spiritual principality that attacked the dignity of all human beings. So the allusion to White supremacy as a primary weapon in the artillery of the evil one was a notion that went far beyond anything they had previously considered.

To their credit, being caught off guard did not lead to defensiveness. Instead, it actually made them curious. The connection between the presence of evil and the ideology of White supremacy opened up a new vista for them by which they could examine the principalities that work to sustain the construct of race. And when the event ended, many of them reported back to the president their gratitude for developing a more deeply biblical framework for White supremacy, and some even repented for putting up so much resistance to the organization's important shift to prioritizing the confrontation of White supremacy as part of their growing sense of mission. It was an important moment.

This event also ended up being a pivotal point in my own journey. Though I had long seen White supremacy as being sustained by supernatural evil, I had failed to include this in a meaningful way when talking about race in front of people of faith. This experience changed that. I had witnessed firsthand the way entire dispositions changed once people took a step back and considered the supernatural dimensions of race. It was then that I realized I could never talk again about confronting White supremacy without also talking about the need to duel with the devil.

Over the course of the rest of this chapter, I'm going to

marry together two different big ideas. I'll finish the chapter with quotes from prominent politicians, using them as a means to make the case that the narrative of racial hierarchy continues to be a lie that persists in an almost unchallenged manner. But to get there, I first am going to explore what the Bible says about the nature of evil and about the devil specifically. That's not exactly everyday dinner conversation, but I'm convinced that our theological foundation remains dangerously weak without a sufficient understanding of the devil. Therefore I'm going to dive deeper into theological reflection in this chapter than I will in any other and ask that you come along with me on this journey.

What the Bible Says about the Devil

How does the Bible depict the devil? To frame the answer to that question, let me first point to the work of C. S. Lewis. When you search for resources within the broader Christian tradition on the nature of the devil, it's amazing how frequently his name comes up.

The British professor, theologian, and author was able to connect to a broad swath of humanity as it relates to the contest between good and evil and the devil's role in it. His most popular work on the subject was The Chronicles of Narnia, a series of seven novels that became an instant classic in the genre of children's literature. Lewis took his readers on an imaginative journey into the land of Narnia and helped us see good, embodied through Aslan, and evil, embodied through the White Witch. As a result, hundreds of thousands of people developed a deeper appreciation of the way our individual choices are shaped by, and ultimately impact, the larger spiritual battle happening all around us.

The place where C. S. Lewis most directly explored the nature of the devil, however, was in his book *The Screwtape Letters*, a story about a senior associate demon named Screwtape, who mentors his younger nephew Wormwood (another demon) on the ways of evil. The book is filled with interesting lessons throughout, but it's actually the book's preface that provides a helpful framework on this matter:

> There are two equal and opposite errors into which our race[1] can fall about the devils. One is to disbelieve in their existence. The other is to believe, and to feel an excessive and unhealthy interest in them. They themselves are equally pleased by both errors . . .
>
> Readers are advised to remember that the devil is a liar.[2]

This quote carries two different and important ideas. The first is the warning about having an imbalanced view of the devil—either disbelieving in devils or feeling an unhealthy interest in them. During my high school years, I was in a highly charismatic environment and had firsthand experience with the second half of this imbalance. While that environment certainly formed me in a lot of positive ways, I regularly ran into folks who seemed to be overly consumed with the presence of the devil. They suspected demons as the catalyst behind everything from traffic jams to kids who cursed too much.

While I think that imbalance represents a legitimate caution, and one to consider if you are from an environment like that, the other end of the spectrum seems far more common—and, honestly, more dangerous. When it comes to the challenge of confronting White supremacy among people of faith, I find that the error of disbelief reigns.

This disbelief manifests differently, depending on whether one is in a progressive or a conservative faith community. In progressive circles, there tends to be a much sharper understanding of the problem of White supremacy, at least at an intellectual level. But if someone suggests that dark powers and principalities are what ultimately sustain White supremacy, the bearer of that opinion risks being labeled as completely archaic in their thinking.

In conservative circles, it is not nearly as outlandish to point to the reality of the devil. Most people in these communities already possess a strong theology of supernatural evil, at least at a theoretical level. But when one attempts to demonstrate the link between the devil and White supremacy, it is almost always dismissed. In conservative circles, the bearer of that message risks being labeled and dismissed as too social, political, or liberal. In both cases, what we see is a form of the error of disbelief.

Let's take Lewis's framework to the biblical text. Consider the writing of the apostle John, who brings an interesting vantage point, because he lived so much longer than any of the other disciples. With the exception of Judas, who tragically hung himself, John was the only one of the original twelve who averted martyrdom.[3] Historians believe that he lived into his nineties before dying peacefully in the city of Ephesus. As a result, he had the opportunity to train multiple generations of disciples in the way of Christ. And when he did, he grounded his teachings in the cosmic conflict between good and evil.

In his opening account of the life of Jesus, for instance, John refers to this cosmic conflict right from the jump: "In him was life, and that life was the light of all mankind. The light shines in the darkness, and the darkness has not *overcome* it" (John 1:4–5, emphasis added). The Greek word translated "overcome" can also be translated "apprehended," with either term effectively pointing to this very active fight between light and darkness (with a resounding reminder that light wins!).

John didn't stop there though. He noticed the way Jesus regularly talked of the ongoing battle with the devil and recorded three different occasions where Jesus referred to him as the "prince of this world" (John 12:31; 14:30; 16:11).

The apostle Paul planted most of the churches referred to in the New Testament, and he too was a clear believer that Christianity was set against this backdrop of a cosmic battle between good and evil. He talked of "fighting the good fight" (2 Timothy 4:7), described the devil as "the ruler of the kingdom of the air" (Ephesians 2:2), and personally lamented that a "messenger of Satan" had been sent to torment him at one point (2 Corinthians 12:7). He also famously talked of the need for believers to put on the full armor of God, because our battle is not against flesh and blood but against "the powers of this dark world and against the spiritual forces of evil in the heavenly realms" (Ephesians 6:12).

Once we develop a more robust understanding of the devil, as the apostles did, we can then move on to ask the question of how the devil works. When the apostle Paul talked of the need to put on the full armor of God, he said it was "so that you can take your stand against the devil's *schemes*" (Ephesians 6:11, emphasis added). This is the Greek word *methodeia*, from which we get the English word *methods*. Learning to precisely identify the schemes or methods of the devil is arguably one of the most important skills a Christian can develop.

Fortunately, the devil does not possess a large artillery. In fact, the Bible depicts him as being largely a one-trick pony. C. S. Lewis affirms this reality and defines it with clarity in the second part of his quote: "Readers are advised to remember that the devil is a *liar*."

That's it. It's no more complicated than that. The devil is a liar. Consider three biblical accounts where a lie is told:

Example 1: The Garden

The first time evil enters the biblical picture is in the Garden of Eden. In chapters 1 and 2 of Genesis, we see the overwhelming glory that comes from the goodness of God, and we bear witness to the perfect harmony that existed spiritually (Adam and Eve had an intimate and uninhibited relationship with God), relationally (Adam and Eve were able to fully reveal themselves to each other with no reservation), psychologically (being right with God meant Adam and Eve felt no sense of shame or of being less than), and with creation. But as the page turns to chapter 3, God's creation comes under siege. We are not told precisely where the evil came from or how it found its way into the garden, but we do see that the garden is under attack.

When evil finds its way into the garden, it's interesting to notice what form it takes. It does not come in as some type of medieval dragon threatening to incinerate the garden with its powerful flames. If that would have been the case, the entire created order would have felt its presence and would have immediately worried about its safety. Instead, evil comes as a serpent, which is not a particularly powerful animal. It's a slithery, sneaky, deceitful creature. So when evil shows up, the animals of the garden don't run for cover. The devil[4] is not a fire-breathing dragon; he's a lie-spitting lowlife.

When I reflect on this account and on the schemes of the devil, I start by considering what the voice of evil does *not* say to Adam and Eve. The serpent does not say, "So, that's the garden God made for you, huh? That's an okay garden. But now, come see the garden *I* made for you. You'll never want to come back to this garden after you see mine." Of course, the serpent doesn't say that. He doesn't have anywhere near that kind of power. The devil never could, and never will be able to, go toe-to-toe with God.

Instead, the evil one utilizes his singular trick. He *lies*. He calls into question the character of God. He attacks the previously unchallenged confidence that Adam and Eve had in the goodness of God. He plants the seed of a lie, insinuating that if they took power into their own hands, they would be gods themselves.

A helpful way to think about this comes from Tinasha LaRayé, one of my spiritual mentors on the subject of evil. Tinasha is a pastor at Bethel Church in Redding, California, and when speaking about the nature of evil, she often reminds me of Amos 3:3, where God corrects the Israelites and reveals to them the path back to reconciliation.

Through Amos, God says, "Do two walk together unless they have agreed to do so?" Tinasha uses this language of *agreement* to clarify the way human choice aligns with the light of God or the darkness of the devil. When we "agree" with truth, we align with the power of God's light and life. When we instead "agree" with lies, we abdicate the power given to us by God and transfer that power to the forces of evil.

That's what happened in the garden. Up to the time they met the serpent, Adam and Eve had agreed with the truth of God. As a result, they experienced the zenith of God's goodness. Then the serpent showed up, with no power outside of its ability to lie about God's character. At that moment in history, Adam and Eve were still the ones who possessed all the power. That's important to remember. If they had continued to agree with the truth that was in God, they would have walked away victorious, as Jesus would later do in his duel with the devil. Instead, they agreed with the lie of the devil. And we all know what happened next.

That's why Genesis 3 is such an important resource for understanding how evil works. It reminds us what the devil can and cannot do. Said optimistically, the devil has very limited power, particularly in contrast to the power we possess as Spirit-filled, image-bearing human beings. The devil is unable to affect our physical surroundings or create some type of alternative reality. All he can do is lie. And yet, said pessimistically, we must never underestimate how powerful lies can become once we agree with them. When we choose to reject truth and agree with lies, we place all of God's creation at stake.

Example 2: The Temptation of Jesus

The Bible gives little information about Jesus before his launch into public ministry as an adult. We know a lot about his birth, and we get one passage about Jesus talking with the religious leaders in the temple as a boy, but outside of that, the Bible is quiet. When it finally comes time for Jesus to step into his mission, though, all four Gospels start their account with his baptism by John the Baptist in the Jordan River. What happens there is beautiful on every level. Here is Matthew's version:

> As soon as Jesus was baptized, he went up out of the water. At that moment heaven was opened, and he saw the Spirit of God descending like a dove and alighting on him. And a voice from heaven said, "This is my Son, whom I love; with him I am well pleased."
>
> *Matthew 3:16–17*

No other passage more beautifully represents the truth found in the gospel (at least in my opinion!). As Jesus comes out of the baptismal waters, the voice of the Father drenches him in the transformational truth that he is God's beloved. Jesus is reminded that he is a son, that he is loved, and that God takes great pleasure in him.

This is a sermon for another day, but I'm convinced there are no words known to humankind more powerful than these. I believe the most transformational change that can happen to us comes when we "agree" with the truth that God has spoken over each of us about who we truly are.

For the purposes of this chapter, what happens next is of vital importance. Immediately following Jesus' baptism, the Spirit sends Jesus to the wilderness to duel with the devil (Matthew 4). In the same way that the Garden of Eden sets the template for how to think of evil in the Old Testament, so it is with this temptation by the devil in the New Testament. Jesus has fasted for forty days and nights when the devil finally deems it time to attack Jesus. And when he attacks, he again uses the singular weapon at his disposal—he lies.

Jesus undergoes three separate temptations, each with their own particularity. But what is interesting is the consistent lie that seems to bind them all together. The devil knows that Jesus has *just* heard the blessing of love spoken over him by the Father. This is the truth that has coronated Jesus as God's Son, and it is the truth that sends him into mission. The devil can't create an alternative truth for Jesus. In fact, the devil knows there is *nothing* he can ultimately offer that could compete with the riches of God's love. All he can do is attack the truth Jesus is basing his life on. All he can do is lie.

The devil begins the first temptation with an attack on the truth that Jesus just heard at his baptism. The devil says, "If you are the Son of God, tell these stones to become bread" (Matthew 4:3). Notice the importance of the word that starts this temptation: "*If* you are the Son of God." The lie of the devil hinges on the word *if*. The blessing of God did not come down conditionally on Jesus at the Jordan River as an *if*. That blessing was unwavering, unconditional, industrial-strength truth. All the devil can do is try to weaken Jesus' resolve by tempting him to agree with a lie.

The second temptation then hinges on the same lie. After taking Jesus to the highest point of the temple, the devil repeats the exact same lie: "*If* you are the Son of God, throw yourself down." The third temptation doesn't use that same word *if*, but it is still rooted in the devil's deceitful attacks on the truth found in God's words. Isn't it interesting that despite however much time has elapsed between the Garden of Eden and the temptation of Jesus, the devil's schemes haven't changed one bit?

Example 3: Jesus' Teaching on the Devil

The place where Jesus most directly names the devil and most clearly describes the devil's schemes comes in John 8. The backdrop of the chapter is a lengthy and tense conversation with the Pharisees. Jesus is frustrated that despite their knowledge of the Hebrew Scriptures, they remain unable to accurately identify the Son of God who stands right before them. "I am the light of the world," he plainly says to them. "Whoever follows me will never walk in darkness, but will have the light of life" (John 8:12).

The Pharisees continue to resist, however, so Jesus raises the stakes of the conversation by invoking the name of the devil. In doing so, he draws a direct connection between their inability to grasp the truth before them to the active choice they are making to align and agree with the lies of the devil. Consider the seriousness of these words:

> Jesus said to them, "If God were your Father, you would love me, for I have come here from God. I have not come on my own; God sent me. Why is my language not clear to you? Because you are unable to hear what I say. You belong to your father, the devil, and you want to carry out your father's desires. He was a murderer from the beginning, not holding to the truth, for there is no truth in him. When he lies, he speaks his native language, for he is a liar and the father of lies."
>
> *John 8:42–44*

117

There are a couple of immediate and important notes to make about Jesus' rebuke to the Pharisees here. First, it reinforces the notion that at the core of his DNA, the devil is a *liar*. Jesus says it three different ways: the devil is a liar; he speaks his native language of lies; and he is the father of lies. It would be hard to find a more emphatic way to state this than Jesus does here. The devil wants to kill, and the way he does so is through lies. Period.

Second, it opens us up to the terrifying idea that a group of people can love God, be highly familiar with the Bible, and yet still be under the influence of the devil. "You are unable to hear what I say," Jesus says to the Pharisees. "You belong to your father, the devil." If someone were to read this verse in isolation, it would sound like Jesus was talking to a group of Satan worshipers. But these are the Pharisees! Nobody knew the Bible better than they did. In fact, they were so committed to the precepts of the Hebrew Scriptures that they added six hundred–plus additional laws just to ensure that their lifestyle of holiness was seen as above reproach. And yet we discover that having an intellectual knowledge of Scripture is not the same thing as actually *agreeing* with truth. It is quite possible to have a knowledge of the Bible and still be in functional lockstep with the lies of the devil.

I want to stop for a moment and reflect on the gravity of that. What a sober reminder that at a supernatural level, the agreements I make here and now, and the choices that spring from these agreements, directly affect whom I am aligning with. When I agree with truth, I align with the supernatural force of light, which is how Jesus describes himself in this passage. When I agree with lies, I align with the supernatural force of darkness. Do I get that? Do you? It's very serious.

That leads to the last implication of this passage—the point that moves us back into a direct exploration of the relationship between the devil and White supremacy. Notice how Jesus finishes his warning to the Pharisees. He tells them the devil is not just a liar; the devil is *the father of lies*. Both parts of that phrase are critical.

First, Jesus refers to the devil as a *father*. This is significant, because "father" is the primary way in which Jesus refers to God. "Our Father" is how he teaches his disciples to begin their prayers. "Father" is how he most often talked to God in his own personal prayer life. As such, the term *father* clearly is meant to impact our sense of identity. This is consistent with a broader understanding of the gospel, since a Christian is one who knows that the most defining thing about their identity is that they are a daughter or a son of Almighty God. Through the death and resurrection of Jesus, we can know we are forgiven, beloved, and delighted in. Therefore, Jesus' description of the devil as also being a father points to the way that lies represent a direct assault on our identity. The devil is always trying to attack the *imago Dei*, which is one of the reasons that White supremacy is so seriously dangerous.

Second, Jesus refers to the devil as a father of *lies*. A single lie told to a single individual already represents a direct threat to that person's well-being. But when Jesus turns this word into the plural and says the devil is the father of *lies*, he is pointing to something very revelatory about the way the devil works.

There is something about the accumulation of lies that represents a whole new frontier of risk. Whatever threat level a single lie represents, the threat level increases exponentially when it turns into a cluster of lies. Said another way, if we want to know what a principality looks like (as the apostle Paul referred to it), or if we want to know where the devil and his legions are most active at a given time in history, we don't have to look very hard. We just need to go to where the historic, accumulated, clustered set of lies lives. Where lies have turned into a swarm.

Once we find that, we will find the father of lies, hovering above it, guarding, protecting, and nurturing those lies. The devil has been a murderer since the beginning, and he will not rest until these lies kill more people.

And this is precisely where I see an undeniable connection between the supernatural reality of evil and the social problem of White supremacy. As we explored in both chapters 3 and 4, White supremacy is built on a set of *lies* about human value. The narrative of racial hierarchy, which is the operating system of White supremacy, is really not much more than one ongoing lie.

It is a lie that attempts to deceive and harm people of every background, telling them their value is directly tied to their racial background and not to their divine birthright. The narrative lies to White people, and says they are inherently superior because they have been placed at the top of the hierarchy. It lies to Black people and says they are inherently inferior because they have been placed at the bottom of the hierarchy. It lies to Native people and says they no longer matter and are forever irrelevant within race conversations. It lies to Latino and Latina people, Asian American people, and Middle Eastern people and tells them they can only hope to achieve worthiness by getting proximate to Whiteness.

When an individual agrees with the lie of the narrative, this is already a matter of obvious danger. But what happens when it is no longer just an individual who agrees with that lie? How much more powerful does the lie become when it is agreed with by an entire family? Do you see how quickly the power increases when it begins to become a cluster of lies? And then what happens when it is not just a family that agrees with the lie of the narrative, but a whole community agrees with it? What happens when a whole city agrees with it? What happens when a whole nation agrees with it?

Do you see how and why the lies that sustain White supremacy become the devil's breeding ground? Do you see why the father of lies would be so keenly interested in the narrative of racial hierarchy? Can you see how and why White supremacy has become a well-guarded, well-sustained principality of darkness?

This is what we're getting at when we talk about White lies. This swarm of lies around human value has infected the very air we breathe. We cannot live or move in this atmosphere without inhaling these lies. We must, therefore, contend with these White lies.

Tinasha LaRayé, whom I quoted earlier, summarizes the link between the father of lies and the narrative of racial hierarchy like this: "White supremacy represents four hundred years of agreement with lies. A massive force of people—believer and unbeliever alike—not only agreed with this lie but made a pact with it. Now the ability to separate truth from the lies has become so complex because of this great length of time that the pact with this lie has occurred and continues to occur. The ability to disentangle our nation from these lies begins to feel almost impossible. The agreement with the lie is so entrenched, which is why confronting White supremacy feels so overwhelming."

The Devil and White Lies

The narrative of racial hierarchy, when viewed in a timeline, is painful and grueling. But it is critical to lay bare the cluster of lies that has dominated our discourse on race for more than four hundred years in America. This lie has been durable and unrelenting. We will see how it has infected the hearts and minds of individuals from every philosophical leaning and political persuasion. I want to show how the lie has impacted both the "bad" people and the "good" people alike. In this way, we will clearly see the supernatural principality of White supremacy.

In our society, few places carry more social power than the political office. Elected officials represent at least 51 percent of the populace at any given time. For this exercise, I have chosen quotes from American politicians. This will show us how consistent and how far-reaching the narrative has been. As you'll see, no political party has a corner on the narrative of racial difference. Democrats and Republicans have taken turns being the primary ones to communicate its message. I have notated the party of each person to show the balance.

I am grateful to live in this country and believe that healing and forgiveness can be applied to the deep generational wounds. But I also believe that for this to happen, we must collectively improve at telling the truth and exposing the power of lies. This is one exercise aimed at doing so.

An important disclaimer. While the contents of this book are written for a White reader, I realize that many who are not White will be reading this too. I've learned that it's important to give fair warning before stepping into painful and degrading conceptions of humanity, which is what we are about to do. I lament that this type of dehumanization has been such a norm in our society, and I lament needing to talk about it so openly right now. I lament that you need to be reminded, yet again, of just how far and how deep the dehumanizing rhetoric stretches within our collective history.

All that being said, I want to share seventeen quotes that span from the early days of our republic all the way to our present day. Many things have changed in the almost 250 years represented by these quotes, yet *the presence and power of the narrative of racial hierarchy have remained unbreakable over that era.* I pray these quotes will help paint a picture of how and why supernatural evil is deeply invested in protecting this cluster of lies.

1783: George Washington
First President of the United States

> [Indians and wolves are both] beasts of prey tho' they differ
> in shape.[5]

In chapter 3, we examined the ways in which the lie of the narrative of racial hierarchy was used to depict Native people as "savages," with sociologists Keith Kilty and Eric Swank noting that eliminating "dangerous savages" became less of a moral problem than eliminating human beings. By starting our timeline with George Washington, the nation's first president, we see just how far back that narrative goes. Natives were regularly referred to in dominant culture as some combination of vermin and human refuse; as untamed, cruel, bloodthirsty, and merciless; as "red devils"; and as deadly predators. In this quote they are depicted as beasts of prey. This sustained attack on the *imago Dei* of Native people is the foundation of the lie in America.

1814: Thomas Jefferson
Founding Father, Third President [*Democratic-Republican Party*]

> Their [Black people's] amalgamation with the other color
> produces a degradation to which no lover of his country, no
> lover of excellence in the human character can innocently
> consent.[6]

Just as the Pharisees believed in the truth of God while simultaneously succumbing to the lies of the devil, we see this same duality in one of our founding fathers. The same man who helped pen the words "we hold these Truths to be self-evident, that all Men are created equal" was also under the bondage of the lie of the narrative. His views on amalgamation (intermarriage or child-rearing between White and Black people) would eventually contribute to the legal precedent of what would come to be known as the one-drop rule: any person with even one drop of sub-Saharan African blood was to be considered Black.[7] The message sent through this quote was similar to what Jefferson conveyed in his *Notes on the State of Virginia*: "The blacks . . . are inferior to the whites in the endowments both of body and mind."[8] Again, highlighting the duality of belief in a truth and bondage to a lie, Jefferson "amalgamated" with some of his six hundred–plus slaves, fathering a number of biracial children.[9]

1823: James Madison
Founding Father, Fourth President [*Democratic-Republican Party*]

> [In response to the question, "What is their (the free Blacks') general character with respect to industry and order, as compared with that of the slaves?"] Generally idle and depraved; appearing to retain the bad qualities of the slaves with whom they continue to associate, without acquiring any of the good ones of the whites.[10]

James Madison represents a long line of leaders in our history who knew that slavery was wrong and yet who couldn't stop themselves from subscribing to the lie that allowed for slavery to happen in the first place. Madison referred to slavery as a "dreadful calamity," yet in quotes like this he perpetuated lies about the character of Black human beings, using theological terms like *depraved* to describe them. In contrast, he depicted White people as those who were granted the "good" qualities endowed to the pinnacle of the racial hierarchy.

1833: Andrew Jackson
Seventh President [*Democrat*]

> That those tribes can not exist surrounded by our settlements
> and in continual contact with our citizens is certain. They
> have neither the intelligence, the industry, the moral habits,
> nor the desire of improvement which are essential to any
> favorable change in their condition. Established in the midst
> of another and a superior race, and without appreciating the
> causes of their inferiority or seeking to control them, they
> must necessarily yield to the force of circumstances and ere
> long disappear.[11]

Among many Native people, Jackson is often referred to as
the "removal president" because he signed the Indian Removal
Act that took millions of acres of lands from tribes and led to
forced removal from tribal ancestral lands west of the Mississippi
(the campaign commonly referred to as the Trail of Tears). When
you hear him describe Native people like this, it's not difficult
to see how the rationale for these policy decisions was formed.

1857: Roger Taney
Supreme Court Chief Justice

> [Persons of African descent] had for more than a century . . .
> been regarded as beings of an inferior order, and altogether
> unfit to associate with the white race either in social or
> political relations, and so far inferior that they had no rights
> which the white man was bound to respect.[12]

As the United States continued to expand west, laws
around slave ownership became increasingly blurred. The

ambiguity around a slave's ability to become free came to a head with the 1856 *Dred Scott v. Sandford* case in the Supreme Court. Dred Scott was born into slavery in 1795, and after his first owner died, Scott spent time in two free states working for several subsequent owners. Shortly after he married, he tried to buy freedom for himself and his family. Scott won his suit in a lower court, but the Missouri Supreme Court reversed the decision.

Eventually it went all the way up to the United States Supreme Court and was finally decided in 1857. The Dred Scott case became a landmark decision, as the Supreme Court ruled that all African Americans living in the United States—slaves as well as free persons—*could never become citizens.* Seven of the nine justices agreed that Dred Scott should remain a slave (five of whom were former slave owners themselves), but Roger Taney, who wrote the majority opinion, did not stop there. He also ruled that as a slave, Dred Scott was not a citizen of the United States and therefore had no right to bring suit in the federal courts on any matter. In addition, he declared that Scott had never been free, due to the fact that slaves were personal property and had always been regarded as "an inferior order."

This decision was so controversial that many believed it to be "a harbinger for Abraham Lincoln's Emancipation Proclamation and inevitably of the Civil War."[13] It also represents one of the most important moments in United States history when examining the fortification of the narrative of racial hierarchy. The act of labeling Black people as inferior, subhuman, and legal property of White people could no longer be dismissed as a narrative that belonged exclusively to fringe racists. The highest court in the land had now appealed to the narrative to make its landmark decision about slave ownership.

1858: Abraham Lincoln
Sixteenth President [*Republican*]

> There is a physical difference between the white and black races which I believe will forever forbid the two races living together on terms of social and political equality. And inasmuch as they cannot live, while they do remain together there must be the position of superior and inferior, and I as much as any other man am in favor of having the superior position assigned to the white race.[14]

Lincoln is thought of as one of the presidents who accomplished the most good for Black people, but that doesn't mean he was untouched by the lie of the narrative of racial hierarchy. In this quote we see that he politically acquiesced to the reality that in order for our society to function, the White "race" needed to be placed in the superior position of the hierarchy.

1860: Jefferson Davis
Senator, Mississippi [*Democrat*]

> This Government was not founded by negroes nor for negroes, but by white men for white men . . . We recognize the fact of the inferiority stamped upon that race of men by the Creator, and from the cradle to the grave, our Government, as a civil institution, marks that inferiority.[15]

This quote stands out as a particularly illuminating version of the lie of the narrative of racial hierarchy. When Davis used the metaphor of being "stamped," he was directly evoking the language of divinity. One human being cannot stamp another human being—this is an authority that rests with God alone. To claim that inferiority was stamped on the

Black race from the beginning was to overtly subscribe to and perpetuate the lie that God's very self was responsible for the hierarchy.

It is sobering to remember that this appalling portrayal of human dignity—this view that we have been stamped from the beginning—was not held by some fringe extremist group, as many would have us believe. On November 6, 1861, Jefferson Davis was elected as president of the Confederacy.[16] Hailed as a "champion of a slave society" who "embodied the values of the planter class,"[17] Davis brought the full measure of this lie into the DNA of his leadership over the eleven states that seceded from the United States in 1860–1861 following the election of President Abraham Lincoln.

1862: Horatio Seymour
Governor, New York [*Democrat*]

> The scheme for an immediate emancipation and general arming of the slaves throughout the South is a proposal for the butchery of women and children, for scenes of lust and rapine; of arsen and murder unparalleled in the history of the world.[18]

When promoting the lie of the narrative, it has never been enough to simply talk of racial differences. The bottom end of the hierarchy needed to be depicted as fundamentally dangerous to the upper end of the hierarchy. Natives were painted as savages, and Black people were painted as intrinsically dangerous, oversexualized, and predatory to White women. This quote from Seymour, who in 1868 ran for president on the Democratic ticket as the "White man's candidate," is one of the clear cases of injecting increasing levels of inflammatory material into the already existing narrative lie.

1865: Andrew Johnson
Seventeenth President [*Democrat*]

> It is vain to deny that [Black Americans] are an inferior race—
> very far inferior to the European variety. They have learned
> in slavery all that they know in civilization.[19]

Some quotes are so self-explanatory that they barely need
commentary. The narrative of racial hierarchy is that White
people (of European ancestry) are inherently superior and that
Black people are inferior and that all other people of color find
their value between these two poles. President Johnson articu-
lates this here about as clearly as it can be said.

April 9, 1865: *The End of the Civil War*

1895: Theodore Roosevelt
Twenty-Sixth President [*Republican*]

> A perfectly stupid race can never rise to a very high plane;
> the negro, for instance, has been kept down as much by lack
> of intellectual development as by anything else.[20]

Once again, we encounter derogatory and inflammatory language depicting how Black people were fundamentally perceived.

1912: Woodrow Wilson
Twenty-Eighth President [*Democrat*]

> I stand for the National policy of exclusion. The whole
> question is one of assimilation of diverse races. We cannot
> make a homo-genous population out of people who do not
> blend with the Caucasian race . . . Oriental Coolieism will

give us another race problem to solve and surely we have had our lesson.[21]

President Wilson gave voice to the way that the lie began to shift from a narrative that historically had measured just Native and Black people against White people to a narrative that mapped the human value of other ethnic groups onto this hierarchy. Notice how the defining trait of Asian Americans here is the way they "blend" with the Caucasian race. The idea of tainting White blood with colored blood was not a new one; applying the idea to Asian people was.

1946: Theodore G. Bilbo
Governor, Senator, Mississippi [*Democrat*]

> It is indeed a sorry white man and white woman who when put on notice of the inevitable result of mongrelization of their race and their civilization are yet unwilling to put forth any effort or make any sacrifice to save themselves and their offspring from this great and certain calamity.
> YOU MUST TAKE YOUR CHOICE!
> Personally, the writer of this book would rather see his race and his civilization blotted out with the atomic bomb than to see it slowly but surely destroyed in the maelstrom of miscegenation, interbreeding, intermarriage, and mongrelization.[22]

A self-admitted, lifelong member of the KKK, Bilbo was a favorite in White supremacist circles. He wrote an influential book called *Take Your Choice: Separation or Mongrelization* in which he urged White America to recognize the threats of sexual relations between Black and White people. He was an unashamed proponent of the narrative of racial hierarchy. In a

1938 filibuster against antilynching legislation, Bilbo said on the Senate floor that the bill would "open the floodgates of hell in the South" by encouraging Black men to rape White women.[23] In their 2018 report titled *Segregation in America*, Equal Justice Initiative noted that "in 1946, after four white men beat a black Army veteran for attempting to register to vote, Senator Bilbo delivered a radio address urging every 'red-blooded Anglo-Saxon man in Mississippi to resort to any means to keep hundreds of Negroes from the polls in the July 2nd primary.'"[24]

1949: Allen Ellender
Senator, Louisiana [*Democrat*]

> The Negro himself cannot make progress unless he has white leadership. If you call that 'supremacy,' why suit yourself. But I say that the Negro race as a whole, if permitted to go to itself, will invariably go back to barbaric lunacy.[25]

A senator for almost thirty-five years, Allen Ellender was deeply committed to racial separation and consistently supported segregationist policies. When describing the lie of the narrative here, he uses a familiar approach of appealing to the inherent superiority of White people and the inherent inferiority of Black people. This quote also highlights another dimension of that same lie—one that became commonplace throughout the various justifications used to support slavery. Black people were described not only as inferior, which was horrible enough, but also as a people who were naturally oriented toward "barbaric lunacy." This, in turn, meant that White people were not just superior, which was a horrible enough conclusion, but had been endowed with a godlike responsibility of leading Black people into the vision of human progress.

1954: Thomas Pickens Brady
State Supreme Court Justice, Mississippi [*Democrat*]

> You can dress a chimpanzee, housebreak him, and teach him
> to use a knife and fork, but it will take countless genera-
> tions of evolutionary development, if ever, before you can
> convince him that a caterpillar or a cockroach is not a deli-
> cacy. Likewise the social, political, economical, and religious
> preferences of the negro remain close to the caterpillar and
> the cockroach.[26]

One of the consistently dehumanizing tactics used to promote the narrative of racial hierarchy was to compare those
deemed as inferior to animals instead of viewing them as human
beings. This is one of the more inflammatory examples of a state
Supreme Court justice demeaning Black people. In contrast, he
painted a picture of supremacy as well, at one point saying that
a "Southern white woman" was "the nearest thing to an angelic
being that treads this celestial ball."[27]

1960: Leander Perez
Judge, District Attorney, Louisiana [*Democrat*]

> Don't wait for your daughters to be raped by these Congolese.
> Don't wait until the burrheads are forced into your schools.
> Do something about it now.[28]

One of Louisiana's fiercest foes of African American civil
rights, Leander Perez demonstrates the tactic of arousing White
fear by likening Black people to sexual predators. Perez reminds
us that these lies of White supremacy are not restricted to White
people—people of any ethnic background can and have subscribed to and perpetuated them.

April 4, 1968: *Assassination of Martin Luther King Jr.*

1973: Richard Nixon
Thirty-Seventh President [*Republican*]

> I know, I know. I admit. I mean there are times when abortions are necessary—when you have a black and a white [interracial pregnancy] . . . or rape.[29]

President Nixon was in office when the Supreme Court legalized abortion, and he confessed that he saw two reasons for morally seeking an abortion: in the case of rape and in the case of a child of sexual relations between a Black and White person. This admission demonstrates how deep the lie goes—that someone could see the basis for killing a child because he or she was mixed race. This quote also serves as a reminder of how long the idea behind the one-drop rule governed popular thought. We saw Thomas Jefferson espouse this view in 1814, and we see that it was just as operative in 1973.

2018: Donald Trump
Forty-Fifth President [*Republican*]

> Why are we having all these people from shithole countries [places like Haiti and Africa] come here? We should bring in more people from countries like Norway.[30]

Regardless of one's view of President Trump, most observers agree that he regularly utilized the narrative of racial hierarchy to validate his political positions. Whether it was telling U.S. Congresswomen of color in a tweet to go back to the "totally broken and crime infested places from which they came,"[31] referring to Mexican immigrants in a tweet as "all of these people" who "invade our Country,"[32] or referring to a Black-dominant city in a tweet as a "disgusting, rat and rodent infested mess,"[33] Trump regularly referenced groups of color in relation to their White counterparts. I chose the lead quote as the primary example, however, because it so clearly illuminates the meaning of the narrative of racial hierarchy. By alluding to immigrants from Black countries and continents like Haiti and Africa as unwanted, and to immigrants from White countries like Norway as being more desirable, he paints as precise a picture of the narrative of racial hierarchy as one possibly could.

A Commission from Jesus

In chapter 4, we paid close attention to Bryan Stevenson's work of illuminating the far-reaching power of the narrative of racial hierarchy. He said, "That ideology [the narrative of racial hierarchy], which set up White supremacy in America, was the most poisonous and destructive consequence of two centuries of slavery. And I do believe that we never addressed it. I think the North won the Civil War, but the South won the narrative war. The racial-equality principle that is in our Constitution was never extended to formerly enslaved people, and that is why I say slavery didn't end in 1865. It evolved."[34]

The seventeen quotes above show us the clear link between the presence of evil, the weaponizing of lies, and the poisonous and destructive consequences that have come from this sustained attack on human dignity.

The selection and commissioning of the twelve disciples provide us with a moral and spiritual template for courageously standing up to the forces of evil. Mark records the selection of the disciples like this: "Jesus went up on a mountainside and called to him those he wanted, and they came to him. He appointed twelve that they might be with him and that he might send them out to preach and to have authority to drive out demons" (Mark 3:13–15).

After calling these twelve disciples to himself, Jesus focused on growing their spiritual capacity first for learning to be "with him" and then for learning to be "sent out" by him.

What were they sent to do? First, they were sent out to preach the gospel, which is probably what we would expect Mark to say. But in tandem with that call, they were also sent out to have authority to drive out demons. Is that a bit surprising?

We have examined the need to duel with the devil throughout this chapter. I hope Jesus' commission to drive out demons makes more sense than ever. The devil is a liar, and lies are powerful. We cannot effectively bear witness to the truth found in Jesus without also challenging the lies found in the presence of evil.

Jesus sent out the disciples with authority to drive out dark powers, and his intention is to send us out as well.

Are we ready to tell the truth?

Tell the Truth

O ne of the more memorable conferences I've participated
in was built around a small gathering of pastors on the
East Coast. Their city had experienced a series of traumatic,
race-based incidents, and as a result, social tensions had escalated
to a near boiling point. A well-known foundation in the area
was looking to do something in response. It offered a new grant
that focused on developing leaders who could serve as change
agents, particularly with regard to the problem of race. One of
the subcategories of leaders they were looking to develop was
clergy, and through the grant a cohort was formed that accepted
thirty applicants to take part in a rigorous training program. As
part of the curriculum, I was brought in to facilitate a one-day
session around the question of how churches can meaningfully
organize themselves to confront White supremacy.

We had a great day together, and the content of the session
revolved around the five practices we've covered up to this point
in the book. In our final session, we focused on John 8, the same
passage we looked at in the last chapter. We reflected on the
importance of Jesus characterizing the devil as the father of lies,
examined the way White supremacy represents one of the most
powerful cluster of lies in American history, and pinpointed the

narrative of racial hierarchy as the operating system of this cluster of lies. And then we reflected on the importance of Jesus' characterization of himself as the remedy to these lies. In this majestic and beautiful promise, Jesus reminded his listeners that we can find true freedom only when we come to know the truth that is in him: "To the Jews who had believed him, Jesus said, 'If you hold to my teaching, you are really my disciples. Then you will know the truth, and the truth will set you free'" (John 8:31–32).

These are two of my favorite verses in the Bible, and I used them to bring our time to a close. I reminded these pastors that at the end of the day, their primary job description can be simply summarized with three words: *Tell the truth*. These three words don't just represent this sixth practice; they represent one of the core dimensions of discipleship. Could Jesus say it any more clearly? To be his disciple is to know the truth, and to know the truth is to be set free.

Truth and freedom are what we need badly, especially when it comes to race. The White lies of race represent a form of captivity on so many levels—spiritually, emotionally, socially, communally. I beseeched these pastors to take that captivity seriously and to commit themselves to seeking the necessary deliverance from the serious effects of White supremacy at every level—in their own personal lives, in their pastoral leadership, in their churches, in their city, and in our nation. We prayed to that effect and then concluded our time together.

When the session ended, one of the young pastors immediately came over to me. It was clear that the Spirit had provoked something meaningful inside him, and he asked if he could have five minutes to share what had been illuminated in the final session.

We grabbed some chairs in the corner, and he began to passionately share his testimony. He had been an intellectual prodigy in high school and was recruited by almost every big-name school in the country. Eventually he accepted a full-ride scholarship to an elite private college in his city, and his collegiate career started off strong. Unfortunately, he found his way into a social circle that experimented heavily with recreational drugs, which evolved into increasingly stronger substances. In time, he fell into a full-fledged drug addiction, and his life went quickly off the rails. The next five years were marked by one disastrous decision after another that culminated with his friends and family arranging an intervention.

The intervention ended up being just the spark he needed, and he moved into a Christian halfway house for six months. There his life was completely turned around. He found freedom from his drug addiction, placed his faith in Christ, and even discovered a pastoral call on his life. He wasted no time pursuing this call, and as soon as he was affirmed as sober, he left the halfway house and enrolled in seminary. Three years later, he graduated and was ordained by his denomination to plant a church, and now, five years later, he is highly regarded as one of the most active and trustworthy pastors in his city.

I was glad to hear the testimony just for the sake of the story, but he also wanted me to know he had a larger purpose for sharing it with me. He said that something in the final session had brought him right back to that critical time in his life in the Christian halfway house. One of his fondest memories of that era was the case worker who walked closely with him in his addiction and who ultimately helped him get to the other side. This case worker loved Scripture and would often share verses in hopes of providing encouragement. His favorite was John 8:32: "The truth will set you free." He believed that the temptation of drugs relied on a set of lies that drew someone into the need for escapist behavior and was convinced that the pathway to freedom was always tied to an experience of the truth of Jesus, made manifest in transformational ways.

So when we spent our final session looking at John 8, this young pastor knew that God was up to something. He had come into this session feeling a burden around racial injustice and his lack of substantive confrontation of it, but admitted he had no idea what to do in response. It was beyond his wildest imagination that the path forward to confronting White supremacy would so closely resemble the same liberation path he had taken to get free from the grip of drug addiction. But in a moment, it had all become so clear. Exposing lies and telling the truth had been his pathway to freedom from drugs, and now he could see that exposing lies and telling the truth represented the pathway forward to freedom from White supremacy.

He was overjoyed at the clarity he now felt and was ready to immediately pursue this new pathway in his home church. He asked if I'd be open to being a support partner, and I gladly agreed. We spent some time praying for the journey ahead, and as he left, I found myself feeling very hopeful about the impact he could have. The healing journey he had been on was a unique resource for this new journey he was about to embark on, and I was determined to do whatever I could to support him as he challenged his church to come along for the journey.

This young pastor wasted no time. As soon as he got home, he requested a meeting with his elder board, and there he shared his enthusiasm for this new direction. His concern about race had been growing for a while, so this news wasn't completely unexpected. But even still, they felt uneasy about the congregation taking such a substantial step forward. However, the repeated allusion to his personal testimony of being freed from the lies of addiction and its connection to the freedom the congregation needed from the lies of White supremacy was finally enough to convince them. They gave him the blessing to move ahead.

Armed with the conviction that the basis of his testimony represented a helpful parallel to the transformation waiting for his church, he developed a six-week series titled "Telling the Truth." Before sharing it with his congregation, he vetted it with a variety of mentors who understood the complexities of racial justice, and they confirmed the theological and historical accuracy of his material. As the series neared, he told his church how excited he was. He believed the journey they were about to embark on was of critical importance and would be a series that forever changed their church.

It turned out he was right, but for all the wrong reasons.

The first week of the series was an immediate harbinger of bad things to come. Though the content was mostly introductory in nature, it still opened the floodgates to a torrent of angry emails. Some were concerned that their pastor had been swept up by current affairs and was no longer committed to Scripture. Some were concerned that he was going down the "slippery slope of social justice." Some were just plainly offended by the subject matter and voiced displeasure about being made to feel guilty at church just because of their racial background.

This young pastor was staggered by the negative response and wasn't sure what to do next. We talked a number of times that week, and I told him that, generally speaking, I believe it is important to listen to our critics, as a grain of truth can often be learned from them. As such, we combed through the emails to see what we could learn. But the more we read them, the more the hard reality began to set in. The criticism he received revealed less about the content of his sermon and more about where the congregation was. This was not a group that was ready for the truth about White supremacy.

The enthusiasm that had marked this pastor's demeanor a couple months earlier was quickly evaporating, but he still felt it was important to follow through on the series. He carefully preached each of the remaining five weeks and pleaded with his congregation to open their eyes to the far-reaching nature of

White supremacy. He referenced his personal journey throughout and talked of the power that comes from exposing lies and chasing truth. He told them that freedom is what lives on the other side of this journey and urged them to come to experience that for themselves.

A handful of people responded well to the series, but those success stories were largely washed over by the tremendously negative response of the congregation as a whole. Families had begun to trickle out as early as the second week of the series, and by the time the damage was done, it had turned into a near exodus. Incredibly, 25 percent of the congregation left the church because of this six-week series on race. And to compound matters further, a large percentage of those who left had been major donors, turning their departure into a full budget crisis. As a result, giving dropped significantly and the church had no choice but to ask two staff members to step down.

The pastor weathered the disappointment from this experience for a little while, but he didn't last long. He became discouraged to the point that he felt he could not continue, and six months after the completion of this series, he resigned. In his farewell letter, he told the congregation that he loved them dearly and was thankful for the opportunity to serve them, but that it had become clear there were irreconcilable differences between the vision he had sensed for this church and the vision they had sensed for themselves.

Once again, telling the truth came at a tremendous price.

A Broken Foundation

The Bible contains a well-known saying from Jesus about the need for his followers to "count the cost." The phrase comes from Luke 14, where Jesus highlights the intense commitment that is expected from those who accept his invitation to become a disciple. Emphasizing the larger point, Jesus says that absolutely nothing should come between us and him—not parents or children, not spouse or siblings—not even our own life! It is a hard-core passage.

The phrase "count the cost" is typically thought of in terms of individual application, but by the time Jesus uses it, he has actually shifted to a meaning that goes beyond the need to count the cost of following him at an individual level. He uses the term in a more concrete manner, in terms of needing to count the cost of what will be required to carry out a major project. In this case, Jesus paints the picture of a construction process that will result in the eventual building of a tower: "For which of you, desiring to build a tower, does not first sit down and *count the cost*, whether he has enough to complete it?" (Luke 14:28 ESV, italics added).

The word that Jesus uses here has an accounting feel to it. In *Strong's Concordance*, the synonyms for the verb *count* are "compute" and "calculate." Jesus is issuing a literal instruction or warning to the builder: Before setting out on an important project, make an accurate appraisal of what it will take to complete the project! Jesus uses a question that borders on humor, asking why someone would even set out on a project like this without the assurance that the necessary supplies were already in place, and then he concludes, "For if you lay the foundation and are not able to finish it, everyone who sees it will ridicule you, saying, 'This person began to build and wasn't able to finish'" (Luke 14:29–30).

I have reflected on this passage frequently over the past few years, particularly in the context of engaging White Christians with the need to confront White supremacy. This image of laying the foundation is particularly noteworthy, since foundation imagery is recurrent throughout the Bible.[1] Some big questions arise out of this biblical imagery with regard to the mission of confronting White supremacy. What is required to lay this foundation in a way that ensures the project can actually continue its progress toward eventual completion? And just as importantly, what is currently missing from the foundation that prevents it from doing so?

One of the gifts that has come from *White Awake* has been the opportunity to travel and visit a variety of predominantly White institutions across the country. In the process, I've been introduced to a broad and diverse network of leaders who have been tasked with building the foundation for these conversations within their institutions. It has been incredibly valuable to gain a panoramic view of these foundation-building exercises and to learn their perspectives on "counting the cost" of what is required to accomplish this task of cultivating conversations on White supremacy from a biblical viewpoint. In each setting, I've been determined to learn as much as I can, and one of the enlightening realities has been this consistent feeling across the country that something is fundamentally broken in the foundation of most of the White Christian institutions in our country. What is broken? *The ability to engage with truth.*

I confess that when I first heard this, I was slow to believe it. Some of the inability to believe it is on me, and I completely own that. But some of the reason this answer was so hard to believe is that truth should be the most fundamental, unmovable piece of the Christian foundation. How can we follow the One who defines himself as truth and yet lack the ability to engage with truth?

And yet the more I thought about it, the more the critique made sense. To be clear, the inability to engage with truth is not universal in its application. In fact, in just about every other arena, Christians seem to be doing just fine at engaging with truth. But something in the atmosphere shifts when the subject matter turns to White supremacy. Our ability to hear truth seems to immediately weaken. Grounding our worldview in biblical truth suddenly becomes an elusive task. Stated simply, when it comes to White supremacy, our foundation for engaging with truth is broken.

Let me illustrate this in a couple of ways, starting by recalling the opening story of the pastor who had such a difficult experience with his church. The tremendous unrest that his sermon series created, as well as the accompanying fallout, makes little sense at a rational level. The pastor loved Jesus. He loved his church. His motivation was nothing more than for them to grow in their ability to see truth—both the truth of who Jesus is and the lies that stand in the way of the truth of Jesus being clearly seen in our current moment in society.

Why would a series called "Telling the Truth" be so threatening to a group of Christians? What could possibly be so threatening about saying that the truth of God's view of humanity is found in the doctrine of the *imago Dei* and that Christians need to build their theological knowledge about race on the sure foundation of this truth? What could possibly be so threatening about saying that the lie of the devil is what animates White supremacy and sinfully assigns human value based on someone's position in the racial hierarchy? It is illogical on every level.

We can safely assume that if the pastor's series called "Telling the Truth" had been focused on any other subject matter, it would have gone over fine—probably even would have been applauded. But when he focused the gaze of truth telling onto the specific arena of White supremacy, he initiated a level of unrest that led to the near demise of that church. Unfortunately, his story is not an anomaly. I hear accounts like this all the time. It is a vivid reminder that when it comes to conversations about White supremacy, something in our foundation is broken. We can't engage with truth.

A second illustration comes from a more personal place.

What used to be a theoretical analysis has now become hardened by reality for me. I am often asked to speak about the Bible and White supremacy, and I regularly run into this problem of an inability to engage with truth. This inability can manifest in a variety of ways. Sometimes it manifests in the form of people becoming offended and walking out in the middle of a presentation. Other times it manifests through a torrent of angry letters sent to the administration before or after I'm brought in to speak. In one Christian college I spoke at, an entire row of students wore "Make America Great Again" hats and T-shirts to express their displeasure with the chapel director for inviting me to address this topic.

One response in particular summarizes the sentiment of what I am trying to convey here. I had been invited by a Christian college to speak on the need to develop a biblical framework for addressing and confronting White supremacy. At the conclusion of the presentation, students were invited to ask questions. A White woman in the audience had been obviously disturbed by the content of the presentation at multiple points throughout. By the time it was over, the emotional turmoil she was feeling had translated into a physical state of shaking. She blurted out, "Fine. Let's say White supremacy may have been real at one point in American history. I don't think that's the case anymore. All someone has to do is look around to see that it's no longer the case. I don't think you can point to any definitive proof that it still exists."

It wasn't exactly a question, but I decided to treat it as such. I began to share some of the many ways that White supremacy still manifests itself, alluding to key statistics in health care, home ownership, household incomes, life expectancy, and incarceration rates. But with each indicator I cited, her irritation only increased. When she could no longer take it, she just blurted out, "Why are you even here!" And then she walked out.

I was surprised by the outburst and debriefed afterward with the administrator who had invited me to speak. I felt bad that this had happened and apologized if inciting such a reaction made him look bad.

But he quickly said, "Oh, don't apologize. That response wasn't due to what you said; it's a result of a faulty foundation. We find that our White students are able to wrestle with challenging truths in just about every other area of the Christian life. But when the topic shifts to race, the entire mood changes. This is actually why we brought you to speak to this as a White pastor. When I talk about White supremacy as a Black man, I know the students struggle with the truth. But many of them find a way to dismiss it because I'm Black. They'll say something like, 'Well, that's just a Black person who has had a hard life and who is angry at White people for it.' And then they move on. But when you say the truth as a White male, it creates a different level of disruption. They can't dismiss the truth by saying it's just you being an angry Black man. I'm glad you spoke to the truth of White supremacy, and I'm glad she was honest about how disgusted she was by that truth. I don't think transformation can happen until this resistance to the truth comes out into the open."

Experiences like this have led me to join the chorus of conviction that so many BIPOC leaders convey when their attempts to engage their White counterparts with honest conversations about race fail. The sobering reality is this: In no current environment in the United States is it more difficult to tell the truth about White supremacy than in White, Christian, Bible-believing spaces. Those of us who follow the One who is "the way and the truth and the life" (John 14:6) are the ones who currently have the hardest time interacting with truth—at least when it comes to race.

As I say this, I hope it's also clear what I am *not* saying. I am not saying this is true of every White Christian. In fact, it's quite the opposite. One of my joys in this work is seeing the growing number of White Christians who, though raised with a sense of obliviousness to the lies of White supremacy, refuse to allow that obliviousness to be the prevailing reality any longer. They now hunger to tell the truth and expose the lie of the narrative of racial hierarchy. They hunger to understand the ways that the lie has impacted them and how it has impacted the society we live in. They are eager to go out into the world, sent by the Spirit, to participate in the work of Jesus in dismantling this lie. That's an important part of the story—a part I celebrate.

When it comes to this sixth practice of telling the truth, the applications are closely aligned with Jesus' teaching to "count the cost." There is a personal level of counting the cost and a collective, missional level of counting the cost.

First, at the personal level. Because it's so difficult for White Christians to engage with the truth of White supremacy, being the one who initiates these conversations will always carry a risk. I don't want to overstate that risk, as leaders of color have been doing this work for decades and at much greater risk. But I don't want to ignore it either. The opening story of the pastor illuminates some of the very real risks we take when we plainly pursue the truth.

Second, at the collective, missional level. It is here that we remember Jesus' words, "For which of you, desiring to build a tower, does not first sit down and *count the cost*, whether he has enough to complete it?" This is the accounting side of the equation. It is making an accurate appraisal of the current condition of the foundation. To assist in that task, I want to spend the remainder of the chapter simply exploring the question, "Why is it that White Christian spaces have such a hard time telling the truth?" There are at least four big reasons, and each provides a resource for moving forward into a renewed sense of telling the truth.

Reason 1: Telling the Truth Confronts History as We Have Come to Know It

When I reflect on my own nascent encounters with truth, the visceral feelings that accompanied those early experiences come rushing back quickly. For instance, when I was in my early twenties, one of my truth encounters came as a result of an ongoing uneasiness I felt with the Thanksgiving story I was taught. In an attempt to expose me to a more whole history, a friend shared a magazine article that outlined some of the truth around settler colonization. Even though I asked for it, I still found myself with an almost immediate onslaught of feelings such as shock, outrage, and defensiveness.

It was shocking to discover that the United States government had authorized more than fifteen hundred wars, attacks, and raids on Native Americans—the most of any country in the world against its indigenous people. It was shocking to discover the racist words used by President Andrew Jackson (see the previous chapter), and the sixty thousand Native people removed from their homes on the "Trail of Tears." It was shocking to discover that President Abraham Lincoln, after defeating the Dakotas, ordered military officials to hang thirty-eight of the captives on the day after Christmas 1862.

The fact that I had never been taught these history lessons was already enough to set me up for the inevitable whiplash that came from these discoveries. But it went deeper than that. This story of settler colonialism was not just unfamiliar; the truth contradicted history as I had come to know it. I was taught that relations between European settlers and Native Americans were kind and cordial, with Thanksgiving representing the culmination of this happy alliance. How could that version peacefully coexist with what I knew now? I was taught to view President Lincoln as the greatest crusader for racial equality our country had ever seen. But how was I to reconcile that teaching with the historical reality that he had authored the largest mass execution in American history? This was more than new information; it felt like an assault on the history I had come to know.

I carry a similar set of intense feelings from when I first encountered the severity of slavery. One of the few Black friends I had in my twenties felt embarrassed on my account for my lack of historical understanding, and rather than getting into an intellectual debate where he'd try to convince me of its veracity, he urged me to watch the miniseries *Roots*. Written by Alex Haley, *Roots* tells the story of Kunta Kinte, an eighteenth-century West African who was captured as an adolescent, sold into slavery in Africa, and eventually auctioned into chattel slavery in Annapolis, Maryland. There he experienced one horror after another, ranging from being repeatedly whipped and maimed so he wouldn't try to escape to having his daughter ripped away from him and sold. The show then continued to explore the lives of Kinte's descendants in the United States all the way down to the generation of the author who had written it.

While *Roots* gave me just a beginning glimpse into the brutal nature of slavery, it was still more than enough to create substantial disequilibrium. This new degree of revelation was not only challenging the highly inaccurate version of slave history I had picked up in the curriculum of my public school upbringing; it was directly confronting the lies I had picked up along the way in Christian spaces as well. Whether it was the false notion that slavery removed Africans from a culture that practiced witchcraft or that slavery graciously brought heathens to a Christian land where they could hear the gospel or that the benefit of Christian masters providing religious instruction for their slaves somehow canceled out the brutality of slavery, it was clear I would have to contend with a series of deceitful validations if I was going to have any chance of continuing down the road of truth.

While these accounts represent just my own personal experience, I believe they are also emblematic of what happens to most White Americans when they encounter the full truth. There tends to be a monstrous gulf between the truth they are now hearing for the first time and the version of history they had come to know until then. And crossing that gulf requires more than just the consumption of information; it requires the ability to manage the shock, outrage, and defensiveness that accompany the discovery and reckoning of these contradictory versions of history.

So what can we do about that?

An important starting point is the command that God repetitively gave the Israelites throughout the Old Testament, summarized in one word: *remember.* They were to remember that God had delivered them from slavery (Judges 8:34). They were to remember that God spoke to them at Mount Horeb and gave them the Ten Commandments (Deuteronomy 4:10). They were to remember that God tested them in the wilderness for forty years (8:2). They were to remember the commands that God had given them as a result (8:11). They were to remember the covenant that God had made with them (8:18). In sum, common memory was an indispensable resource for moving the Israelites into the future that God had for them.

One of the more prolific truth tellers in modern times used this exact tactic to accomplish his task of getting the dominant culture to reckon with an honest appraisal of White supremacy. Georges Erasmus was born to a Tlicho (Dene) mother and a Cree-Métis father in a small Tlicho community in Fort Rae in the Northwest Territories of Canada in 1948. Erasmus eventually emerged as one of the most well-respected spokespersons for Indigenous peoples in his country. He demonstrated unusual ability as both an organizer and a public intellectual from an early age, and he eventually rose to the ranks of national chief of the Assembly of First Nations, which has established itself as the "undisputed voice" of Indigenous peoples in Canada.[2]

His vision for truth telling was built around the necessity of a community *remembering*. Erasmus believed that in order for a community of people to move into a new future together, there must first be a concerted effort to develop a shared and agreed-on history. Here is his most famous quotation on this, which he borrowed from H. Richard Niebuhr: "Where common memory is lacking, where people do not share in the same past, there can be no real community, and where community is to be formed common memory must be created."[3]

There are many from the dominant culture who long for a new future absent of racism, but they are still unwilling to engage in the process of recovering a common memory. The process of doing so is painful at times and requires courage and resilience from those who have learned only revisionist history. But as Niebuhr and Erasmus remind us, and as the Bible historically has taught, there is no moving into the future without first remembering the past. We must create a common memory.

Reason 2: Telling the Truth Reveals a Fragmented Discipleship Framework

I was speaking with a group of student leaders at a prominent evangelical seminary in the Midwest, and we were discussing the importance of developing a biblical framework for confronting White supremacy.

After the presentation, the moderator opened the space for Q&A. A young woman immediately ran to the mic. "Seeing White supremacy as a principality, sustained by a set of lies, makes so much sense. And in light of that, seeing the role of Christians as one of truth tellers not only makes sense, but seems so obvious. It sounds so simple . . ." She paused, almost as if she had gotten temporarily lost in another world. Finally she sighed and finished her thought. "But as straightforward as it seems to be, I still find that I can't talk about it openly in my home church. They can't hear it. Any mention of White supremacy just shuts the conversation down. Why is it so hard to talk about White supremacy in White Bible-believing spaces?"

I affirmed that when it comes to truth telling, this is indeed the million-dollar question. I then shared the first of these four points—that truth is hard to hear because it confronts history as we've come to know it. She responded positively to that answer but felt like there must be even more to it. "I understand why these opposing versions of history can be difficult to reconcile," she said, "and I can even appreciate how listeners may feel initially threatened by this. But at the end of the day, we are people of the truth. It shouldn't be this hard for White Christians to expose the lies they've been told and to pivot to the truth. There must be more to their resistance."

I wholeheartedly agreed. While the confrontation with history is important, the issue indeed goes even deeper. I was ready to share the second major obstacle we face in White Bible-believing spaces. To get there, I first asked her and the group a question: "What is discipleship?"

To bring greater definition to the exercise, I asked them to focus their answers specifically on how they had been taught to think of discipleship in their church upbringings. For those of you who grew up in similar settings, you can probably guess some of what they said. The most common answers were daily Bible reading, prayer, moral purity, the fruit of the Spirit, confession, evangelism, and service.

Once they had exhausted their answers, I asked them to look over the list and reflect on their collective responses. I then asked them to respond to this question: "If you had to pick one of these discipleship qualities as the representative answer as to why

Christians should be motivated to confront White supremacy, which would you choose?"

These student leaders cared deeply about White supremacy and were eager to find a connection. But the more they tried to find one, the more they faltered. Finally, after a period of unsuccessful attempts, it became clear to them that there was no clear connection point between the question, "What is discipleship?" and the question, "Why should we be concerned about White supremacy?"—at least based on the answers they came up with.

A collective mood of depression began to sink over the room. The reason most of them had chosen to enroll in seminary in the first place was to learn more about discipleship, as well as about how they could become church leaders who grew disciples. But what were they to do if there was no connection between the two? I didn't want them to remain in a state of despair, but I did believe it was important they counted the cost of the path they were potentially preparing to embark on.

After a couple of minutes of silence, the eyes of one of the students lit up, and it was obvious something had been clarified for him. He jumped up to the microphone, eager to share his revelation. "It's not that there is no connection between discipleship and White supremacy. The problem is that we have *too small* a view of discipleship. If we learned to think of discipleship in a more holistic way, then this connection would suddenly become much more obvious!"

"Amen!" I instinctively shouted. This was exactly the point I was hoping they would arrive at.

The prevailing view of discipleship in most White, Bible-believing spaces importantly includes many of the nonnegotiable elements that come with devotion to Jesus, particularly around personal obedience and transformation. But with that being said, the prevailing view is also fragmented profoundly. When our vision of discipleship understates (or full-out rejects) any combination of critical pieces of the puzzle such as the *imago Dei*, truth versus lies, the ministry of reconciliation, the unity of the body, the coming of Jesus' kingdom, or authority over evil (among others), a grossly imbalanced vision forms that leaves followers of Jesus off-kilter, unprepared, and vulnerable to being "tossed back and forth" by the deceitful scheming of the lies of this age.

This is the exact imagery used by the apostle Paul with the church in Ephesus when talking about the need to build mature communities of believers. He warned of remaining like "infants," who were "tossed back and forth by the waves, and blown here and there by every wind of teaching and by the cunning and craftiness of people in their deceitful scheming" (Ephesians 4:14). His solution to that problem is the same as what we've discussed all chapter long—to tell the truth! Paul said it like this: "Instead, speaking the truth in love, we will grow to become in every respect the mature body of him who is the head, that is, Christ" (Ephesians 4:15).

This is one of the reasons that this memory with the student leaders stands out as such a bright spot. They were deeply motivated to do just what Paul exhorted—to find ways we could speak the truth in love in spaces populated by White Christians who profess allegiance to Scripture and yet whose practice leaves them vulnerable to stagnation and immaturity.

My friend David Swanson defines discipleship in his book *Rediscipling the White Church* as "following Jesus in order to become like Jesus to do what Jesus does."[4] This is a helpful way to connect discipleship with the call to racial justice. The students spent the next twenty minutes filling in the list with other important but neglected themes from Scripture. By the time we were done, this group of young leaders felt equipped to deepen the conversation on discipleship. This is a critical piece of the puzzle when it comes to telling the truth in communities and organizations of White Christians.

Reason 3: Telling the Truth Reveals a History of Christian Complicity

The "skeleton in the closet" is a familiar phrase that paints a picture of the risks that come with untold secrets. It has a bit of a grisly origin, as the phrase is literally derived from the imagery of . . . well . . . a skeleton in the closet! The idea was that if a human corpse was left hidden in someone's home for a long enough period of time, the flesh would decompose all the way to the bone.

One of the reasons it is so hard to tell the truth about White supremacy among White Bible-believing Christians is that it brings attention to some of the ugliest skeletons hidden in the collective Christian closet. We suffer from the reality that White supremacy lives and breathes in large part because of our collective complicity.

What types of skeletons come out of the Christian closet when we talk about White supremacy?

Christian theology. Despite the obvious contradictions between the narrative and *imago Dei*, which locates human value within the likeness and image of God, Christian theology has been repeatedly used to defend and even reinforce and nourish the narrative of racial hierarchy.

Dr. Willie Jennings, whom I refer to in the introduction, is an associate professor of systematic theology and Africana studies at Yale Divinity School. He is the author of *The Christian Imagination: Theology and the Origins of Race*—one of the strongest theological treatises I've read on the subject. The title itself gets to his premise: the collective Christian imagination should be informed by the Bible, and this imagination should shape the way we see the glory of the *imago Dei* reflected in human beings. But because of sin, pride, power, and greed, our imagination has been warped, and we have adopted a viewpoint of human worth that functionally aligns much more closely with the lies of White supremacy than with the truth of Scripture.

Here Dr. Jennings is talking about the origins of race and tracing the beginnings of the narrative of racial hierarchy all the way back to the mid-1400s and the emergence of Prince Henry, a Portuguese colonizer. It is here that Dr. Jennings sees the beginnings of Christian complicity in what he calls a "cosmic horror" and a "catastrophic theological tragedy":

> The christological pattern of his [Zurara, Prince Henry's royal chronicler] narrative illumines the cosmic horror of this moment and also helps the reader recognize the unfolding of a catastrophic theological tragedy. Long before one would give this event a sterile, lifeless label such as "one of the beginning moments of the Atlantic slave trade," something more urgent and more life altering is taking place in the Christian world, namely, the auctioning of bodies without regard to any form of human connection. This act is carried out inside Christian society, as part of the *communitas fidelium*. This auction will draw ritual power from Christianity itself while mangling the narratives it evokes, establishing a distorted pattern of displacement.
>
> Christianity will assimilate this pattern of displacement. Not just slave bodies, but *displaced* slave bodies, will come to represent a natural state. From this position they will be relocated into Christian identity . . . An unchanging God wills to create Christians out of slaves and slaves out of those black bodies that will someday, the Portuguese hope, claim to be Christian.
>
> Slave society was not the new reality appearing here . . . The new creation here begins with Zurara's simple articulation of racial difference: "And these, placed all together in that field, were a marvelous sight; for amongst them were some white enough, fair to look upon, and well proportioned; others were less white like mulattoes;

others again were as black as Ethiops [Ethiopians], and so ugly, both in features and in body, as almost to appear (to those who saw them) the images of a lower hemisphere." Through comparison, he describes aesthetically and thereby fundamentally identifies his subjects. There are those who are almost white—fair to look upon and well-proportioned; there are those who are in between— almost white like mulattoes; and there are those who are as black as Ethiopians, whose existence is deformed. Their existence suggests bodies come from the farthest reaches of hell itself. Zurara invokes, in this passage, a scale of existence, with white at one end and black at the other end and all others placed in between.[5]

I wish I had time to build an entire chapter around just this quote. But for now, let me focus on a couple of the key phrases Dr. Jennings uses to get to the heart of Christian complicity with the narrative of racial hierarchy. To start, notice how he uses the evocative language of a "cosmic horror" to describe the "theological tragedy" of the narrative. I would strongly suggest we consider using that same type of language when we talk about the historical relationship of the church with the narrative of racial hierarchy.

Second, notice the important ways Dr. Jennings demonstrates that the narrative was the precondition for slavery. He uses phrases such as something even "more urgent" than the Atlantic slave trade—something that was "more life altering" taking place in the Christian world. The auction of bodies that led to slavery in the first place would "draw ritual power from Christianity itself while mangling the narrative it evokes." And before finishing with the explicit way in which Prince Henry's royal chronicler describes the meaning of these perceived physical differences, Jennings says "the new creation" begins not with slavery, but with the "simple articulation of racial difference" (a synonym for the narrative of racial hierarchy).

To summarize in my own words what Jennings is saying, it comes down to this stark reality: *The narrative of racial hierarchy could not have survived without the support and sustenance of Christian theology.* This is a hard truth to hear, but it is one we must reckon with. We must allow the weight of that truth to sink in. And then we need to tell the truth about Christianity's historical complicity with this narrative.

The Slave Bible. Perhaps the most poignant example I have encountered of how Christian theology was used to manipulate the narrative, particularly for the purposes of justifying transatlantic slavery, is the Slave Bible. Published in 1807 in London, it is now on exhibit in the Museum of the Bible in Washington, DC.[6] The missionary organization that helped design and distribute the Slave Bible did so under the guise of introducing slaves to Christianity, as well as educating and uplifting them. The only problem is that before the Bible was distributed, edits were made to ensure that the slaves were not incited to rebel against their masters. As such, every passage considered to be dangerous was removed.[7]

The result? An absolute mutilation of God's Word. For instance, the Slave Bible starts with the creation story and then skips the entire story of Moses leading the slaves out of Egypt. It picks back up with the story of Joseph in slavery, with the insinuation that this worked out well for him and his family. And in case the motivation behind those edits wasn't initially clear, it became undeniable when the Slave Bible deleted the *entire* book of Exodus. Can you imagine deleting an entire book of the Bible? The risk of showing a God who intervenes on behalf of those who have been oppressed was clearly seen as a risk too great to take.

Deleting the book of Exodus may have been the most egregious example of the mangling that happened, but it certainly wasn't the only one. Passages that emphasized equality between groups of people were also excised, including this one: "There is neither Jew nor Gentile, neither slave nor free, nor is there male or female, for you are all one in Christ Jesus" (Galatians 3:28). The Slave Bible also doesn't contain the book of Revelation, which tells of the punishment of evil and the establishment of a new heaven and earth. In contrast, one of the passages that remained was one that proponents of slavery loved to cite: "Servants, be obedient to them that are your masters according to the flesh, with fear and trembling, in singleness of your heart, as unto Christ" (Ephesians 6:5 KJV).[8]

Anthony Schmidt, associate curator of Bible and Religion in America at the museum, summarizes the final damage like this: "About 90 percent of the Old Testament is missing [and] 50 percent of the New Testament is missing. Put in another way, there are 1,189 chapters in a standard protestant Bible. This Bible contains only 232."[9]

When I contemplate the depth of this sin, I reflect on my own church upbringing. I was raised in a household that placed tremendous reverence on the Scriptures. It was regularly instilled into us that no human being was allowed to add or remove anything from God's Holy Word, with verses like Deuteronomy 4:2 often cited: "Do not add to what I command you and do not subtract from it, but keep the commands of the LORD your God that I give you." When I discovered the skeleton in our closet called the Slave Bible, all those early lessons came rushing back. The sadness of what we did to the Bible in order to justify the narrative and the horrific system of slavery built on it was almost more than I could bear.

To make matters even worse, the history represented by the Slave Bible is in direct contrast to the Christian propaganda that often accompanies the distorted retelling of history. I regularly heard that slavery was actually some type of gift to the African peoples, as if it introduced them to the God of the Bible. Can you see the sinful hubris in the suggestion that Europeans are the ones who introduced Africans to Christianity? Not only do we have clear biblical accounts of African encounters with Christianity, such as the Ethiopian eunuch in Acts 8:26–40, but we have all kinds of historical scholarship pointing to Christianity arriving in Africa anywhere from the late first century to the early second century.[10]

This is just one more painful example of a skeleton in the Christian closet. Not only has the truth of what we did to the Bible been hidden, which is bad enough, but we have also added counternarratives on top of that lie to make it look better. In the words of the apostle Paul, we have "exchanged the truth about God for a lie" (Romans 1:25).

Bob Jones University. A more recent example of a skeleton in the closet is the Christian complicity with segregation in America. Robert "Bob" Jones is an iconic example of this stain on our collective Christian record. One of America's most famous evangelists in the early 1900s, he preached to millions of people across the United States, before founding Bob Jones University in Greenville, South Carolina. The school was started with money from the Ku Klux Klan, and in accord with that value system, Bob Jones University opened in 1927 as a private, Christian, all-White college. African American students were banned from the university for the entirety of his lifetime and weren't finally allowed to be admitted until 1971. Even then, the principle behind the "one-drop rule" was still legislated by the university, with interracial dating banned until a visit from George W. Bush drew press coverage that forced the school to withdraw the policy in 2000.[11]

The desire to portray the actions of one racist minister as an aberration will always be a temptation, but telling the truth necessitates that we demonstrate the ways in which Christian leaders like Jones accurately represented the spirit of the day. For instance, when Bob Jones wanted to explain why he was so committed to segregation, he appealed to his Christian belief system. When we remember that he was one of the most famous evangelists of his generation, it's both embarrassing and appalling that on Easter Sunday in 1960, Bob Jones preached a sermon titled "Is Segregation Scriptural?" In the sermon, which was widely distributed to students at Bob Jones University well into the 1980s, Jones made the case that God was the author of segregation, and that to oppose segregation was tantamount to opposing God.[12]

More examples could be shared, but these three drive home the essence of this third point: *It is not possible to tell the truth about White supremacy without also telling the truth about the ways in which Christian complicity helped enable White supremacy to survive and even thrive.* It may be hard for people to hear, but it is the truth nonetheless. We have to trust that there is freedom in truth, even when it is hard to hear.

I will finish this third point with a quote from one of the truth tellers whom I avidly follow—the Reverend Dr. Charlie Dates, the senior pastor of one of the most historic Black churches in Chicago, Progressive Baptist Church. He is one of the most dynamic preachers I know, and I admire the way he so consistently speaks the truth in love about White supremacy.

In addition to his congregation in Chicago, Dr. Dates has a large social media following. One time he visited the historic Emanuel AME Church, where the fateful Charleston shooting happened, and he was showing pictures of the slave quarters that had been memorialized there.

While there, Dr. Dates received a question from one of his African American followers. Given the content we just covered, it's a question we should all be prepared to answer: "A lot of this was done in the name of the Bible. How can you be a Christian, knowing that the Bible was used as a weapon of the state?"

In reply, Dr. Dates said this: "You are absolutely right. The Bible was used as a weapon of the state. But what I have to say is that you don't judge the value of something based upon its worst abusers. You don't do that with anything else. The gospel is still true although it was hijacked and used inappropriately to enslave millions of people, and for that, people will give an account before God. But God is gracious, his Word is true, and Christ is our Redeemer, nonetheless. I'm still a believer."[13]

We must find a way to strike this kind of balance, especially among White, Bible-believing communities. We first must be ruthlessly honest about our historic complicity with White supremacy. Then we must demonstrate an authentic posture of confession and repentance. Finally, as Dr. Dates does here, we can help people see that Christ is still Redeemer, even in the midst of such a sinful and turbulent history of intermixing the truth of the gospel with the lies of White supremacy.

Reason 4: Telling the Truth Confronts the Idol of White Nationalism

This fourth reason is perhaps the most challenging of all, and it's also the most complicated. Numerous threads need to be untangled in order to clearly see the idolatry that manages to hide in plain sight. The two biggest threads can be summarized under a pair of headings: *nationalism* and *manifest destiny*.

Nationalism. The dictionary defines *nationalism* as "a sense of national consciousness exalting one nation above all others and placing primary emphasis on promotion of its culture and interests as opposed to those of other nations." This definition highlights how nationalism, even as an isolated force, can become dangerous quickly. Whereas *patriotism* describes one's affection for or commitment to their country (which I am not critiquing here), *nationalism* describes a view of one's nation as *above* others. It emphasizes the superior traits of that particular nation and promotes those traits over the traits and values of another.

From the perspective of a Christian worldview, nationalism is problematic for multiple reasons. Besides the obvious problem of seeing one's nation as fundamentally superior, nationalism endorses values that are contrary to Jesus' teaching about being members of the kingdom of God. While we indeed recognize that God has established earthly authorities, and we are urged to submit to those authorities (Romans 13:1), we also must remember that our ultimate allegiance is never to a nation. Rather, Christians are to think of themselves as "God's elect" who are "exiles" (1 Peter 1:1) and "foreigners" (2:11) in this world. Our certificate of naturalization comes through the gospel, and our primary citizenship is located in the kingdom of God. It's not a bad thing to love one's country or honor those who serve it. But we are temporary residents passing through this world (1 Peter 1:17), and our kingdom identity is meant to inform our national identity—not the other way around.

Manifest Destiny. *Manifest Destiny* is the term used to describe the Christian precept that helped fuel colonialism and territorial expansion during the formative years of our country. Taken literally, the term means "the obvious will of God," and those who subscribed to Manifest Destiny essentially bought into three basic beliefs about God's will for America: (1) the Christian morals, values, and institutions of the United States were both righteous and superior; (2) God had tasked this country with the responsibility to spread these ideas for the benefit of the world; (3) God had blessed America to succeed in this task, and that success (particularly economic success) was an ongoing confirmation of that blessing.

There is a vast amount of scholarship on Manifest Destiny, and many trace its origins back to papal bulls written by Pope Alexander VI in the late 1400s. In the American context, nearly every scholar I've studied agrees that the doctrine was most clearly annunciated by John Winthrop in 1630. Winthrop was an English attorney who led the largest original venture ever attempted in the English New World. As his ship prepared to land in America, he penned a sermon for the nine hundred congregants he would provide spiritual guidance to in the Massachusetts Bay colony. Already chosen governor, Winthrop offered these words to describe his dreams and goals for the colony:

> We shall find that the God of Israel is among us, when ten of us shall be able to resist a thousand of our enemies; when he shall make us a praise and glory . . . For we must consider that we shall be as a city upon a hill. The eyes of all people are upon us. So that if we shall deal falsely with our God in this work we have undertaken, and so cause him to withdraw his present help from us, we shall be made a story and a by-word through the world. We shall open the mouths of enemies to speak evil of the ways of God, and all professors for God's sake. We shall shame the faces of many of God's worthy servants, and cause their prayers to be turned into curses upon us till we be consumed out of the good land whither we are going.
>
> I shall shut up this discourse with that exhortation of Moses, that faithful servant of the Lord, in his last farewell to Israel, Deut. 30. *Beloved, there is now set before us life and death, good and evil, in that we are commanded this day to love the Lord our God, and to love one another, to walk in his ways and to keep his Commandments and his ordinance and his laws* and the articles of our Covenant with him [Winthrop's addition], *that we may live and be multiplied, and that the Lord our God may bless us in the land whither we go to possess it.*[14]

165

This quote reveals the theological heresy used to propagate Manifest Destiny. Winthrop highlighted God's promises to Israel and then drew a straight line to the promises God had applied to the incoming European immigrants. He co-opted Israel's narrative. He may have been one of the first voices to do so. It quickly became a common practice during the colonial era. Passages like Joshua 24:13 would often be quoted as a justification for the unrelenting march toward progress in America: "So I gave you a land on which you did not toil and cities you did not build; and you live in them and eat from vineyards and olive groves that you did not plant."

In the context of American history, we have something historically unique, at least when viewed through a theological lens. We have a historical witness of a group of immigrants who framed their conquest of a new land through a biblical narrative that was co-opted from the Israelites and wrongfully applied to themselves (ourselves). We took the Old Testament narrative of God's choice of Israel as the nation that would be God's channel of blessing to the world and then pulled a bait and switch, swapping out Israel for the United States of America. We anointed ourselves as the singular heirs to that promise and used that stolen blessing to justify all future actions through this God-ordained lens of Manifest Destiny.

This wasn't the only time in his speech that Winthrop used a theological bait and switch. In his next line he moved from the Old to the New Testament and urged his followers to remember that they "shall be as a city upon a hill." This was a direct allusion to the opening image of Jesus' Sermon on the Mount and planted the seeds for Manifest Destiny's first cousin to emerge: *American exceptionalism.* American exceptionalism is not the same as saying the United States is different or unique from other countries. Exceptionalism points to a deeper ideology—a sense of one's self as being more or better. It's a belief that the United States follows a path of history that is different from other countries, and that because of its exceptionalism, it is destined by God to bring freedom, liberty, democracy, and the superior American values to the world.

Putting these together, we see that a distorted version of Christian theology was quickly emerging that attempted not only to make sense of the coming domination but also to validate it spiritually. A vision was solidifying that viewed the United States of America through the Old Testament prism of being God's chosen people, uniquely tasked with carrying out God's destiny.

Art often has the ability to communicate complex ideas in a more effective manner than words, so I'll finish this description with the most famous painting of Manifest Destiny. Titled *American Progress*, this John Gast painting shows an angel leading the way west across the vast plains of America. Behind her lie the industrialized eastern cities. Before her lie the great Rocky Mountains and the Pacific Ocean. Indians and bison are shown, quite appropriately, fleeing in fear. The angel is leading the way for new technologies with a train nipping at her heels and a length of telegraph wire in her hands. That is what Manifest Destiny sounded and looked like.[15]

White nationalism. The book of Acts provides a helpful reminder of how dangerous nationalism can be, especially when it gets intermixed with religion. It also presents us with a real-life model of what it can look like for an individual to courageously rise up and speak the truth in love when this unholy alliance forms.

The backdrop begins in Acts 6 when Luke (the author of Acts) details the appointment of the first deacons to the early church. Seven people were recognized as being filled with the Spirit and with wisdom and were commissioned to take on new levels of leadership. Stephen was one of those seven, and Luke tells us he made an immediate ministry impact. He was "a man full of God's grace and power" who "performed great wonders and signs among the people" (6:8).

Unfortunately, it didn't take long for the religious authorities to become uncomfortable with his presence and to design a fictitious smear campaign to silence him. Acts 6 ends with Stephen being taken into custody, and chapter 7 opens with Stephen being put on trial. Stephen is then commanded to give a defense for the alleged charges. But rather than rightly defend himself, Stephen chooses to recognize this as an opportunity to preach an important sermon to a captive crowd. He has a public audience that includes everyone from the high priest to everyday citizens, and he decides to leverage this moment to prophetically speak truth.

Stephen gives an amazing speech, which takes up fifty-two valuable verses in the book of Acts. In it, he repeatedly challenges the dangerous ways his people have intermixed religion and nationalism. Partly to establish credibility and partly to illustrate the consistency of this troubling trend, Stephen meticulously catalogs key moments throughout the chronological timeline of Israel's history in which God had revealed himself to them.

Stephen's point seems to be that instead of correctly interpreting these visitations from God as part of the larger picture of God's mission for them, they used them to further solidify the idol of nationalism. The ultimate sign of this idolatry came in the form of their missing the "Righteous One" (Jesus), despite the clear and consistent prophecies they were given about him in the Hebrew Scriptures (Acts 7:52). Stephen finishes his speech with the reminder that this idolatry ultimately led to Jesus being betrayed and murdered, an act that demanded an immediate reckoning with truth.

While I'm not suggesting that the form of nationalism that Stephen confronted in Acts 7 is exactly the same as the form of White nationalism we're up against today, I do think there are a lot of important parallels. The nationalism Stephen confronted was largely a by-product of theology that had gone awry, and it had gotten so mixed up with religion that the typical observer could no longer distinguish the religion/nationalism hybrid from the gospel itself.

We are facing a similar problem in the United States right now. The mainstream understanding of White Christianity is so mixed up with nationalism and Manifest Destiny that the typical observer can no longer distinguish the distorted hybrid from the gospel itself. This is the reason we so badly need the truth. We badly need to get back to being what the apostle Paul called "children of light" who "have nothing to do with the fruitless deeds of darkness, but rather expose them" (Ephesians 5:8, 11).

As much as I would love to say that the truth-telling task of exposing this darkness is an easy one, I think it's nonetheless wise to continue to remember that there is an element of counting the cost as we embark on this endeavor. This is especially important when speaking the truth about White nationalism.

Going back to the story of Stephen, we are left with the sobering reality that despite his being filled with the Spirit and being a man full of God's grace and power, his words were still unable to pierce the hard hearts of those who were listening. Surely God's hope was that the religious leaders would be convicted by the plain way in which Stephen laid bare the truth, but the opposite happened. Luke tells us that "when the members of the Sanhedrin heard this, they were furious and gnashed their teeth at him" (Acts 7:54).

I hope and pray that we will get to a point in American history where the truth is easier to hear about the way White nationalism has become an idolatrous force in our country. But at this point in time, I suspect the response will more often sound like that of the Sanhedrin than like a warm reception of the honest truth.

Bring It Out in the Open

In his "Letter from a Birmingham Jail," Dr. Martin Luther King Jr. famously challenged the failure of White pastors to stand up in solidarity for justice. At the heart of his appeal was the need to speak the truth and trust the redemptive process that comes with the necessary exposure:

> We who engage in nonviolent direct action are not the creators of tension. We merely bring to the surface the hidden tension that is already alive. We bring it out in the open, where it can be seen and dealt with. Like a boil that can never be cured so long as it is covered up but must be opened with all its ugliness to the natural medicines of air and light, injustice must be exposed, with all the tension its exposure creates, to the light of human conscience and the air of national opinion before it can be cured.[16]

Speaking the truth is not an easy practice. Even doing it in the right way and in the right manner is no guarantee of positive reception. And yet as Dr. King reminds us, until the truth is brought out into the open, no healing can occur. My prayer is that we will become a generation of courageous truth tellers—instruments of God's purposes to bring increased levels of healing and deliverance to our nation.

Choose Your Friends Wisely

White folks, please don't ask me to do your work. When you ask me to teach you about race or explain to you the world as it really is, you end up reopening a wound that I'm working hard to heal from. On top of that, you abdicate your own responsibility when you ask me to do your work. It's not *my* job to educate you on race; that's *your* job."

I attended a conference with a sense of great expectation. I was still early in my own racial awakening process and was desperate to find a place where I could find greater exposure to voices that extended beyond the White evangelical world I was entrenched in. A number of people encouraged me to attend this conference, largely based on its reputation for challenging White ministers in the area of biblical justice. So there I was, ready and eager to learn.

I looked forward to a panel discussion. Each participant was an esteemed thought leader on faith and race. I was hoping to walk away with concrete next steps in my own journey. The moderator asked a couple of introductory questions and then jumped into the topic of White cultural identity development.

He probed the panelists for advice to give to the folks in attendance, and particularly to the White ministers. I moved to the edge of my seat and began to record their answers verbatim. He asked a direct question about White cultural identity: "When a White person in your larger community experiences a racial awakening, are you open to supporting that new journey? Or to ask it more specifically, what is your reaction when a White person asks you for insight or advice as it relates to issues of race?"

The woman who fielded the question was an African American activist. The quote at the beginning of this chapter is her response.

I can still remember how disoriented I felt. At an intellectual level, her words made sense. While I hadn't yet thought about it as much as I should have, I could now see the way my well-intentioned questions could have the unintended effect of reopening wounds—wounds that were almost certainly inflicted by White folks in the first place. But even as I intellectually made sense of it, I was nonetheless contending with what felt like an emotional letdown. The reason I was at this conference was that I knew I didn't understand race well enough. I also knew my social network was embarrassingly monolithically White, and I was hoping to expand that.

But her comments challenged my line of thinking. In a way I hadn't considered before, I was beginning to see how abdicating my own responsibility would unfairly shift the bulk of the educational burden onto the very relationships I was seeking. Therefore, in that moment, I made what felt like a really big commitment—to no longer make attempts to engage the wisdom that came from my friends and mentors who carried the lived experience of navigating the system of race. I realized they already faced a big enough challenge to overcome the impact of White supremacy in their own lives. I was not willing to add to that.

One year later, at the very same conference, my thoughts would get turned upside down again. A nearly identical panel was on the schedule, once again composed of thought leaders on faith and race. The faculty, however, was all new. I was eager to see what new topics of conversation would come with that. To my surprise, the moderator once again quickly zoomed in on this exact same question. He issued a nearly verbatim form of the question to this new slate of panelists: "When a White person in your larger community experiences a racial awakening, are you open to supporting that new journey? Or to ask it more specifically, what is your reaction when a White person asks you for insight or advice as it relates to issues of race?"

I smiled smugly, because I already knew the answer to this one. *We should never attempt to access their wisdom*, I thought to myself. *Doing so only abdicates our responsibility to take ownership of this learning process.*

But in this case, this wasn't how the panelist responded. In fact, her answer sounded about as opposite as it could have from the response a year before. "I'm happy to support the journey of a White person in my community," she answered. "If I have a White friend or colleague who is actually serious about learning about White supremacy and is humbly ready to learn, I will almost always support that journey."

She then paused as if she was trying to decide whether to add additional commentary. She then said this: "I might go even further. If a White person is *not* learning from leaders of color—especially if it's a White minister—I would say they are perpetuating a colonized theological framework. How could a White leader hope to do the work to confront White supremacy without learning from those who actually have lived under that very system? Of course they need to learn from us."

As I listened to her, I found myself having a serious déjà vu moment. For the second year in a row, the answer to this question had caught me off guard, but each time for different reasons. Last year's speaker had challenged my blind spot of erroneously asking friends to do the work only I should do. But this year the speaker was challenging my blind spot of perpetuating a monolithic worldview whose blind spots and distortions remained untouched.

Her logic made absolute sense, but it also created a new level of confusion for me. I hungered to grow, and I wanted to find wisdom wherever I could. But now I felt less clear than ever about whether I could or should seek out friends and mentors to support that learning process. I was quickly coming to realize that this question was going to become one of the most important ones of my journey. If I didn't figure out how to develop this practice of choosing my friends wisely, I was going to risk doing damage to both myself and those I was hoping to learn from.

To Engage, or Not to Engage?

I'd like to wrestle with this question: When it comes to the White learning journey, is there a point where it becomes appropriate to seek guidance from friends, mentors, or communities that are knowledgeable about White supremacy—particularly those whose knowledge has been formed through the painful lived experience of surviving White supremacy?

This is a complicated question that represents one of the most controversial questions in the field of racial awakening work. As the opening story points to, there is a wide range of perspectives on this question. As the first speaker illustrated, some voices underscore the high degree of risk that carriers of this knowledge expose themselves to when sharing their wisdom among White communities and therefore would discourage this course. As the second speaker illustrated, under the right circumstances and with the right precautions, some voices are willing to make themselves available for this type of access and engagement.

I have taken this topic, and the questions it provokes, very seriously at every stage of my racial awakening journey. I have asked a variety of questions of my mentors and friends over these years, but no question has been asked more frequently than this one. At a personal level, it has been important for me to understand if, when, and how my mentors and friends prefer I seek to engage with their wisdom. As I've done increasing amounts of training with other White people, it has been important to understand how mentors and friends want me to talk about this important subject matter at a broader level.

Their insight has been so valuable. As I have sat under their tutelage, I have learned that the answer to whether we should seek to engage with the wisdom that comes from the lived experience of mentors and friends is, "It depends." As the contrast of the perspectives in the opening story alludes to, there are times when we should, and then there are times when we shouldn't.

To illustrate, let's take the first of those responses, where the speaker emphasizes the importance of White people doing their own work. Here is one manifestation of this—one that has been universally agreed on by every person I've talked to on this subject. One of the clearest examples of a White person abdicating the work we should be doing is when we ask our friend to *prove* that racism is real.

This happens on a nearly daily basis in cross-cultural relationships, and it goes something like this. As a White person, I see a clip of police brutality. Or I read an article about structural inequalities in the workplace. Or I have a colleague at work who describes a personal experience of racism. Part of me is drawn into their story and wants to believe them. But part of me still feels skeptical, since I've never seen this type of mistreatment firsthand.

So what do I do? I reach out to my Black (or insert other ethnic background) friend and share my conflicted feelings. I first tell them about my new discovery and invite my friend to build on this new knowledge. However, I follow up by also telling them of my ongoing skepticism and ask my friend to help me reach a verdict on the veracity of the claim.

When we make a request like this, I imagine we do so under the guise of our coming with a sincere posture, ready and eager to learn. And yet the very act of doing so demonstrates how far we still are from clear sight.

When reading this, one of my Black colleagues gave a hearty amen and then shared a story of a friend at work who had just done this very thing. It had really hurt his feelings, and he was debating whether he wanted to let his friend know. I asked what he would say, if he were to decide to, and he responded, "When you as a White man ask me as a Black man to prove to you that racism is real, it hurts on multiple levels. First, it says you don't really see me. Don't you realize how painful these systemic realities are for me? Don't you realize what it has cost me to survive and even thrive in this system, despite the daily assault on my humanity? Don't you realize that by asking me to prove it, you're asking me to prove my very existence? Second, it says you have little to no regard for my personal welfare. When you ask me to prove that racism is real, what I actually hear you saying is this: 'Put your pain on display for me, and then I'll decide for myself if it's real or not.'"

The lament he shares points us back to the statement the woman in the opening story made: "It's not *my* job to educate you on race; that's *your* job."

To ask it in the form of a question: When as a White person, I discover that I am still unresolved about the actual threat of racism, whose job is it to give me clarity? Answer: It's my job! An abundance of resources is easily accessible to help me sort through something like this. To ask a friend or mentor to convince me of the veracity of racism is inconsiderate at best and cruel at worst.

The Limits of Self-Guided Learning

We have just named the importance of doing our own work, which is an important piece of this learning puzzle. But with that being said, we also need to acknowledge that this can never be a comprehensive learning strategy in and of itself. A self-guided path has inevitable limitations and will not produce the full dimension of transformation. Why? Because the whole dilemma of the White learning journey is wrapped around the need to grapple with a dual reality: White supremacy is everywhere, *and* I can't see it as clearly as I need to.

The words of Dr. Chanequa Walker-Barnes shed light on this point: "In any society, the most marginalized people best understand the rules of the system, because they need to know the politics and dynamics in order to avoid being crushed by them."[1] What she describes is the profile of those who see the system with the greatest levels of clarity. They are the ones who have lived under its crushing weight, and they are the ones who possess the greatest levels of understanding about it.

By way of contrast, then, it is those of us who live within the system, often as inside participants, who see it the least clearly. That is the primary reason a *self-guided* journey down the road of blindness-to-sight will always be insufficient. Living on the inside doesn't just handicap our ability to see the system clearly; it also handicaps our ability to see what we don't see!

So once again, we come back to this question: When it comes to the White learning journey, is there a point where it becomes appropriate to seek guidance from friends, mentors, or communities that are knowledgeable about White supremacy—particularly those whose knowledge has been formed through the painful lived experience of surviving White supremacy?

For anyone who wants to be serious about this journey, I think the answer has to be yes. There is just no way to gain meaningful wisdom about the full dimension of White supremacy without the guidance and support of those who know it well from the inside.

And yet this is a risky proposition in every way, particularly for those on the other end of this learning journey. That is why we, as the White students, need to be conscientious in our preparation for this aspect of the journey. The power dynamics that come with this type of engagement are significant, and failure to attend to these will almost always inflict unnecessary pain and hurt.

Therefore, in advance of exploring three concrete actions we can take in this practice of choosing our friends wisely, I would like to reflect on a passage of Scripture that has been enormously helpful in my own journey of wrestling with this question.

The Apostle Paul as a Guide

Learning how to negotiate power dynamics in the context of community, as well as how to healthily engage with those we desire to learn from, can be a tricky path to walk. We need some guideposts to help illuminate this path. The story of the apostle Paul can provide those guideposts. His conversion story, told in Acts 9, is a well-known account in most Christian circles. Yet even with the familiarity many of us have, I would contend that some critical dimensions of the story often get missed. A key piece to implementing this seventh practice, as well as to unlocking the deeper dimensions of the text, comes when we consider the cultural starting point of Luke, the author of Acts. Luke is the only New Testament author who was not a Jew, and that fact played a significant role both in his account of the life of Jesus (the book of Luke) and in his account of the early church in the book of Acts.[2] That unique vantage point comes through in this account as well.

The central theme of this story is the conversion and call to ministry of the apostle Paul (who is referred to by his Hebrew name Saul in this account). But as Luke tells us of this life-changing encounter between Saul and Jesus, he makes sure to emphasize a couple of additional and important themes regarding spiritual transformation that not only illuminate details about Saul's story but also form a foundation for exploring the key question of this chapter.

The first of these themes is the emphasis that Luke places on the significant role that *community* plays in the transformation process of Saul. We discover that without the courageous and risky decision by Ananias to step into the story, the ending could have been very different. The second of these themes comes through Luke's examination of the power differentials represented within the social profiles of these two individuals. They represent the extreme and opposite poles of social power, and Luke invites us to consider how risky an equation Jesus leaned into when intertwining the journeys of Saul and Ananias.

Let's begin with Luke's introduction to the story:

> Meanwhile, Saul was still breathing out murderous threats against the Lord's disciples. He went to the high priest and asked him for letters to the synagogues in Damascus, so that if he found any there who belonged to the Way, whether men or women, he might take them as prisoners to Jerusalem.
>
> *Acts 9:1–2*

White Lies

In these verses, we see Luke describe the profile of Saul, one that represented a social location defined by high levels of privilege and power. One of the typical markers of privilege is access to social networks, which is the first detail that jumps out here. In the Jewish system of that day, the high priest played an incredibly prominent role in the religious landscape. It was a position of tremendous social status. The fact that Saul had direct access to someone like this is an important detail.

The access that Saul possessed was then directly linked to his ability to exercise power, as privilege almost always is. In this case, access to the high priest translated to Saul's being able to act in an official and nearly unilateral capacity for the Jerusalem establishment. With signed letters in hand, he no longer has to worry about being labeled as a wild fanatic or lone ranger as he sets out to hunt, imprison, and even kill followers of the "Way" of Jesus.

After highlighting Saul's privilege and power, Luke goes on to tell us of the voyage to Damascus, the capital of modern Syria, where Saul will continue his inquisition. It is on this road to Damascus where Saul is confronted by Jesus:

> As he neared Damascus on his journey, suddenly a light from heaven flashed around him. He fell to the ground and heard a voice say to him, "Saul, Saul, why do you persecute me?"
>
> "Who are you, Lord?" Saul asked.
>
> "I am Jesus, whom you are persecuting," he replied.
>
> *Acts 9:3–5*

Finally, as the encounter with Jesus comes to an end, Saul discovers he has been left blind:

> Saul got up from the ground, but when he opened his eyes he could see nothing. So they led him by the hand into

182

Damascus. For three days he was blind, and did not eat or
drink anything.

Acts 9:8–9

It is here that Luke is going to show us how central a role
community will play in Saul's transformational journey of moving from blindness to sight. The point is made as strongly by
what Jesus *doesn't* allow for Saul to consider as a remedy for his
blindness as by what he does.

Notice first that there is no option for Saul to consider his
upcoming transformational journey as a *solo affair.* Luke has
already established that Saul is familiar with having some degree
of social power and privilege. But when it comes to finding a
remedy for his blindness, it is apparent that access to those very
privileges now has no value. Saul is not going to be able to solve
this problem on his own or with his own resources. He is going
to have to rely on community.

Notice also that there is no option for Saul to consider his
upcoming transformational journey as a *me-and-Jesus affair.*
Of course, Jesus *could* have healed Saul on the spot. There are
multiple instances throughout the Gospel accounts where Jesus
did just that. But doing so would have come at the risk of Saul
missing the bigger lesson about community that Jesus had in
store for him during this season of his development. Saul is going
to be introduced to a new paradigm of transformation—one in
which his own liberation and healing are going to be tied to his
ability to vulnerably submit himself to community.

The Disciple Named Ananias

After Saul spends three days abstaining from food and water,
Luke turns the camera and shifts the focus onto Ananias. Here
we learn some key details about the man who played such a pivotal role in Saul's story:

In Damascus there was a disciple named Ananias. The Lord called to him in a vision, "Ananias!"

"Yes, Lord," he answered.

The Lord told him, "Go to the house of Judas on Straight Street and ask for a man from Tarsus named Saul, for he is praying. In a vision he has seen a man named Ananias come and place his hands on him to restore his sight."

"Lord," Ananias answered, "I have heard many reports about this man and all the harm he has done to your holy people in Jerusalem. And he has come here with authority from the chief priests to arrest all who call on your name."

Acts 9:10–14

The most important detail we learn about Ananias is that he is a "disciple" of Jesus, the same term used for the twelve disciples, as well as for the broader groups of disciples who had committed themselves to the cause of Christ. It seems that Luke wants to emphasize this fact, as Ananias is remembered again in Acts 22:12 as "a devout observer of the law and highly respected by all the Jews living there."

Building on that foundation, Luke then paints a picture of the social profile of Ananias. We see that his social position is one that closely aligns with what Dr. Chanequa Walker-Barnes described in her earlier quote: "In any society, the most marginalized people best understand the rules of the system, because they need to know the politics and dynamics in order to avoid being crushed by them."

In this system—where Jews who professed their allegiance to Christ became immediate targets for persecution—Ananias indeed represented the margins. As such, he needed to know the politics and dynamics of this system so he could avoid being crushed by it.

It is at this point that we discover Jesus' plan for Ananias's transformation story is going to take a sharp turn in the opposite direction of Saul's. Whereas Saul's transformation journey was to be framed around the liberation path of moving from blindness to sight, Ananias's journey was going to be framed around forgiving and learning to love his enemy. At first glance, his story may not be remembered in as dramatic of terms as Saul's, especially since the encounter wasn't accompanied by blinding lights or a falling onto the ground. But in many ways, his encounter was every bit as dramatic as Saul's, if not more.

We get a glimpse of the stakes in Ananias's response to Jesus. When he says, "I have heard many reports about this man and all the harm he has done to your holy people," you can almost feel the rawness of his emotion oozing out.

Which part of this request was worse? That Jesus was asking Ananias to put his life in danger by voluntarily searching out Saul? Or that Jesus was asking Ananias to forgive Saul for tormenting fellow disciples? Or that Jesus was asking Ananias to reclassify Saul from enemy to friend? Or that Jesus was asking Ananias to play a principal role in his healing process? Every one of these scenarios must have stirred emotions that ranged from panic to anger.

And yet, despite every human instinct telling him to run like Jonah, Ananias chooses to obey the Lord:

> Then Ananias went to the house and entered it. Placing his hands on Saul, he said, "Brother Saul, the Lord—Jesus, who appeared to you on the road as you were coming here—has sent me so that you may see again and be filled with the Holy Spirit." Immediately, something like scales fell from Saul's eyes, and he could see again. He got up and was baptized, and after taking some food, he regained his strength.
>
> *Acts 9:17–19*

Ananias proceeds to lay his flesh-and-blood hands on Saul's flesh-and-blood head. He looks Saul in the eye and, using the life-and-death power of words,[3] tenderly calls him brother. His gift of words precedes the gift of the Holy Spirit, and the scales fall from Saul's eyes, both in the natural and in the supernatural. It is one of the most magnanimous displays of grace from one human being to another in the entire New Testament. And as a result, Saul will never be the same.

Putting It into Practice

This passage has been an important one in my journey for many reasons, but for the purposes of this chapter, I will focus exclusively on the light it sheds on the big question we've been wrestling with: When it comes to the White learning journey, is there a point where it becomes appropriate to seek guidance from friends, mentors, or communities that are knowledgeable about White supremacy—particularly those whose knowledge has been formed through the painful lived experience of surviving White supremacy?

As I prepare to draw out some of the lessons I've learned from this passage, I will share a quick caveat. I take the task of "handling the word of truth"[4] very seriously and do my best to avoid application of any Scripture beyond its obvious scope. As such, I acknowledge that this is fundamentally a story about Paul's conversion and call to ministry, not a story about a White person on a racial awakening journey.

And yet, with that being said, it is also my conviction that with some theological reflection, this passage can make critical contributions to how we think about (1) the role that community plays in the transformation journey, which is particularly important, since the entire thrust of this chapter is determining when it's time to move beyond self-guided learning and into community; and (2) the role that power dynamics play within this communal engagement, particularly when the learner is coming from a social location vastly different from the location of the guide he or she is seeking wisdom from.

For the sake of simplicity, I will categorize the concrete applications of this seventh practice around three categories of action: preparing to learn, receiving guidance, and discerning mission.

Preparing to Learn

How can I best prepare and posture myself for this type of engagement? Two phrases from Paul's account create very clear guardrails.

"When he opened his eyes he could see nothing" (Acts 9:8). When Jesus blinds Saul on the road to Damascus, I believe there are multiple meanings. The most concrete and immediate is also the most obvious one: Saul is now physically blind. But I think there is a broader, more metaphorical message that Jesus is communicating as well: for Saul, blindness *has always been the problem.*

Let's go back to Acts 7, where Luke first introduces Saul. We covered this in chapter 6, when we looked at the story of Stephen. As you will recall, it was then that Stephen preached a prophetic sermon on the dangers of intermixing nationalism and religion and was stoned as a result. But before the stoning was complete, there was one final and chilling image. The witnesses to the execution began to take off their coats and place them at the feet of Saul (Acts 7:58). Scholars debate the full meaning of this gesture, but I align with the interpretation that this was a recognition of Saul as the emerging leader of this holy war they thirsted for.[5]

That is what makes this image so profoundly scary. It reveals that Saul wasn't just blind; *he was blind to the fact that he was blind.*

Saul was convinced that what he was seeing was the same as what God was seeing, and he had organized his life around a version of reality founded on bad vision. That's why I believe the encounter on the Damascus road had an additional meaning. Jesus was illuminating for Saul just how far his blindness actually went.

Here's how I make the connection from Saul's story back to the White learning journey and what it means for us. As I've alluded to throughout the book, there is a tremendous drive within most of us who are White to prove that, when it comes to race, we see clearly. Whether it is acquiring the label "woke" or showcasing our knowledge of the history of racism or engaging in some other act to demonstrate that we "get it," we feel an ongoing need to establish our credentials. Given this internal pressure, it becomes completely counterintuitive to voluntarily admit just how deep our blindness goes.

And yet that is exactly what we must do. We must be honest that with every new level of revelation we experience, we once again discover just how deep our blindness about White supremacy actually goes. It is the only meaningful pathway forward.

Therefore, as you consider seeking this type of engagement from your larger community, I encourage you to look to Saul's transformation journey as both an example and a resource. If Saul had tried to manipulate the situation to try to show that he was more in control of the situation than he actually was, he would have undermined the very progress God had in store for him. The only way forward was through an embracing of the fact that he was unable to see. It was true in that moment. And as he was discovering, it had been true long before that.

"I am Jesus ... Now get up and go" (Acts 9:5–6). I believe this part of Saul's story represents the single most important resource for us as we prepare to learn.

I recently met with a group of student leaders at a Christian college, each of whom was facilitating a small group with fellow students around *White Awake*. What made this conversation unique, however, was that none of these leaders were White. They were part of a diversity council that was attempting to advance this conversation at their school, and they made the unique and brave decision to experiment with race-training groups led exclusively by student leaders of color. They wanted to see what would happen if they offered their lived experience as a resource for their fellow White students to access and learn from on their racial awakening journeys.

Each of the student leaders shared how the experience was going, and after a Korean American woman shared her experience, she followed up with a question: "What do I do about White fragility in my group? I am already contending with so much ambivalence as it is. But once the subject matter starts to get tense, the members tend to move from ambivalence to fragility. For some, it manifests as shutting down; for others, it manifests as paralyzing shame. How do I get my White peers to toughen up? How can I preemptively address the privilege?"

I knew exactly what she was asking, as would everyone who has experienced this dynamic while facilitating race-based conversations. It is very common. And when she used the term *White fragility*, a phrase popularized by Dr. Robin DiAngelo, it was clear that she had done her homework on working with White folks. It is quickly becoming a universal phrase in this work.

I've done a lot of studying and thinking on White fragility. And it's something I wrote quite a bit about in *White Awake*. So when she asked, I was ready to give her the book answer. But in that moment, the book answer just didn't feel sufficient. While I still agree with the social analysis of White fragility and still stand by what I've written about it, I also believe there's a root cause that Christians, in particular, need to acknowledge more honestly. I gave her my honest opinion: "It's not a fragility problem you are up against; it's a faith problem."

To make the case for that, I had the student leaders open their Bibles to Hebrews 11, the most famous passage on faith in the Bible. I reminded them that the common thread holding the chapter together is the testimonies of men and women who had demonstrated great faith over the course of biblical history. Some of the faith heroes in this passage are famous names, but many of them are not. In fact, some of the most amazing feats of faith came through those who are remembered for their great faith more than for their birth name. Here is how the writer of Hebrews concludes the chapter:

> And what more shall I say? I do not have time to tell about Gideon, Barak, Samson and Jephthah, about David and Samuel and the prophets, who through faith conquered kingdoms, administered justice, and gained what was promised; who shut the mouths of lions, quenched the fury of the flames, and escaped the edge of the sword; whose weakness was turned to strength; and who became powerful in battle and routed foreign armies. Women received back their dead, raised to life again. There were others who were tortured, refusing to be released so that they might gain an even better resurrection. Some faced jeers and flogging, and even chains and imprisonment. They were put to death by stoning; they were sawed in two; they were killed by the sword. They went about in sheepskins and goatskins, destitute, persecuted and mistreated—the world was not worthy of them. They wandered in deserts and mountains, living in caves and in holes in the ground. These were all commended for their faith.
>
> *Hebrews 11:32–39*

We read the passage and then all sat in silence together. The magnitude of suffering that these women and men endured for the cause of Christ is astonishing: torture, jeers, flogging, chains, imprisonment, gruesome executions . . . on and on it goes. We just needed to sit in that for a moment.

Once everyone was ready to engage again, I re-established the conversation about White fragility and why I thought the root problem is ultimately one of faith—particularly the way faith is talked about in Hebrews 11. I realize that *faith* is a big word and is even used flippantly at times, but here faith is described as something very specific and powerful. Faith is the means by which we keep our sight set on the person of Jesus: "Therefore, since we are surrounded by such a great cloud of witnesses . . . let us run with perseverance the race marked out for us, fixing our eyes on Jesus, the pioneer and perfecter of faith" (Hebrews 12:1–2).

I reminded them that great faith is far less about something great we do, and much more about the greatness of Jesus and the life he calls us into. He is the *pioneer of our faith.* He is the one who goes out before us. He is the one who calls us to himself.

As such, our job is not to summon great faith, but instead to faithfully keep our eyes on Jesus. To move when he moves. To respond to him in obedience, just as every great hero of faith who has gone before us has done.

The stories in Hebrews 11 remind us of this truth—the same truth that the testimonies of martyrs throughout the centuries remind us of. When we are connected to Christ and the kingdom by faith, there is no level of challenge we cannot rise to. There is no obstacle too great to overcome. There is no threat so scary as to immobilize us. When Jesus calls and when the Spirit empowers, we are able to join the great faith of this cloud of witnesses.

And this is why I see the root of fragility as being fundamentally a faith problem. From a social science perspective, there are legitimate and helpful explanations as to why White people fatigue so quickly over conversations on race. But from a spiritual perspective, the most fundamental explanation is tied to faith. For many of us, we do not see this learning process as something that Jesus told us to do. We do not see it as critical to the cause of Christ as it actually is. If we did see it this way, we would have the strength to remain steady on the course.

* * *

Saul had every reason to be "fragile" when Jesus told him to go to Ananias. What if Ananias decided this was his opportunity to strike a death blow to the oppressive system Saul was leading? Saul had a far better rationale for fragility than we will ever have on this learning journey. And yet he obeyed, doing as he was asked. Why? *Because Jesus told him to.*

I want to suggest that the motivation behind our learning journey will make all the difference in the world. Tepid interest won't be enough motivation. The pursuit of ways to be more politically correct won't be enough. Self-actualization won't be enough. This road is hard, and you will encounter uncomfortable truths at every step of the journey. I believe there is only one source of motivation that gives us the necessary resolve, resiliency, and courage to stay true to this call. Like Saul, we must hear the voice that says, *I am Jesus . . . Now get up and go.*

Therefore, as you consider seeking this type of engagement from your larger community, I encourage you to root your motivation in the richest soil available to us—the voice of God. We should seek out the additional guidance we need because we can't fully participate by faith in the cause of Christ without it.

Receiving Guidance

I was having coffee with a fellow pastor in Chicago in the early days of River City. I was a big admirer of the work she was doing in our city and was amazed at the ways she gracefully navigated the pressures not only of being Black in America but also of being a woman in a male-dominant church world. She knew that for my journey as a White pastor, a long learning curve lay ahead, and she had graciously made herself available to talk through some of the many questions I was contending with in my early stages of reckoning with race.

The conversation had been going smoothly up to this point. But when I shared one of the pastoral care situations I was currently perplexed by, the tenor of our conversation changed. A Black congregant in my church had shared a painful experience of racism in the workplace, and I was now asking my pastor friend if she had any advice on how I could best provide support in a case like this. She got ready to answer, but then she got very emotional and had to pause.

She took a couple minutes to sit in her sadness and then resumed the conversation. "Thanks for giving me a moment," she said. "When you shared the story of what your congregant went through, it unexpectedly brought back a rush of memories. I've had similar types of experiences at many points throughout my life, and when I heard the story, I could feel the trauma from those memories come rushing back in."

As she spoke, I immediately felt bad that my question caused the resurgence of those traumatic memories. So I began to apologize profusely. She interrupted me and said, "Stop apologizing. I didn't say you did anything wrong. I just needed a minute. I knew what I was getting into when I made myself available as part of your racial awakening journey. This comes with the territory."

She then added a critical piece of commentary. "It does provide an opportunity, though, for you to consider how different the experience of a conversation like this is for you versus for me. For you, this is largely theoretical. I believe you care, and I understand that your desire is to help people. But in conversations like this, it will always risk being impersonal for you—like an onlooker who is trying to make sense of it from the outside. For me, conversations like this are *absolutely* personal. They touch every part of my lived experience. I carry trauma from experiences just like this. I have learned to deal with those traumas and to overcome them, but they are still real. And in order to share my wisdom for your journey, I'm going to need to revisit and often relive those traumas."

As I walked away from this conversation, I was struck by the depth and vulnerability of what she had just shared with me. By this point in my journey, I had come to deeply appreciate the intellectual wisdom invested in me during a coaching session like this. But what I hadn't taken the time to consider was the emotional and spiritual toll it took on someone like her when she imparted this wisdom.

As I reflected on this conversation over the next days, I continued to be struck by how imbalanced the risk/benefit equation was in our learning relationship. On my end, the risks in engaging in this type of conversation were minimal—maybe the risk of saying something stupid or feeling stupid. The potential benefits, on the other hand, were immense—information and knowledge about race that I hadn't yet learned, new wisdom and insights for addressing particular challenges I was facing, sharper skills for navigating cross-cultural environments.

On her end, the equation was completely inversed. The risks in engaging in this type of conversation were significant—being triggered or even retraumatized by something I said, expending valuable emotional and intellectual energy that could surely be used elsewhere, managing the risk that I could exercise my privilege at any moment and leave the conversation. And the benefits? If there were any, they were not obvious to me.

Reflecting on this equation once again brought me back to Acts 9. Isn't this a similar equation to what Saul and Ananias faced? For Saul, there may have been some degree of risk in seeking out Ananias, but it paled in comparison to the potential benefits he could receive—healing and liberation. For Ananias, on the other hand, this engagement was defined by pure risk. He risked being imprisoned or beaten or even killed. And what was the benefit to counteract that risk? It would be difficult to say there was one at all, other than being faithful to the request Jesus made of him.

Addressing this equation becomes an important part of this seventh practice. When we seek out the guidance of someone whose lived experience represents all the risks of living under White supremacy, we need to appreciate how upside down the nature of what we're asking them is. We are asking them to freely share the costly wisdom that has been acquired through the survival of a deadly system. We are asking them to reenter their pain, hardship, and at times even trauma, so that we might in turn increase our own leadership proficiencies. It is a request that, humanly speaking, makes no sense at all.

To build on this point, let me share some data to reinforce just how valuable yet costly the wisdom of lived experience is for those whose very existence has been daily threatened by White supremacy. As the first example, consider an article from the Southern Poverty Law Center titled "Racism Is Killing Black Americans." The editors point to numerous studies over the years that demonstrate the gap in health outcomes between minority groups (Black folks in particular) and White Americans. They note that African Americans have a lower life expectancy than White people and are more likely to suffer and die from chronic conditions such as kidney, cardiovascular, and lung disease. The infant mortality rate is more than twice as high for Black children than for White children—a disparity that is wider today than it was in 1850, when the majority of African Americans were enslaved, and one that is not related to the economic or educational status of the mother.[6]

Or consider the *U.S. News & World Report* article titled "Being Black Is Bad for Your Health." Risa Lavizzo-Mourey and David Williams build on this idea, noting that "researchers have coined a term—'excess deaths'—to explain the sad fact that if blacks and whites had the same mortality rate, nearly 100,000 fewer black people would die each year in the United States." African Americans face sickness and death at a younger age when compared to White peer groups of the exact same social location (level of education, income, etc.), with their skin color being the only point of difference between the two groups. A Black person will live on average about three fewer years than a White person with the same income.[7]

Summarizing the undeniable link between lived experience and the toll it takes on a person's health, the authors put it this way: "Merely being black in America triggers exposure to stressors linked to premature biological aging. Research indicates that blacks get sick at younger ages, have more severe illnesses and are aging, biologically, more rapidly than whites. Scientists call this the 'weathering effect,' or the result of cumulative stress."[8]

*   *   *

I met up again with my pastor friend about a month after our first conversation. The clarity she had provided in our first meeting had touched a deep nerve in me. Before that conversation, I hadn't considered the risks she was exposing herself to in this relationship for no other reason than the sake of my learning needs. And the more I thought about this, the more I wondered why she had made herself available to me in the first place, especially when there was no benefit for her. So I asked, "Why do you meet with me and help me when it benefits me in such clear ways yet represents little more than risk for you?"

Her answer has stuck with me. "First," she said, "you and

I now have a relationship together. I trust you as a person, and I'm willing to invest in your journey because I'm invested in *you*. Second, I trust what I see in your posture for this journey. I trust the humility you've demonstrated so far. I trust your willingness and hunger to learn. And I trust that your faith in Jesus is what drives you. That in turn leads me to trust you. Third," she continued, "I trust that you are willing to take what I said last time to heart. I trust that you will take seriously that any wisdom I have acquired has come at a cost, and I trust that you will take the stewardship of that cost seriously and take the lessons you learn and integrate them in meaningful ways. Fourth, and most importantly, it is because of Jesus." She smiled and finished by saying, "I wouldn't be doing this if he didn't tell me to do it."

As you consider seeking this same type of engagement from your larger community, I encourage you to reflect on the magnitude of what you are asking for and to continually keep that in view.

Discerning Mission

Most of you reading this are going to have a bias toward action, and rightly so. Once we awaken to the profound and far-reaching nature of White supremacy, it makes sense to search for actionable ways to confront it, right?

In the grand scheme of things, the answer to that question is definitely *yes*. But Saul's story, even if an extreme example, reminds us that attempting to tackle a problem we don't clearly see or understand comes with great risk. This is a risk that must be named and taken into account when we find ourselves ready to spring into action mode. While it is important for us to keep growing in our passion for seeing and confronting White supremacy, we must also hold it in tension with the reality that being able to name White supremacy as a problem is not the same thing as being fully equipped for engaging what comes next.

So how do we manage that tension? How do we balance the danger of action without accountability on one side with the need to actively confront White supremacy on the other? The answers remain the same! We must keep our view of transformation permanently tethered to the blindness-to-sight journey, and we must find a way to surrender and submit to community.

For the final part of this practice, I want to apply what we've explored throughout this chapter specifically to the call to action. I want to explore concrete ways we can submit all of our actions to a larger community so as to ensure the needed accountability, support, and guidance.

To do so, I want to come back to Saul's story one last time. We have already spent a lot of time looking at the interaction between him and Ananias. Now I'd like to take a jump forward in his story to Luke's account of Saul being *sent* out into *mission* (from a Latin word meaning "sent," which is why these two words are so closely linked). In the next chapter, I'll spend a fair amount of time developing the importance of the church in Antioch, so I will skip over that for now. For the purposes of this chapter, the relevant passage is Acts 13:1–3, which proposes an interesting model for how a community can send emerging leaders into mission.

In this short yet powerful passage, we see that a dynamic and diverse leadership team has been assembled in the church at Antioch. This was the team that had developed Paul as a leader up to this point and would provide ongoing accountability, support, and guidance. The leadership team is in a time of prayer and worship when God reveals that it's time for Paul and Barnabas to be sent out. God asks the leadership team to "set apart" these two for mission, and the leaders respond obediently. After prayer and fasting, they place their hands on Barnabas and Saul and send them off to the task that God has waiting for them.

This image of a community of leaders that "send" us into

mission is a powerful one. It also represents a model for how we can most effectively safeguard our desires to discover ways to actively participate in the confrontation of White supremacy. At the most fundamental level, I think of it like this: any action I take to confront White supremacy should be tied to being sent by a community of people who know me.

This is the model I have adopted in all my efforts to confront White supremacy. While I badly want to make a difference in the ways I contribute to the fight, I'm also convinced I should never be the one who ultimately determines if I am helpful to the cause.

Those who see White supremacy most clearly and are affected by it in the most devastating ways should determine if I am ready. Ultimately God is always the one who sends us into any mission. But in the same way that God's call on Saul and Barnabas was identified and discerned within the community they submitted to, I want any forms of active participation I engage in to be affirmed in community as well.

I'm often asked what this looks like practically for me, so I'll share some of the ways I submit to a sending community within each sphere I'm actively involved with in the confrontation of White supremacy:

- the local church
- the local neighborhood
- the West Side of Chicago

The local church. When I started River City Community Church with a small team of people in January 2003, I did not yet have a home base of leaders I could submit my ideas to and receive wisdom from. The core was small, and we were all young, so we didn't have the internal infrastructure yet to provide the necessary accountability, support, and guidance. In light of that,

I made a commitment to our core team. I told them that until we had that type of leadership community developed internally, I would look to the clergy in our neighborhood for our accountability.

I spent the next three months asking if I could meet one-on-one with every pastor in Humboldt Park considered to be a vibrant part of the fabric of this neighborhood. Some pastored small churches, and some pastored megachurches. Some were well known, and some were nearly anonymous. Nonetheless, I shared the same speech with each one, telling them I wouldn't even consider joining the fight against White supremacy in our community unless they thought I should. I told them I would not move forward with the church if they didn't feel like they could confidently "send" me into that work. I leaned into the two big points of this chapter and assured them that I saw myself as someone who was very much on the blindness-to-sight journey. I assured them that I had a sense of the cost to invest in me and told them that if they decided to do so, I would never take for granted the gift of that investment. I invited them to share openly with me any blind spots they perceived in me and assured them that this was an open invitation that extended far beyond that moment.

Thanks be to God, every one of them encouraged me to continue in the journey, and without fail, each one prayed over me and commissioned me for the task ahead. Most of them have stayed in regular contact with my development in the years and decades that have since passed.

Eventually our infrastructure did develop to the point that we had a healthy team of diverse, godly, wise, Spirit-led leaders who could serve as my "sending" community. To this day, there is literally not a single idea for engagement that I consider without first submitting it to this team of leaders. I don't trust my own instincts to decide where I should be investing time and where I shouldn't; which causes I should take up and which I shouldn't; where my voice is helpful and where it is unnecessarily taking up space that should belong to others. This team represents one of God's greatest gifts in my life and ministry, and I thank God for this accountability and support on a daily basis.

The local neighborhood. The vision of River City Community Church is organized around three big pillars: worship, reconciliation, and neighborhood development. The neighborhood development pillar represents a distinct form of joining in the fight against White supremacy. Dr. Marian Wright Edelman, one of my personal heroes and the founder of the Children's Defense Fund, often says, "The most dangerous place for a child to grow up today is that intersection of race and poverty."[9] That was the guiding principle for the location of our church, in west Humboldt Park. We felt God leading us to root ourselves at the most intense intersection of race and poverty within our neighborhood.

Even more specifically, we established our church building directly across the street from Cameron Elementary School, which tirelessly serves the children, youth, and families of this neighborhood. Together, our two organizations have entered into a long-term covenant partnership to combat the enduring effects of White supremacy in this part of the city.

This partnership points to the second realm of community that plays an active role in sending me into mission. The principal of the school, alongside other key administrators and leaders there, knows that I will never embark on any action that involves racial justice without first submitting it to community and relying on their collective voice to "send" me into the work they are already doing. They know this is my genuine posture with the leaders in our church, and they know it is my intention for how I want to submit to their leadership. Therefore, our staff and I meet with the principal and his key advisers at the beginning of each school year (1) to be held accountable for our efforts the previous year and (2) to get instructions for how we can be most supportive of their efforts in the next year.

The West Side of Chicago. The topography of Chicago, like many large cities in the United States, has been profoundly shaped by the forces of White supremacy. Both the south and west sides of our city are primarily African American—a direct result of the migration from the South during the height of lynching. As Bryan Stevenson says, "The African Americans . . . did not come as immigrants looking for economic opportunities, they came as refugees, exiles from lands in the South where they were being terrorized."[10] The Great Migration between 1916 and 1970, spurred by the terror of lynching, attracted more than 500,000 of the approximately 7 million African Americans who left the South during these decades.[11] Through homeowner discriminatory practices, redlining, exclusive zoning to single-family housing, and racially restrictive covenants, Black people were kept far from White-dominant areas where they could work, shop, and find transportation. As a result, most of these areas continue to suffer the economic and social impact of those racial practices.

Our church is located on the West Side of the city and, as such, has an obligation to confront this legacy of White supremacy at a broader level than just the six-block radius on which our neighborhood development efforts are focused. With that being said, I would never take direct action in this regard outside of communal guidance.

In this case, my submission to community happens through an established group of Black clergypersons who run a collective on the West Side called the Leader's Network. The three pastors who lead this initiative know I am eager to participate in any ways I can, but also that I fully depend on following their lead.

For the first few years, this meant coming to their meetings, listening, and demonstrating my genuine willingness to follow their lead without needing a defined role that made me feel useful. In more recent years, certain opportunities have arisen where this group has asked me to accompany them to city hall, to pray or speak at a protest, or to serve on a board that influences legislative issues on the West Side. But at the end of the day, this communal principle is what drives all of my activity with them. I never attempt to confront White supremacy on the West Side outside of the context of submission and accountability to community.

I share these examples to remind us that we never outgrow the need for the guidance, support, and accountability that can come only from community. Learning to submit to community, and particularly to those who see the problem through a clearer lens than we ever could, becomes a critical dimension of this practice.

I leave you with some questions to that very end. Do you have these types of relationships as part of your larger community? If not, what are some steps you can take to begin to cultivate those kinds of relationships? If yes, what are some growth steps you can take to deepen those relationships? In what ways can you communicate your understanding of the deep value that comes from their investment in you? In what ways can you more clearly submit to community your desire to be an active participant? In what ways can you enhance the guidance, accountability, and support in your larger community?

Moving Forward

White supremacy is one of the deadliest and most dangerous systems the world has ever seen. We all need to see it, understand it, and then confront it. But we also must be wise about how we prepare for this confrontation. We must beware of the temptation to move with a blind sincerity that risks doing more damage than good.

The Bible gives a vision of community that teaches us how to think and act differently. It gives a vision for collectively resisting the temptation to conform to the patterns of this world and experiencing transformation through the renewal of our minds (Romans 12:1–2). How is God asking you to participate? Where is God providing a community for you? What are the next steps as you consider seeking engagement with that community? My prayer is that you will surrender to this beautiful vision of community and allow it to lead you into the necessary and transformative work that prepares you for joining the fight.

Interrogate Power

It was winter of 2003, and the core group of our eventual church plant was beginning to take form. Much of what we envisioned for ourselves was what churches universally aspire to—loving God, loving people, teaching the Bible, building community, caring for the hurting, and so on. But in addition to those common virtues, we sensed that God had also called us to a very specific priority: to become a multicultural church that addressed racial divisions both internally, within our church, as well as externally in the world.

As clear as this mission felt, the question still loomed: "Where should we begin?" Though our core group was culturally diverse, we nonetheless realized we were still bound by the common experience of growing up in culturally homogeneous churches. We had folks who could speak to the African American church experience, the Asian American church experience, the Latino and Latina church experience, and the White church experience, but none of us could effectively speak to what should happen when we attempted to create something new together. We needed help.

Determined to answer this question, our group decided to engage in a pair of learning activities. First, we would visit a different church in a different part of the city each Sunday morning, and then we'd meet back up that evening to debrief on what we had learned. Second, we would read a different book on faith and race each month and try to piece together themes from the book into our emerging strategy.

One of the books we found helpful during this stage was *Divided by Faith* by Michael Emerson and Christian Smith, as well as Emerson's follow-up book titled *United by Faith*.[1] These two books helped us create common language around the difference between the individual and systemic impacts of race and introduced us to some national models that were experimenting with approaches to building multiracial congregations. Just as we were finishing *Divided by Faith*, we discovered that Dr. Emerson, who at the time was a sociologist at Rice University, was coming to Chicago to give a lecture at a local Christian college. We reached out to see if he would be willing to do a training for our group while in town, and we were delighted when he agreed.

When the day of the training finally came, we excitedly crammed into the classroom we were renting from a local nonprofit in our neighborhood. Dr. Emerson began by sharing his enthusiasm that we had embarked on a project like this and told us how much he believed it was in line with God's heart. He then gave a short presentation that summarized the contents of his books and opened the floor for questions.

One of the young leaders in our core group jumped in. "I think everyone in this group resonates with what you just presented, and we believe this is the direction God has called us to go in. But we all come from such different backgrounds, and we all have so many different ideas of where we should start. Can you help us with this? From all you've seen, do you have any suggestions on what we should prioritize as we set off in this direction?"

Dr. Emerson answered without pause. "Power," he said. "The kind of multicultural vision you all are envisioning is the kind where White, dominant culture is going to come into contact with non-White, subdominant cultures, and that inevitably means there are going to be all kinds of power differentials that emerge. Learning to identify and navigate that power differential will be imperative. I'd go so far as to say that the success or failure of this aspect of the church's mission will almost certainly come down to how you all learn to operate within these immanent power dynamics."

Emerson's clarity regarding the role that power would play within a vision like ours caught me off guard. Looking back, I realize it shouldn't have, as it was absolutely the right place for him to start the conversation. But in the moment, the contrast between his definitive conviction that power was the priority and my lack of consideration of power was uncomfortably vivid. So I began to wonder, *Why did I think about power so little?*

I wondered if some of it could be explained by my age and background. I was twenty-nine years old at the time, and up until that moment, I had genuinely never thought of myself as an even remotely powerful person. During my growing-up years, I battled depression and for the most part lived within a self-imposed social isolation all the way through high school. Even as a young adult, I had never occupied a social space that left me feeling particularly powerful. It was a topic I had never considered in any arena of my life. It wasn't necessarily surprising that I hadn't thought about it within the context of this church plant.

Yet even as I tried to attribute my lack of thoughtfulness to my upbringing, it also became apparent that my disconnection from the notion of power went deeper. I was beginning to realize I had subscribed to some type of voluntary oblivion when it came to race and power. I suspected another major transition from blindness to sight was on my horizon.

As has often been the case in my transformational breakthroughs, community played an instrumental role in the next level of awakening. Our core group continued to intentionally discuss power after the training with Dr. Emerson, and we started by interrogating it at an individual level. In ways I had never noticed, the other members of our group illuminated the differences that a White person and a BIPOC person can encounter in almost any everyday experience. When it came to something as simple as walking into a grocery store or a new restaurant or even a new city, the differential of power was almost palpable to them. To be White, and in my case a male, was to be able to enter into a public space feeling completely empowered. I didn't need to worry about how I was being perceived or whether I was welcome or whether my safety was at risk. It didn't matter if I actually *felt* powerful. The ability to walk through life with a carefree oblivion highlighted the fact that it was there nonetheless.

They then helped me grapple with the reality of power at an organizational level. In ways I had never seen before, they illuminated the different experiences that a White person and a BIPOC person tend to have when functioning within a White-dominant organization. For instance, one of the African American women in our group shared about the exhaustion that came from the contradictory double message she continued to receive in her workplace. Her supervisors told her they valued her presence and wanted to hear her opinions on how and where the company could better address race. But each time she shared, no matter how carefully she said it, she would be told she was making people uncomfortable and needed to find ways to say it more gently. One of the African American men told of an experience in which he shared an idea at work for his team to consider, only to receive a cool reception. Minutes later, a White colleague picked the idea back up, and it swiftly gained traction. This wasn't the first time he had failed to successfully sponsor an idea to his team, only to have the same idea find new life when it came at the suggestion of a White person instead.

As I listened to these stories, it became increasingly obvious how little I had thought about power over the course of my life. Unlike me, every BIPOC person in this circle talked of power dynamics as something that needed to be navigated on a daily basis. I was beginning to see just how much courage, resilience, and intelligence were required to do so. Soberingly, it also became clear that they assumed these same dynamics would be present in our church, just as they were in the other spaces they navigated on a daily basis. The difference here, at least they hoped, would be that the White folks would be serious about understanding these power dynamics, which would perhaps create a different reality of living, serving, and ministering together.

As this gap between the level at which they saw power and the level at which I saw power grew more evident, I made a commitment to never again underemphasize this important theme. I was determined to become a student of power and to learn how to interrogate it both personally and organizationally.

Learning to Interrogate Power

Power is a vast and far-reaching topic. We find within any organization a number of arenas where differences in power play out in a significant and often harmful way. Gender inequality, for instance, continues to foster glaring and terribly imbalanced power differentials. Another critical arena is money. The manner in which wealth directly impacts the dynamics of an organization is always a foundational backdrop in any conversation on power. By focusing on power through the lens of race, I don't mean to understate how important these other arenas of conversation are as well. But with this book's focus oriented toward the equipping journey of the White person who looks to challenge and confront the system of White supremacy,

I will spend the rest of the chapter examining power exclusively through that lens.

One of the reasons it is so important to specifically examine and interrogate power through a racial lens comes as a direct result of the specific intentions behind the original construction of the system of race. White supremacy has always been rooted in a thirst for power. From its very origins, its agenda was to coalesce and protect power for White people and White communities and then to quarantine, control, and even dominate those who were viewed as a threat to that arrangement. So there is literally no way to talk about confronting White supremacy without also learning to confront the power structures that continue to perpetuate that system.

So how do we learn to interrogate that power?

I will focus my answer on interrogating power in organizations. But before getting there, we should consider the personal dimension of this practice. Consider the opening story. Even though I was very motivated to participate in a multicultural community and to confront White supremacy, I still had never spent any meaningful time reflecting on the way I personally carried power with me into every setting I entered. This was a blind spot—an important one for me to acknowledge and understand. It was unrealistic for me to understand and interrogate power dynamics in an organization if I wasn't first committed to doing so in my personal life. I had to be on a parallel learning track of understanding and interrogating power at a personal level.

I encourage you to make a similar commitment in your journey. Start with personal reflection. Ask yourself questions:

- Do you think about power much?
- Are you aware of the power you possess as a White person in a society built around the system of race?

- Do you see the ways the narrative of racial hierarchy assigns a superior set of qualities to your personhood?
- Do you see the ways your perspective may be deemed more valuable in certain settings because you are White?

From there, we can interrogate power in organizations. Most of you are reading this because you're connected to an organization that is attempting to address race. For some of you, it's your church; for others, it's your workplace; and for still others, it's a nonprofit or an educational institution. If we are genuinely committed to challenging the system of White supremacy, we need to learn how to collectively address its impact on the organizations we participate in. Having a stated commitment to diversity, inclusion, or equity is a great starting point for any organization, but it's ultimately not enough. To learn to interrogate power—particularly the power wielded by White stakeholders within the organization—is the next important step.

Back to our church-planting story. The interrogation of power became the basis for our framing of the learning process for our core group as we moved closer to our launch. While we recognized that people of every cultural background possess and exercise power, we wanted to be especially conscientious of the way White people possessed and exercised power in our environment. We were sober-minded about the historic dominance intrinsic to White culture and longed to find practical ways to assess and interrogate the ways these patterns of dominance were demonstrating themselves within our community. So we studied every model we could find that explored these power dynamics, particularly organizations that explored power dynamics and race. We also spoke to mentors whose wisdom included past experiences of navigating spaces like these and culled every lesson from them we could. We processed our experiences within the group and drew principles from these discussions as well.

The process involved a lot of trial and error, as well as consistently responding to real-time feedback. Those efforts eventually helped us develop an index of seven areas that needed to be continually interrogated. Let me give a handful of disclaimers before diving into these: (1) As important as these seven are, the list is not as exhaustive as it could be. (2) Within each of the seven, my description will only scratch the surface. Much more can and should be said about each. My goal here is to name and index them more than to comprehensively describe each. (3) My organizational focus in this chapter will be church-centric, since that is the environment in which I have most directly worked with interrogating power. I am confident each of these seven is more broadly applicable. I hope you'll be able to find the necessary bridges to your organization in each one:

- how mature Christianity is defined
- how decisions are made
- how hiring practices occur
- how voices that shape the church are decided on
- how the needs of White congregants are attended to
- how public acts of racism in society are corporately addressed
- how racial justice is described

How Mature Christianity Is Defined

Let me come back to the story of when Dr. Emerson led a training with our core group. After Dr. Emerson repeatedly emphasized the importance of identifying and navigating power dynamics, one of the guys in our group asked a follow-up question. He said, "I believe that power is as important as you say it is. But I also admit I don't have a well-developed instinct for identifying power when it is being exercised—especially if it is being exercised in an imbalanced way. Can you tell us what an overt example of exercising power might look like in a church like ours?"

Dr. Emerson drew us all in with the way he set up his response: "Do you want to know what the most powerful thing is that happens in every church?" Our entire group reflexively edged to the front of our seats. Of course we wanted to know what the most powerful thing was that happened in every church!

"At some point, Daniel will get up in that pulpit, or one of the other pastors will get up there, and they will talk about discipleship. They will talk about Christian maturity. And when they do that—when they tell the congregation what it looks like to be a growing, mature Christian—you will witness power being exercised at its highest level."

The response was not what any of us were expecting, and it initially felt fairly anticlimactic. *Defining discipleship* is the most powerful thing that happens in a church?

But as we continued to reflect on his answer, it quickly became profound. If the whole purpose of being a Christian is to convert by grace to Jesus and faithfully follow him, then it would make sense that defining mature discipleship is one of the greatest exercises of power in a faith community. Regardless of how aware one is of their power in that moment, when someone in a position of spiritual authority gets up in front of a congregation and emphasizes what a disciple should or should not do, they have set a corporate vision for what full devotion to Christ looks like. That is powerful.

This all comes back to Dr. Emerson's original point. When a White disciple of Jesus sees no need to care about White supremacy, much less join in the fight against it, they are exercising a significant form of power that has been passed down by spiritual authorities who exercised that very same power.

Let's consider again the words of Dr. Martin Luther King Jr. in his "Letter from a Birmingham Jail," this time from a different angle. The basis of that letter was his disappointment with White pastors, whom he labeled as the "white moderate" and whom he openly questioned as possibly representing a greater stumbling block to Black freedom than even the White Citizens' Counciler or the Ku Klux Klanner. Chief among his basis for such a claim was the way that the white moderate "paternalistically believes he can set the timetable for another man's freedom; who lives by a mythical concept of time and who constantly advises the Negro to wait for a 'more convenient season.'"[2]

This quote summarizes one of the greatest expressions of unhealthy power in White churches. When we define discipleship as either not needing to care at all or not needing to care in any kind of an urgent manner, we have exercised a tremendous amount of power.

How Decisions Are Made

In the last chapter, we looked at the unique vantage point that the evangelist Luke brought to his writings. As the only non-Jewish author in the New Testament, Luke often observed important details that otherwise may not have been seen by those within the cultural norms of Jewish culture. In the book of Acts, in particular, Luke is fascinated by the multicultural dynamics that came into play when this exclusively Jewish movement suddenly came into contact with Gentile groups of all different backgrounds. Demonstrating his own cross-cultural competency, Luke places a prioritized focus on the power dynamic among these various groups. It's one thing to get culturally diverse groups in the same room together; it's a whole different thing to learn to share power together. That's the timeless sign of authentic cross-cultural community.

As could probably be expected, it didn't take long for differences in power to erupt. Only a little while after the dawn of the church, an ethnic-cultural power issue flared, as recorded in

Acts 6. In a spirit of caring for the vulnerable, the apostles had instituted a food-sharing program for the widows of the community. The program served widows of two different cultural backgrounds, and they were having very different experiences with the food giveaway (Acts 6:1). The widows in the first group were of Hebrew origin, and as such they had direct access to the church's dominant culture of the time. The widows in the second group were of Grecian origin, but they felt that their outsider status was resulting in marginalization when it came time for the food to be distributed.

Based on the way Luke tells the story, it seems that he wondered how the early church would respond. Would they be attuned to the significance of this power differential? Or would they be dismissive of the complaints? Whichever path they chose was going to set a trajectory for the church in regard to its cultural competency. To Luke's presumable delight, the situation was handled delicately and thoughtfully. The apostles indeed recognized that important issues of power were at play, and they crafted a structural solution that responded accordingly. Though the marginalized group did not yet have a full seat at the decision-making table, the apostles created a pathway whereby their needs could be meaningfully addressed. The apostles invited the Grecian widows to elect seven reputable leaders to take on this important task of *service* (the word we translate as "deacons"), a proposal that "pleased the whole group" (Acts 6:5).

As important as this power dispute in chapter 6 is to the narrative of Acts, it remains only a preview of what was to come. The city of Antioch was about to take center stage, and the church planted there would become the mother church for every future faith community in the New Testament. Antioch was no ordinary city. A port and a transportation hub, Antioch was the third largest city in the Roman Empire. It was also the most culturally diverse. In his book *The Rise of Christianity*, respected sociologist Rodney Stark shares how he discovered evidence of up to eighteen different nation groups that lived there, each divided into its own separate ethnic quarters.[3] Can you imagine how diverse that city was? But also how culturally charged it was?

That is what makes Acts 13:1 such a uniquely important verse. Every church in the New Testament had a leadership team that oversaw it, yet not once, outside of here, do we get a window into the makeup of that leadership team. But here in Antioch, Luke wants to make plain that a large part of the church's success was due to the culturally diverse team of pastors who learned how to successfully share power together. On the team was Simeon called Niger, who was from sub-Saharan West Africa. Next was Lucius from Cyrene, a city near the northern coast of Africa in what today is Libya. Third was Manaen of Palestine, who also had the backroom power politics of Rome on his résumé. Fourth was Saul, a European-trained Jew from Asia Minor. And then there was the ringleader and architect of the group, Barnabas from Cyprus. Luke wants us to pay close attention to this remarkable achievement. A team of five pastors, teachers, and prophets from three continents shared leadership and power, ultimately under the authority of Christ. It's no wonder Antioch was the first place where the term *Christian* was used (Acts 11:26).

Sharing power across cultural lines was a foundational reality in the early church. It's anything but a modern invention. The most important church in the New Testament—and the church that every other church was modeled after—was defined largely by the ability to develop a cross-cultural, power-sharing leadership team. In some ways it could be argued that this was one of the greatest miracles of all in the book of Acts.

This picture of the leadership team in Antioch is the necessary vision for any organization that aspires to address issues of race and confront White supremacy. When organizations continue to be led by all-White leadership teams in our modern context, as they typically are, they find themselves compromised on many levels. Their ability to live out the corporate vision is compromised, since they are only able to marshal a single cultural vantage point as they attempt to move in that direction. Their impact is compromised, because like the apostles in Acts 6, they are not able to understand or respond intelligently to the needs of those who are marginalized in their system. And their credibility is compromised. When organizational patterns of all-White leadership teams are continuously accepted as the norm, it reveals an inability or unwillingness to model the same type of cultural power sharing displayed in the early church.

I strongly advise every church I talk with (and every organization, for that matter), to make the examination of their decision-making systems one of their highest priorities when interrogating power in their organization. In accordance with this model of the church in Antioch, I advise them to make three commitments as quickly as they can: (1) the church commits to a vision of pursuing authentic power sharing across cultural lines, even if they aren't yet there;[4] (2) the church commits to a concrete plan for pursuing and implementing this vision; (3) even as they move toward this plan, the church commits to never making decisions that impact marginalized groups without following the model of the apostles in Acts 6 and finding ways to meaningfully involve those who will be affected most in the process.

How Hiring Practices Occur

One of the most concrete expressions of power in any organization occurs during the hiring process. In the same way an organizational budget reflects the genuine priorities of the institution, so the composition of the staff reflects the genuine commitment to the pursuit of diversity and the confrontation of race. When an organization fails to make meaningful changes in how it recruits, retains, and develops a diverse staff, both the integrity and effectiveness of its mission are at risk. Failure to hire racially conscious, diverse candidates in an organization (and not just at entry-level jobs) leads to at least three areas of compromise:

1. Inability to expose blind spots. In chapter 2, when exploring when diversity works right, I made the case that those of us who are White desperately need the presence of those who can see the racial dynamics we typically cannot see. Diversity helps us see God more clearly, see ourselves more clearly, and see the world more clearly. In most organizations, the leadership staff is what sets the tone. Failing to hire staff who can play this role puts the entire culture of the organization at risk.

2. Inability to fully live out mission. In Matthew's version of the Great Commission, he records Jesus' final words to the disciples: "Therefore go and make disciples of all nations, baptizing them in the name of the Father and of the Son and of the Holy Spirit, and teaching them to obey everything I have commanded you" (Matthew 28:19–20). As we noted earlier, the Greek word for "nations" is *ethnos,* from which we get the words *ethnic* and *nationality.* We live in an extremely diverse society—one in which God has brought all the "nations" into the proximity of most of our churches and organizations. In the same way that the church in Antioch best fulfilled their mission through the development of a culturally diverse leadership team, our churches need to move beyond all-White teams that are attempting to carry out the diverse mission that Jesus has entrusted to them.

3. Inability to develop a leadership pipeline. One of the dynamics often overlooked by those of us who are White is the immense role that social networks play in every stage of our professional development. Not only do these social networks often help us gain initial access to the field in which we work, but often they are key to finding professional mentors who play a role in our ongoing nurture and support. When the hiring practices of our organizations fail to recruit and retain a diverse pool of candidates, we adversely affect both the would-be candidates and the future of our organization. The would-be candidates suffer from the loss of access to entire social networks that could have otherwise played a significant role in their professional support and career advancement. The organization also suffers, since the best leaders are almost always grown within the pipeline of an organization where emerging leaders are identified and developed from early on in their career.

For these reasons and more, it is important to interrogate the power dynamics in the way hiring practices occur in the organizations we are part of.

How Voices That Shape the Church Are Decided On

On October 15, 2019, gospel music star Kirk Franklin won the Gospel Artist of the Year from the Dove Awards—his second time to win this prestigious award for that category. As he accepted the award, he acknowledged the tragic death of Atatiana Jefferson, a twenty-eight-year-old Black woman who was killed in her home by a White police officer. She had been in her Fort Worth, Texas, home playing with her eight-year-old nephew when it happened. After a neighbor made a call, the officer showed up on the scene and ultimately fired the deadly bullet through her window (he has since resigned and been arrested and charged with murder). For everyone paying attention, it was a national tragedy that again highlighted the many layers of threat faced by Black people in our country. When a Black woman playing with her nephew in her own home is shot and killed, many are left wondering if there is any place that is truly safe.

Therefore it made sense that when Kirk Franklin accepted the award, he would acknowledge the fear and distress so many were feeling. "When we don't say something, we're saying something," he prophetically reminded the audience. While directly addressing an inflammatory subject that could easily arouse charged feelings, Franklin chose to be quite delicate. He simply said, "This past weekend, a young twenty-eight-year-old lady, a young girl by the name of Atatiana Jefferson, was shot and killed in her home by a policeman. And I am just asking that we send up prayers for her family and for his, and asking that we send up prayers for that eight-year-old little boy who saw that tragedy."[5]

When TBN (Trinity Broadcasting Network) aired the Dove Awards five days later, they deleted the section of his speech in which he addressed the shooting of Atatiana Jefferson. Sadly, this wasn't the first time that had happened. Kirk Franklin had won the same award three years earlier and addressed recent shootings of unarmed Black men then too, acknowledging the tragic loss of both Philando Castile and Walter Scott. When TBN aired the awards show, they deleted his comments then too. After the first offense he voiced his complaints to TBN and the Dove Awards committee, and while the former never responded to him, Franklin said the latter promised such an incident wouldn't happen again.[6]

After experiencing the underside of power for a second time, Kirk Franklin met with his pastor, Dr. Tony Evans. He weighed his advice, prayed on it, and then made this public statement:

> In 2019, history repeated itself. I was humbled to win the same award and during my speech, I brought attention to the murder of Atatiana Jefferson, in her home by a white police officer. Last week, during the airing of the awards on the same network again that part of my speech was edited out. So now . . . I've made the decision . . . to not attend any events affiliated with or for the Dove Awards, Gospel Music Association or TBN until tangible plans are put in

place to protect and champion diversity, especially where people of color have contributed their gifts, talents and finances to help build the viability of these institutions.[7]

In his explanation, Franklin also said, "I am aware that the word *boycott* often has a negative connotation and finality to it, but my goal will forever be reconciliation as well as accountability. It is important for those in charge to be informed. Not only did they edit my speech, they edited the African American experience."[8]

TBN and the Dove Awards may have "edited the African American experience" on a stage that is much more public than ones you and I will ever occupy, but this particular demonstration of power is in no way unique to them. BIPOC folks of all different backgrounds can attest to the ways their stories have been edited in White spaces, whether it was the sanitizing of their words to make the message more palatable or simply the muffling of their voices once they are deemed as a threat to the status quo.[9] Therefore we must consistently interrogate the power dynamics that are exercised in determining whose voices shape our organizations and how. Here are three places to continually check:

1. Who preaches and teaches at the church. As referred to in the first point of this checklist (how mature Christianity is defined), one of the most powerful exercises of power in a congregation happens in the teaching and preaching ministry. The declaration about who God is and what God is like represents one of the most important activities that happens for those in spiritual leadership positions. When the pulpit is occupied by exclusively (or mostly) White voices, there is a massive imbalance of power that needs to be addressed.

2. Whose books are read at the church. This is a derivative of the point above but stretches out even further. Most White churches have some type of small group or Sunday school ministry in which books about spiritual growth are either read through together or recommended for ongoing study. After the preaching and teaching ministry, this tends to be the second most powerful way in which people in the congregation receive spiritual formation.

3. Whose voices are invited to shape the church. One of the most important but fragile activities that an all-White leadership team will embark on is the search for diverse voices to speak into the life of the congregation. One danger in this pursuit has already been named in the Kirk Franklin anecdote—the active editing and deleting of constructive voices because of the discomfort their messages create for the dominant culture. The other big danger that consistently crops up in White-dominant settings is the search for voices in the BIPOC community that have been conditioned to align with the viewpoints of majority culture people, and the subsequent weaponizing of those voices to undercut the important critiques coming from those who are racially conscious and are rightly challenging organizational norms. This is one of the most critical dynamics to watch for and to interrogate.

How the Needs of White Congregants Are Attended To

In an authentically multicultural church, the vision is dependent on a belief that not only will each cultural group experience a degree of *contentment* within the experience of diversity, but each group will also need to make some type of *sacrifice* in order for that vision to be realized. One of my favorite voices on this contentment and sacrifice quotient is Dr. James Forbes, who made history in the world of multicultural churches when he became the fifth senior minister of the historic Riverside Church in New York City. His installation in 1989 made him the first African American senior minister of one of the largest multicultural and interdenominational congregations in the United

States,[10] and from that position he wrote and spoke quite a bit about multicultural ministry. When he talked about the contentment and sacrifice quotient necessary in a diverse congregation, he often called it the 75 percent rule:

> A truly diverse congregation where anybody enjoys more than 75 percent of what's going on is not thoroughly integrated. So that if you're going to be an integrated church you have to be prepared to think, "Hey, this is great, I enjoyed at least 75 percent of it," because 25 percent you should grant for somebody's precious liturgical expression that is probably odious to you; otherwise it's not integrated. So an integrating church is characterized by the need to be content with less than total satisfaction with everything. You have to factor in a willingness to absorb some things that are not dear to you but may be precious to some of those coming in.[11]

One can debate whether the proposed ratio of 75/25 is the exact percentage for what a cultural group (particularly a historically marginalized group) should subscribe to as part of the contentment and sacrifice quotient, but let's put that debate to the side for now. For the purposes of this point, let's assume 75/25 is a fair baseline to hold every cultural group to. In this theoretical exercise, if a church agreed to this 75/25 quotient as a standard, then each cultural group would have a clear measure by which to gauge their experience within the church. If 75 percent of their church experience was enjoyable and fulfilling and led to overall contentment, it would mean the multicultural vision was actually working. And while 25 percent of their experience would still feel like a cultural sacrifice—maybe even a loss—at least they would still be able to translate that sense of personal loss as a win for the collective vision.

If a multicultural church committed to this 75/25 quotient and if White people were part of this church, then it would be only natural that the White community would be held to the same contentment/sacrifice standard as every other cultural group. If 75 percent of their church experience brought growth, enjoyment, and overall contentment, they should see this as a big win and be happy about it. And if 25 percent of their church experience brought discomfort and sacrifice, then at a minimum, they should be able to recognize that they are sacrificing at the same baseline as everyone else.

Unfortunately, that is almost never what actually happens.

Instead, what nearly every study of multicultural churches reveals is that the White community is the group that gives up the least and demands the most. Consider the work of Dr. Korie Edwards as an example. A professor of sociology at Ohio State University, she conducted one of the broadest studies of interracial churches ever done in *The Elusive Dream: The Power of Race in Interracial Churches.* Her studies showed that the standard for mixed-race churches is to adhere strongly to White norms. The research demonstrated that African Americans in multiracial settings, in particular, tend to adapt their behavior to make White congregants comfortable (i.e., submitting to culturally White time preferences, restricting their expressiveness so as not to create discomfort for White worshipers, and adapting to preaching styles that are culturally normative in Euro-Christian traditions). Her blunt assessment is that to make interracial churches work, Black people must adjust their behavior to accommodate the predilections of Whites. Sadly, they must conform to White expectations in church just as they do elsewhere.[12]

Whether it's the unconscious expectation that comes from being so consistently centered in society at large or the outright demand that our felt needs be directly and immediately responded to, we as the White community are the cultural group that most consistently disrupts the contentment and sacrifice quotient. Though many would contend that due to historic power differentials it should be the White community that sacrifices the most to help achieve a multicultural reality, it is almost always the exact opposite.

When it comes to interrogating power in a church setting, ask this set of questions:

- To what degree is each cultural group being required to sacrifice in order to make this multicultural vision a reality?
- Are those sacrifices equally distributed among the different cultural groups?
- Are the needs of the White community at a commensurate level with the needs of other cultural groups? Or do the needs of White people in the congregation take an unfair share of the attention and prioritization?

How Public Acts of Racism in Society Are Corporately Addressed

On March 9, 2018, Campbell Robertson of the *New York Times* wrote an article that was widely spread titled "A Quiet Exodus: Why Black Worshipers Are Leaving White Evangelical Churches."[13] In it, she first explored the growing number of Black congregants, many motivated by a vision of racial reconciliation, who had decided to participate in White-majority churches during the first decade of the turn of the twenty-first century (White evangelical churches had a greater spike than White mainline churches during this period, so she especially focused on them). This participation peaked in 2012, when according to a report from the National Congregations Study, more than two-thirds of those attending White-majority churches were worshiping alongside at least some Black congregants, a notable increase from a similar survey in 1998.

But as the title foreshadows, that high point was short-lived. From that point forward, White evangelical churches began to experience an exodus of Black worshipers. The article examined the causes and found that much of it had to do with the refusal of White churches to talk honestly and openly about instances of racism in society. "Black congregants . . . had already grown uneasy in recent years as they watched their white pastors fail to address police shootings of African-Americans," says Robertson. "They heard prayers for Paris, for Brussels, for law enforcement; they heard that one should keep one's eyes on the kingdom, that the church was colorblind, and that talk of racial injustice was divisive, not a matter of the gospel. There was still some hope that this stemmed from an obliviousness rather than some deeper disconnect."

But this hope never materialized. "As the headlines of the outside world turned to police shootings and protest, little changed inside majority-white churches. Black congregants said that beyond the occasional vague prayer for healing a divided country, or a donation drive for law enforcement, they heard nothing." At one of the White megachurches profiled by Robertson, she noted, "Black worshipers would discreetly ask one another if they were the only ones who noticed that one could talk about seemingly anything but racism, a feeling one former congregant described as an out-of-body experience."

Robertson focused in on Tamice Namae Spencer, who used to attend a mostly White church in Kansas City, as an example of what happens when churches actively avoid addressing racism in society. When Trayvon Martin, a Black teenager, was killed in Florida at the hands of George Zimmerman in 2012, the Black community across America was grieving. Not only did Spencer's church fail to address this national mourning (a decision most White churches in America made at the time), but she found that none of her White congregants had ever even heard his name.

And when she attempted to educate them on the significance of his death, the White church members asked why she was being divisive. "It's not even on your radar and I can't sleep over it," she remembered thinking. "And now I'm being vocal, you think I've changed."

This exodus reminds me of the words of the apostle Paul in 1 Corinthians 12:26, when speaking to the theme of unity in the church: "If one part suffers, every part suffers with it." That is one of the key descriptors of a healthy diverse church. But in too many of our White churches, this is a rarity. Instead of acknowledging the suffering that so many BIPOC collectively experience when racism rears its ugly head in a highly visible manner, White church members often exercise power in the form of silence and indifference.

As the Black folks who were quoted in Robertson's article point out, it's not as if there is no basis for bringing attention to collective suffering when it happens in other settings. Whether it is a tragedy in the law enforcement community or a terrorist attack in a European country, or even damage to a historic European icon like the Notre-Dame cathedral, there are plenty of examples where White churches demonstrate a willingness to suffer with those who are suffering (as they should). However, the fact that White churches instinctively bring attention to these while actively avoiding race-based suffering makes the omission all the more glaring.

To conclude, let me draw a link between these last two exercises of power. The fifth area of power was the degree to which the needs of White congregants are attended to, and that really affects this sixth one. As my friend Rev. Julian DeShazier, a Black pastor and activist on Chicago's South Side, says, one of the most powerful forms of privilege comes in the ability to walk away from that which we don't want to engage. When an act of public racism happens, it rarely has much impact on the everyday experience of a White person, so there is immense power in simply being able to indifferently shrug our shoulders and proceed with life as normal, even as brothers and sisters in the body are mourning.

And as important as it is to name power in the form of the ability to walk away, it goes even deeper yet. A big part of the reason White-dominant churches choose not to corporately lament public displays of racism is that we inherently know how uncomfortable it will make our White congregants.

As an example of this, my church had an extended time of lament after the exoneration of George Zimmerman in the Trayvon Martin case, and Darren Wilson in the Mike Brown case. In both instances, we lost White families who thought our lament was excessive and imbalanced. I say that with grief and sadness. I also say it with an acknowledgment that the fears many of us have about the way White congregants may respond to these collective laments may be well-founded. But even as we acknowledge the risk, we still must name the fact that choosing to ignore racist acts is an exercise of power. Each time we come to the crossroad of choosing to shield White congregants from the realities of racism in society or choosing to suffer with those who are suffering, we are at an important power juncture.

How Racial Justice Is Described

In chapter 2, when discussing the risks of diversity, I made the case that when attempting to understand the problem of race, those of us who are White tend to operate from a flawed theory of change. We have been conditioned to identify the core *problem* of race as segregation, and therefore the core *solution* to race as the pursuit of diversity. I shared my own awakening to this flawed theory of change, as well as my realization that while segregation is both real and serious, it is still just a symptom of a much larger problem. The deeper problem behind race is the ideology of White supremacy—an ideology that created extremely powerful and durable structures that continue to systematically target BIPOC. Diversity will always be a secondary solution to a primary problem. The only chance we have for authentic transformation is to attend to the systems created by White supremacy, as well as to the narratives that sustain them.

Here's how this directly links to power in a congregational setting. When a pastor like me gets up in front of a congregation and preaches about the sin of the system of race, that's a good start. But if I then follow that up by saying the best way to respond to this sinful system is by making the effort to befriend people of other cultural backgrounds, I have just exercised power in a harmful way. It may be a sincere mistake, but I have still reinforced a flawed view of the problem of race (segregation) and have misled White people to believe that as long as their social network carries some level of cultural diversity within it, they have taken the necessary and meaningful steps to confront race.

Diversity represents something important, but it should never be held up in our organizations as the primary pathway to pursuing solutions to the problem of race. While I think it's a great idea to have friends of all backgrounds and that our churches should be as diverse as they can be, pursuing diversity still doesn't mean we've taken any meaningful steps toward confronting White supremacy. Instead, we need to frame the forward-moving journey in terms of racial justice. Isaiah 58 says it like this:

> "Is not this the kind of fasting I have chosen:
>   to loose the chains of injustice
>   and untie the cords of the yoke,
>   to set the oppressed free
>   and break every yoke?
> Is it not to share your food with the hungry

and to provide the poor wanderer with shelter—
when you see the naked, to clothe them,
and not to turn away from your own flesh
and blood?
Then your light will break forth like the dawn,
and your healing will quickly appear;
then your righteousness will go before you,
and the glory of the LORD will be your rear guard.
Then you will call, and the LORD will answer;
you will cry for help, and he will say: Here am I.

"If you do away with the yoke of oppression,
with the pointing finger and malicious talk,
and if you spend yourselves in behalf of the hungry
and satisfy the needs of the oppressed,
then your light will rise in the darkness,
and your night will become like the noonday.
The LORD will guide you always;
he will satisfy your needs in a sun-scorched land
and will strengthen your frame.
You will be like a well-watered garden,
like a spring whose waters never fail.
Your people will rebuild the ancient ruins
and will raise up the age-old foundations;
you will be called Repairer of Broken Walls,
Restorer of Streets with Dwellings."

Isaiah 58:6–12

There is a lot in this passage that is worth developing further, but I will use the opening and closing phrases to seal this point. Isaiah starts by talking about the fasting that God has chosen: "*to loose the chains of injustice.*" The passage then finishes with a picturesque way for the Israelites to remember the justice-seeking aspect of their collective identity: "*Your people will rebuild the ancient ruins . . . you will be called Repairer of Broken Walls.*"

I always want to be cautious about extending a passage beyond its appropriate application, but I honestly can't think of a more holistic way to theologically frame the path of racial justice for White congregants than this. We need to be Spirit-formed, Spirit-filled people who fast *and* who seek to loose the chains of injustice. We need to be a people who rebuild the ancient walls. We need to identify ourselves as repairers of broken walls.

Until we adopt a justice-centric framework as the primary motif for how we think about the problem of White supremacy, we will continue to be at risk of holding up a "kumbaya, everyone-hold-hands" vision. And what I'm stressing here is that a diversity-centric solution is not just inadequate; it is an exercise of power.

Following in the Footsteps of Jesus

Many commentators would say the most poignant account of Jesus' relationship with power comes in Philippians 2, where the apostle Paul describes the *kenosis*, or self-emptying, of Jesus' will for the purpose of becoming entirely receptive to God's divine will. I often come back to the beginning of this passage as a way to remember the importance of tenderness, compassion, and humility as we embark on this journey. I pray it will encourage you as well as you set out on the task of interrogating power:

> Therefore if you have any encouragement from being united with Christ, if any comfort from his love, if any common sharing in the Spirit, if any tenderness and compassion, then make my joy complete by being like-minded, having the same love, being one in spirit and of one mind.

> Do nothing out of selfish ambition or vain conceit. Rather,
> in humility value others above yourselves, not looking
> to your own interests but each of you to the interests of
> the others.
>
> *Philippians 2:1–4*

practice nine

Repent Daily

A s I have alluded to throughout the book, I believe there is a uniquely Christian path for exposing the White lies behind race and for exposing and resisting the racial systems that divide us. While the system of White supremacy has done unspeakable damage at almost every level of society, the case can still strongly be made that its roots are more deeply spiritual than social. That is why it's important to remember that White supremacy represents not only a societal ill, but also a principality of darkness and a stronghold of evil. Any attempt to expose, confront, and by God's grace dismantle White supremacy must be established in a spiritual power that is greater than the evil that works to preserve it.

Therefore, it is of primary importance in this work that we concentrate on becoming Spirit-sensitive, Spirit-filled people who learn how to get in touch with that power of the divine. The Bible makes the astounding promise that this is indeed possible. In one of the most beautiful prayers ever said over a community, the apostle Paul prays that the believers in Ephesus would come to know the same power that God exerted when raising Jesus from the dead—the same power that God used to place Jesus far above every principality (Ephesians 1:18–21). We really can live with access to that kind of power!

Each practice in this book has a broad spiritual meaning. Each one has specific applications for confronting White supremacy as well. I've tried to show the connection between the two in each chapter. Nowhere is the link more evident than in this ninth and final practice of repentance. I find that it's difficult to make the case for our need for repentance in the journey of confronting White supremacy if one doesn't already see the deep need for repentance in their daily walk with God, so let me start there.

When describing why the practice of repentance is import-ant to me (and why I think it should also be important to you!), I find the most straightforward way to get to its rich beauty is by going straight to the Greek word: *metanoe*. That word is made up of two parts—*meta* and *noeo*.

The especially intriguing dimension is the first part—*meta*—because it is the prefix regularly associated with some of the best ideas we have around transformation. In English, for instance, we talk of the metamorphosis of a butterfly, which describes one of the most stunning transformational processes in the created world. In Greek, the phrase shows up in words like *metamorphoō*, which is used in one of the most famous verses on transformation in the Bible: "Do not conform to the pattern of this world, but be transformed [*metamorphoō*] by the renewing of your mind" (Romans 12:2).

That alone makes the act of repentance a much more excit-ing endeavor than most of us have been trained to think. For a lot of us, *repentance* is a word associated with guilt about bad things we've done, shame about bad things we've thought, or maybe just an overall sense of negativity as we imagine what may be required for us to work off our debts before God and get back in good graces. But that's not the spirit of repentance at all! It's an act we take, by grace, to step into the transformative future that God has for us. And who doesn't long for that kind of transformation?

The second part of the Greek word for repent is *noeo*, which is also intriguing in its own right. *Noeo* refers to the mind and its thoughts and perceptions and purposes. This again highlights something different from what is typically associated with repentance. For many people I talk to, repentance is assumed to be a practice focused on behavior. In other words, when we most badly need to repent is after we've committed some type of offense before God. But the thrust of the word, at least in its etymology, is a transformational shift in mind-set.

One of the ideas in the Bible that has most captured my imagination and drives home this point is the vision to acquire the "mind of Christ" (Philippians 2:5; 1 Corinthians 2:16). It assumes not only that Jesus thinks a certain kind of way—about his kingdom, about people, about the created world—but also that he wants *us* to have that same mind. So when we think about repentance as transformation, we are talking about transformation of our mind-set. This changes everything—how we think, how we see, and how we act in the world.

The idea of a transformed mind-set also clarifies the role that confession plays in the practice of repentance. One way to think of confession is simply as the acknowledgment that we don't currently share the mind of Christ. We don't think like he does. We don't see what he sees. And we certainly don't align our actions with his on a consistent basis. I don't know if that sounds hard to you, but even on my best days, it's clear how far off I am from the mind of Christ. As such, I've come to appreciate the confession part tremendously, especially since it's the most active part of repentance that I can control. Confession is my daily admission that I don't think, see, and act the way Jesus does . . . but that I want to.

What makes repentance so amazing is that it's built on the belief that when I confess and turn to Christ, he is ready to show me the world as he sees it. "The kingdom of God has come near," he says in Mark 1:15. "Repent and believe the good news!" When I repent, I'm telling Jesus I want to experience this kingdom of God that is so near. I'm telling Jesus I want to experience the good news of his love and grace. It is asking Jesus for transformation in how I think. In the same way the laws of nature metamorphose a little egg into a caterpillar and then a butterfly, when I repent, I'm asking God to transform my thought process so that I share the mind of Christ. That is incredibly exciting to me, and something I never tire thinking about.

How will this refreshed understanding of repentance empower us to challenge White supremacy?

Here are three ways the practice of repentance will help you transform your mind:

1. Repentance helps me address my damaged identity.
2. Repentance helps me address my ongoing complicity.
3. Repentance helps me align with the mission of Jesus.

Repentance Helps Me Address My Damaged Identity

One of the most formative preaching series we ever did at River City was titled "Life in (Multicultural) Community." The series had two basic premises, each of which reflects themes addressed in this book.

The first premise is that *diversity can become a valuable method of experiencing transformation in the context of Christian community*, particularly when it serves the larger purposes of seeing God more clearly, seeing yourself more clearly, and seeing each other more clearly. This theme stretched through the entire series, and we continued to examine ways we as a community could more deeply engage with the biblical idea of diversity and translate it into concrete ways people in our body could seek deeper transformation through the realities that diversity can illuminate (see chapter 2).

The second premise is that *the single greatest threat to the unity of the church is White supremacy.* This isn't always as obvious as it should be, but when you look at the American church as a whole, it seems inarguable that race is far more divisive than any other single factor.

To be more specific, we built the whole series around exposing the lie that undergirds the narrative of racial hierarchy. We reminded our congregation that the devil is a liar, and that one of the most powerful lies at his disposal is that human value is ascribed based on where someone falls in this false hierarchy of race. We made the case that this lie represents the single greatest threat to a person's identity journey, as well as the single greatest threat to a community's ability to experience true unity. Without corporate agreement that the lie is real, that it must be exposed, and that it must then be confronted, it is virtually impossible to have unified, authentic participation from the full spectrum of God's people (see chapters 3–5).

It is what we did next that made the series unique. We stressed that in order to be a multicultural community, we needed to understand that the lie of racial hierarchy was the same for everyone, but that *the healing journey was not.*

We asked four different leaders in our church—each representing a different ethnic group in our community—to share a testimony or teaching. Each was assigned the task of building off of this thesis (same lie, but separate healing journey) and talking about how we had been harmed by this lie. Then we would talk about ways in which the truths of identity in Christ had played a direct role in healing from that lie. This exercise illuminated the different healing journeys in a powerful way.

Christine Chang, our executive pastor, went first. While

being careful to stress that she was not trying to represent the experience of all Asian Americans, she explored some of the unique ways the lie had affected her as a Korean American woman. She shared about seasons in her life when she had internalized messages of being "less than" because she was not White. She also shared about times when she had allowed herself to move along with the narrative that depicted Whiteness as the pinnacle of the hierarchy and Blackness as the bottom. She spoke of the need to repent of both complicity and the internalization of the lie, which led to damage to her identity.

Shumeca Pickett went next. With the same disclaimers in place, she talked about ways the lie negatively influenced the development of her identity as an African American woman. She shared some of the conspicuous moments along her life journey when the message of inferiority was used as an assault on her identity, and how she had learned to combat those. She vulnerably shared about ways in which the internalization of that lie eventually emerged as an even more dangerous threat to her well-being than the racist things she heard about herself in society. There was a season in her life when that lie became so powerful that she had trouble accomplishing even basic tasks in her workplace. Finally, she spoke powerfully about the truth found in the words of God. They are the antidote to the poison of the lie. Shumeca told us that coming to a deeper knowledge of who she is in Christ is the only escape from the lie of the narrative of racial hierarchy.

The third speaker in the series was Rebecca Gonzalez—a leader in our church as well as the executive director of operations for our denomination. Rebecca shared the grief that many in the Latino and Latina community feel when they are left out of the conversation on race, and then she spoke to some of the unique nuances that tend to be part of this conversation in her community. For instance, Rebecca highlighted the very important role that family plays in the Latino and Latina culture and how this motif of family tends to be the starting point for race conversations. Like Christine and Shumeca, Rebecca then spoke to some of the ways in which the lie had adversely affected her identity as a Puerto Rican woman, and how the truth of God's words was the healing power for her as well.

I was slated to preach the fourth and final segment. I had been deeply moved by the sermons of each of the women who went before me, and their vulnerable exploration of the impact of the lie ignited new levels of self-reflection in me. But it also had created some confusion. By this point in my journey, I had become familiar with the need to regularly repent of the ways in which I had been complicit with advancing the lie behind the narrative (more on that in the next point). But I hadn't spent as much time as I should have thinking about how my own identity had been adversely affected by the messaging behind the lie. And this was surprisingly difficult to name specifically.

Christine, Rebecca, Shumeca, and I had been meeting throughout the whole of the series to discuss and debrief, and in our final meeting, I shared the confusion I was feeling. Having people like this to process White supremacy with is a gift for which I can never be grateful enough. Once again, they played a transformational role in helping me see what I was having trouble seeing.

Christine responded to my dilemma first. "It makes sense that you're having a much more difficult time with this task than we did. Though the stories of each of us three women were unique in most respects, we still share the common experience of having heard messages of inferiority along the way. Being told you are 'less than' is always an assault on your identity, no matter what form it comes in, so there is a clear need to heal from those assaults. But as a White male, you were never told you were inferior based on your race (or gender, for that matter). You have been told the opposite—that you are superior. And while I know you reject that message, and that you don't want that message to be what functionally shapes your identity, it doesn't change the fact that it is a lie you regularly have heard and still hear, and a lie that does damage. With that said, it's understandable that it requires more effort for you to identify the damage from the lie than was required from us."

Shumeca added to Christine's comments and helped me apply a passage of Scripture to this dilemma in a life-changing way. "Maybe you won't be able to articulate the full damage that this lie has done to your identity by the time Sunday comes," she said, "but at least you have one concrete example. The fact that you cannot yet name the damage done is in itself a form of damage. The fact that you don't even know where the injuries to your identity have occurred is reason enough to say you are in desperate need of healing. So maybe the prework to naming the damage done to you by the lie is to instead confess that you don't know how to find those injuries without the help of God. It makes me think of Psalm 139, where David asks God to search him and to know his heart."

Shumeca's allusion to Psalm 139 proved to be an invaluable resource for this aspect of my identity development journey. One of the reasons this has been a historically beloved psalm is the way that David, through meditation and perhaps even putting his thoughts in song, was able to anchor his identity in the *imago Dei.*

As an image bearer of Almighty God, he believed to the core of his being that his identity was most deeply shaped by his spiritual DNA. "For you created my inmost being," David proclaimed. "You knit me together in my mother's womb. I praise you because I am fearfully and wonderfully made . . . My frame was not hidden from you when I was made in the secret place . . . Your eyes saw my unformed body" (Psalm 139:13–16). On and on he goes, thanking God for the sovereign ways in which God attended to every part of who he was as a human being.

The fact that this psalm is so heavily focused on David and his recall of the wonder of who he is in God makes the final two verses all the more fascinating: "Search me, God, and know my heart; test me and know my anxious thoughts. See if there is any offensive way in me, and lead me in the way everlasting" (Psalm 139:23–24).

I was thunderstruck by the combination of these two realities. I realized that when it came to repentance for the ways that the lie of White supremacy had damaged me, the starting point required a capacity to hold together these same two realities that David testified to centuries earlier. I first needed to remember that who I am in Christ reflects the full glory of my Creator and that I should fully meditate on the joy that comes from that truth.

Second, and just as importantly, I needed to take seriously that the lie of White supremacy had done damage to my sense of identity—sadly, damage I could not always even name for myself. For precisely that reason, I needed to ask God to search me. To know my heart. To illuminate the ways in which the lie of White supremacy had allowed for hints of superiority to remain unchecked inside me. To reveal any offensive ways in which the lie continued to shape the way I viewed image bearers from other ethnic groups.

In short, I needed to learn how to repent for the ways White supremacy had shaped, and continues to shape, my identity.

If the practice of repentance is essentially a transformation of the mind—a confession of the ways we fall short of the mind of Christ and the desire to take on his mind-set—then repentance for the ways our identity has been damaged by White supremacy is something we should do daily. There may be points in your life where you can clearly identify ways you have internalized the lie of superiority. Those points will provide concrete opportunities for repentance.

But let's not forget that we are daily bombarded with messages of the supremacy of Whiteness. Therefore we are never permanently free of its impact, even if it doesn't manifest as overtly racist thoughts bubbling to the surface of our consciousness. Let us repent daily and ask God to search and know our hearts and to see any offensive ways that have begun to form within us. Only by repenting in this way do we position ourselves to continue the desperately needed transformation process of taking on the mind of Christ.

Repentance Helps Me Address My Ongoing Complicity

The first practice we examined was "stop being woke." As we saw in chapter 1, the basis of this practice is built on a recognition that at a human level, we all long to be considered woke—aware of the injustice around us and sensitive to its effects on others. We badly hope for an eventual recognition of having reached an enlightened status about race.

As we discussed, it's important to get out of that make-believe world as fast as we can and firmly entrench ourselves in reality. *Joining the ranks of those confronting White supremacy doesn't mean you are no longer complicit with White supremacy.* The truth is that there will be some moments when you see it clearly and are completely on the right side of the equation. And there will be some moments when you lack clear vision and will be totally complicit with White supremacy. And sometimes you will vacillate between both of these poles on the same day.

In those times when you end up on the wrong side of the equation—when you're accidentally complicit with the ideology of White supremacy—you will find out how much internal fortitude you have developed. If you've bought into the fantasy that there is an arrival point, if you've built your sense of identity on being a perfectly woke person, or if you've adopted a spiritual paradigm that doesn't allow for failure, discovering your complicity will result in an internal collapse.

How do we avoid a collapse? Repentance is the only way. A commitment to repentance leads us first to accept the fact that our own blindness-to-sight journey means there will be moments at every step of the journey when we discover new levels of complicity. There is freedom when we come to grips with the fact that failure is built into the equation, just as it is in the spiritual journey of maturity.

Secondly, repentance reminds us that an enormous part of the transformation journey comes from confession. We confess that we don't think the way Jesus wants us to think, see the way Jesus wants us to see, act the way Jesus wants us to act. Remember that repentance is an invitation into a journey of transformation! Perfection won't lead to deeper levels of transformation. The discovery that we don't currently think, see, and act in accord with Jesus leads to transformation.

This is as true of my journey as it will be of yours. A public and painful example of my own complicity came during a sermon at River City. I was speaking about the narrative of racial hierarchy. Our leadership team had agreed that the narrative is the single most important idea we want our congregation to be familiar with when it comes to challenging White supremacy. We tend to preach on it at least once a year.

During my preparation for this particular sermon, I watched a segment on CNN where Anderson Cooper built on the findings from the famous doll test in the 1940s.[1] In the test, psychologists Kenneth and Mamie Clark designed and conducted a series of experiments to study the effects of segregation on African American children. They used four dolls, identical except for color, to test children's racial perceptions. Their subjects, children between the ages of three to seven, were asked to identify both the race of the dolls and which color doll they preferred. A majority of the children preferred the white-skinned doll and assigned positive characteristics to it; in contrast, they assigned negative characteristics to the darker-skinned dolls.

In this segment on CNN, Anderson Cooper built on the history of the doll test and worked with renowned child psychologist and University of Chicago professor Margaret Beale Spencer to design a study that would evaluate the progress we've made on racial bias since the 1940s. The painful conclusion was that not much has changed. Young children of all different racial backgrounds were once again asked a series of questions and instructed to answer by pointing to one of five cartoon pictures that varied in skin color from light to dark. And once again kids of every background demonstrated what they referred to as "white bias"—ascribing positive characteristics to the cartoons with lighter skin and negative attributes to the cartoons with darker skin.

As I watched this clip, I found myself overcome with sadness. It was another painful reminder about how real the narrative of racial hierarchy is. It was chilling to realize how durable the lie behind that narrative is. Six decades had passed since the doll test, but there had been arguably no change in the deep level of internalization of that lie across a wide spectrum of ethnic groups. I mourned how deeply this lie is lodged in our national consciousness and decided to make this a big part of the sermon.

When Sunday finally came, I taught about the lie of the narrative, as I had planned to, and showed this segment from CNN. The clip I chose was short, but by far the most painful of the entire seven o'clock segment. Its focus was on a participant in the test—a young African American girl who looked to be about four years old. Dr. Spencer invited her to look at the five images on the poster, ranging from lightest to darkest, and asked her to point to which one was the ugly child. In an incredibly painful moment, the four-year-old pointed at the darkest image on the poster. Dr. Spencer then asked her to point to which image was the good-looking child. Heartbreakingly, this dark-skinned four-year-old then pointed to the lightest-skinned image on the poster.

As I showed this clip, I again became overwhelmed with emotion. Wanting to emphasize the seriousness of this, I spontaneously asked that the clip be shown a second time. As we collectively watched the horror of the lie's impact on this young girl, the room fell completely silent. The gravity of the moment was felt by all. And as a result, I felt like I had effectively done my job.

However, not more than two hours after the end of the service, I began to get a steady stream of concerned feedback about the decision to show this clip, particularly from the African American members of our body. I discovered it had impacted some of them to such a level that they were actually starting to wonder if they could stay at River City. I was mortified that my decision to show this clip had impacted our Black community in this way, and I was desperate to find out what had gone so wrong.

Shumeca took on the role of first responder and began to directly reach out to the African American members who had expressed the concern. Through meetings, phone calls, emails, and text messages, she was able to make contact with all of them in a brief window of time. Once she completed the task, we called a leadership team meeting to listen to the report on what she had discovered.

What her conversations unearthed could be summarized by a pair of themes with regard to why this clip had so negatively impacted them. The first theme had to do with my failure to prepare the Black community for the pain sure to be evoked by watching this clip. To watch something this dehumanizing in a public space, in the presence of so many nonBlack people, was painful on many levels. And not only did I fail to warn them or give them an opportunity to exit if they so desired, but I chose to have it played a second time. My ignorance about the retraumatization that would inevitably come with a public experience like that had left many of them feeling understandably *abandoned* in that moment.

The second theme was related but had to do with the back end of the experience. They wondered why I hadn't considered a plan for our Black members to get follow-up pastoral care after experiencing something like that. Presumably the purpose of showing this clip, they figured, was to expose the non-Black community to the seriousness and prevalence of the narrative of racial hierarchy. They could understand why I needed to do that and were glad I was being considerate of the educational needs of those who hadn't yet been exposed. But why had I not extended the same courtesy to them? Why had I not considered what *they* would need? The failure to have a care plan in place exacerbated the feelings of abandonment that showing the clip had evoked in the first place.

When I heard these two themes of feedback, I went through the same sequence of emotions I almost always do when I find out I have been complicit to racial injustice. First, I felt incredibly ashamed. I felt stupid that I hadn't thought about either of these themes, and I grew increasingly angry with myself for being so hopelessly ignorant. In my shameful state, I wanted to hide under a rock and never come out again.

Second, I became overwhelmed with a feeling of disorientation and confusion. I began to replay the many conversations I've had about race and about what my role as a White person should be in confronting White supremacy. The response I most often heard was that I needed to be more vocal. That as a White male I was responsible for finding ways to bring these realities to light for those who never think about them. But wasn't that what I had done here? I had brought White supremacy to light, but it had turned out terribly. Where had I gone so wrong?

At this point of the story, I want to pause and loop in the second practice in this book, where we examined diversity. Chapter 2 explored the dangers of diversity, especially when it becomes an end in and of itself. If the apex of our diversity vision is to broadcast a cosmetic appearance of multiple cultures in the same room, our vision will always fall flat. But I also stressed in that chapter how powerful diversity can be when utilized correctly. When diversity serves the blindness-to-sight process and helps us see God, ourselves, and others more clearly, it is like nothing else in the transformation process.

Having the opportunity to be part of a diverse leadership team played an instrumental role in this story. If this mistake would have happened earlier in my ministry career, chances are high I would have been processing it alone or in the context of an all-White circle of friends. I'm not demeaning that, because it was the only option available for many years. But at this point in my journey, I was surrounded by a team of leaders who believed in the multicultural vision we were pursuing. It was a team of people who understood what I was trying to do, even if it failed, and who were able to process that whole experience with me. Most importantly, *they were able to help me think through what repentance should look like.*

We began by first processing what the personal dimension of my repentance process should look like. As we've discussed, the practice of repentance begins with confession not only for what I've done wrong, but for what I've seen wrong. For where my understanding has fallen short. So that's where we began. The team asked me what I had learned from this experience and how it would serve as a genesis for a deeper level of thinking in the future. We talked through the two specific themes of feedback from the Black community and ensured we would embrace the lessons we needed to learn from these themes.

We then moved to processing the corporate dimension of my repentance process. At this point, I'll loop into this story one more practice. Chapter 8 explored the importance of interrogating power, and the very first index highlighted the unique power that must be stewarded by those who publicly preach and teach. That was a big part of the consideration of what this second form of repentance should look like. In many cases, the mistakes we make as White persons happen at a relational level, and any repair or healing that is needed is interpersonal in nature. But because the pain I caused happened in a public setting, we needed to consider the best way to pursue healing in a public way. So as a leadership team, we evaluated different options as to how to best communicate my sorrow, as well as to offer pathways for moving forward.

Eventually we landed on a plan to communicate directly with the entire Black community of our church. So I wrote a letter that was emailed to every African American member and active participant in the church. Not every one of them had been there for that service, but I nonetheless reviewed all the events. I shared with them what my intentions had been and also acknowledged that, despite my sincere intentions, my blind spots had resulted in pain for a lot of the Black folks in our community. I restated the two themes of feedback they had communicated to me, thanked them for sharing it, and clearly named what I had learned from the mistake. I apologized for hurting them and asked for their forgiveness. I then laid out the four different paths for moving forward that the leadership team had come up with and invited them to choose which one made the most sense for them.

Thanks be to God, the whole process moved forward from there in a really healthy way. A number of important conversations happened as a result of that painful Sunday—conversations that resulted in the development and implementation of some new and important protocols for talking about race in multiethnic settings. And at a personal level, I learned so many valuable lessons. I always lament that my lessons seem to come at the cost of others' pain, but once again I vowed not to dishonor their pain by failing to learn what I need to learn.

And for the purposes of this chapter, the part of the story I want to stress most clearly is the role that the practice of repentance played in this whole saga.

As you move forward in your journey of joining the ranks of those who confront White supremacy, please remember that even if your intentions are pure, you will make mistakes. You will still be complicit. You will falter along the way. It's how the journey of blindness-to-sight works. Every time you experience transformation at one level of sight, you'll then move to the next level of ignorance that must be contended with.

The goal of this journey is not to "win" some sort of contest. The goal is not to prove you are one of the elite reconcilers. The goal is not to become crowned as the woke White person.

The goal of this journey is to have the mind of Christ. To see his kingdom. To participate in his work. To be transformed as you seek transformation.

And the bottom line is this: You cannot deal with your own complicity without embracing the practice of repentance. Confession, forgiveness, and truth telling are indispensable elements of the transformational journey.

Repentance Helps Me Align with the Mission of Jesus

This final point will both draw out a third application of repentance and conclude the nine practices as a whole. To get there, I'd like to come back to the important manner in which Jesus first introduced the idea of repentance, at least according to the accounts of Matthew (3:2; 4:17) and Mark. In Mark's account of the life of Jesus, these are the very first words Jesus speaks when launching his public ministry: "'The time has come,' he said. 'The kingdom of God has come near. Repent and believe the good news!'" (Mark 1:15).

Jesus develops an undeniable link between the kingdom of God and the need to repent. What is the correlation between the two?

The historic orthodox answer to this question is that Jesus' statement here is a pronouncement of the "good news" of the gospel. It's his identification of himself as the Son of God, incarnated into human form, who through a sacrificial death and resurrection will save us from our sins and give us the birthright of being heirs of the kingdom of God. To receive this gift, his listeners needed to repent of their sins and place their faith in the saving grace of God given to us through Jesus.

I am in absolute agreement with this historical position and believe it is the foundation for exploring all other meanings. However, I do believe the link goes even further than that. In fact, this connection between repentance and the coming kingdom of God has been most helpful in deepening my understanding of what it means to participate in the mission of Christ. If I drill down even one more level, this connection also deeply informs my understanding of what it means to be a White Christian who participates in the mission of Christ as he confronts and dismantles White supremacy.

The logic goes like this. When Jesus declared that his kingdom was coming near—a kingdom defined by light, life, and love—I believe this was heard as a warning shot to the sitting kingdom—the kingdom of evil, defined by darkness, death, and lies. If we take the conversation out of the spiritual and think of a statement like this in the natural, isn't that exactly how it would sound? If you were watching a medieval movie that had kings and kingdoms, and a sitting king were to hear a coming king declare that his kingdom was near, wouldn't that be heard as a warning shot? It is a declaration that a change of lordship is on the horizon. And in the case of Jesus, it is a warning to the evil one—the "prince of this world" (John 12:31; 14:30; 16:11)—that his kingdom is on the verge of being dismantled.

Some may say I'm overreaching with this interpretation of the confrontational nature of these words (to evil, not us). But consider how similar it sounds to the way Jesus initially described the church in Matthew 16:13–20 (ESV). Jesus brought the disciples to Caesarea Philippi, a city famous for its pagan idol worship, with the intention of having a conversation about the eternal link between his identity and the identity of the church. He asked them, "Who do people say that the Son of Man is?" To that the disciples replied with the answers they had heard postulated by onlookers: "Some say John the Baptist, others say Elijah, and others Jeremiah or one of the prophets."

From there, Jesus made the question even more personal: "But who do *you* say that I am?"

Peter rightly responded, "You are the Christ, the Son of the living God." Jesus praised Peter for being so in tune with the thoughts of God, and then replied, "Blessed are you . . . Peter, and on this rock I will build my church." Those precious words from Jesus became the basis for how believers over the centuries came to understand the essence of church, namely, to be connected together, bound by this confession that Jesus Christ is the Son of the living God and is Lord over all.

As central as this confession of faith in Jesus Christ is to the identity of the church, Jesus is still not quite done. He has one last thing to add: "I will build my church, and the gates of hell shall not prevail against it." The allusion to the cosmic battle was made once again. Jesus spoke of himself, his church, and, by extension, the kingdom of God as being in a cosmic contest between good and evil.

For those of us who grew up around church, I sometimes wonder if we haven't heard verses like this so many times that we've become anesthetized to the potency of their meaning. Is this not something that should absolutely grab our attention? Is it not noteworthy that Jesus just assumes that the presence of evil is real, active, and determined to harm the work of God? That Jesus just assumes that the mission statement of hell-on-earth is to prevail against the church of Jesus Christ? I believe it should be!

There is far more good news in this statement than bad. Thanks be to God, we know that in the long term, evil will not prevail. Victory belongs ultimately to the Lord. But even as we place our hope in this promise, we should not put our heads in the sand about the clear intentions that Jesus has to place those of us who align with his mission right in the middle of this cosmic conflict. That is a large part of what it means to be the church. We join forces with the kingdom of light, ensuring that the gates of darkness will not prevail.

To put a fine tip on this point, I often reflect on the final prayer of Jesus before he dutifully obeyed his call to the crucifixion. Alluding to the reality of his followers joining him in this cosmic conflict, Jesus prayed this over his disciples: "I do not ask that you take them [the disciples] out of the world, but that you keep them from the evil one" (John 17:15 ESV).

I hear this as a restatement of what Jesus often said when he talked about alignment with his mission: to participate in his mission is to join forces with the kingdom of light and confront the kingdom of darkness. This prayer in John 17 was just one more reminder. For the disciples, following Jesus wasn't going to take them *out* of the cosmic fight; it was going to send them *deeper in*.

Do you suppose the disciples would have been surprised to hear Jesus so bluntly pray for their protection against the forces of evil? I doubt it. After all, when Jesus taught them to pray, this is actually exactly how and what he told them to pray for. Most of us know the Lord's Prayer by heart (Matthew 6:9–13 KJV): "Our Father which art in heaven, Hallowed be thy name." From there we get to the kingdom mandate: "Thy kingdom come, Thy will be done in earth, as it is in heaven." The disciples were taught to pray to join in the efforts of God's coming kingdom, and as such, it should come as no surprise that he told them to finish the prayer this way: "And lead us not into temptation, but deliver us from evil."

That's why I say that Jesus' teaching on the kingdom has helped me understand what it means to participate in the mission of Christ. I can no longer conceive of being a serious follower of Jesus without considering what it means to be aligned with Jesus in this cosmic conflict of good versus evil. And I can no longer conceive of what it means to be part of a church without considering how it is that we stand up against the gates of hell, knowing that their intention is to prevail against the work of Jesus.

And it is from there that I quickly end up back at White supremacy.

Christ as King means Jesus has been declared as supreme over all things. Over *all* things. Therefore, anything that challenges Christ for his supremacy is reflective of an opposing kingdom, of the forces of evil, of the gates of hell. It stands as an enemy to the kingdom of light, life, and love.

I have done my best throughout this book to demonstrate why I believe that White supremacy stands, and has stood for four-plus centuries, as one of the greatest challengers to this very supremacy of Christ. I have done my best to clarify how this system is built on lies about human value and how these lies are fiercely protected by the father of lies. I have done my best to describe White supremacy through a biblical lens and put words to the brawl happening between two warring kingdoms over which one will functionally define God's image bearers.

Now, with my final words, I want to invite us to consider the depth of this final practice of repentance.

When Nicodemus came to Jesus under the cover of night, seeking to know more about the spiritual power that Jesus possessed, Jesus famously responded with these words: "Very truly I tell you, no one can see the kingdom of God unless they are born again" (John 3:3).

This is what repentance means for me. It is a confession that in my current state, I am like Nicodemus. I cannot see the kingdom of God clearly. And when I cannot see the kingdom clearly, I cannot see the King clearly. And when I cannot see the King clearly, I cannot see myself clearly.

This daily confession is good for my soul. It is cleansing. For it reminds me that clear vision is not something I come up with on my own. It reminds me that sight, like grace, is a gift of God. It reminds me that the mind of Christ is not something I go out and get on my own. The mind of Christ is his gift to me, transferred by his Spirit.

So as I conclude this practice of repentance, and as I conclude this book, I will simply do two things.

First, I will remind you of what Jesus has already reminded us all of: "The time has come. The kingdom of God has come near. Repent and believe the good news!" May you be transformed by the good news of a God who loves you more than anything. May you remember that the kingdom of God has come near. May you actively join forces with that kingdom of light, life, and love. And may you actively participate in the mission of Jesus to confront and dismantle the kingdom of darkness.

Second, and finally, I will pray with you and over you the same prayer that Jesus taught us all:

> Our Father which art in heaven, Hallowed be thy name. Thy kingdom come, Thy will be done in earth, as it

is in heaven. Give us this day our daily bread. And forgive us our debts, as we forgive our debtors. And lead us not into temptation, but deliver us from evil: For thine is the kingdom, and the power, and the glory, for ever. Amen.

Notes

Introduction: The Parasite of White Supremacy

1. I first heard Dr. Jennings use this metaphor in a lecture titled "Can 'White' People Be Saved: Reflections on Missions and Whiteness," Fuller Studio, November 1–3, 2017, https://fuller studio.fuller.edu/can-white-people-be-saved-reflections-on -missions-and-whiteness-willie-jennings. His lecture became a chapter in a book with the same title: *Can "White" People Be Saved? Triangulating Race, Theology, and Mission*, ed. Love L. Sechrest, Johnny Ramírez-Johnson, and Amos Yong (Downers Grove, IL: IVP Academic, 2018), 27–43.

2. How we use language is important. After research, reflection, and conversations with BIPOC colleagues and mentors, I decided to capitalize both *Black* and *White* in this book. Capitalizing both terms is a growing trend among those who write for the cause of racial justice, since *Native, Asian,* and *Latino* and *Latina* are capitalized terms. By capitalizing *Black* and *White*, we affirm the inherent value of these racial identities. Also, part of the White supremacy this book addresses is that White people are not often required to consider themselves in racial terms. This capitalization, then, is another step toward removing the parasite of White supremacy from every part of our culture, including language.

3. Chanequa Walker-Barnes, *I Bring the Voices of My People:*

257

A Womanist Vision for Racial Reconciliation (Grand Rapids: Eerdmans, 2019), 30.

4. If you'd like to learn more about River City Community Church, please visit our website at www.rivercitychicago.com.

Practice 1: Stop Being Woke

1. See the introduction for the overview and explanation of the term BIPOC.

Practice 2: Beware of Diversity

1. Cited in Bob Smietana, "Sunday Morning in America Still Segregated—and That's OK with Worshipers," LifeWay Research, January 15, 2015, https://lifewayresearch.com/2015 /01/15/sunday-morning-in-america-still-segregated-and-thats -ok-with-worshipers.
2. I confessed to many of my blind spots in *White Awake* (Downers Grove, IL: InterVarsity, 2017).
3. Michael Emerson cites this benchmark in numerous works, but the place where he gives a complete explanation of the methodology and list of sources that inform this definition is chapter 2 of *People of the Dream* (Princeton, NJ: Princeton University Press, 2006).
4. I want to acknowledge the seriousness of gender inequalities in the workplace as well. I am deeply convicted of the need to address these discrepancies, and I apologize that I'm unable to speak more about that intersection due to the scope of this book.
5. This conversation took place in January 2018.
6. Angela Y. Davis and Ibram X. Kendi, "In Conversation with Jeff Chang," City Arts & Lectures, February 3, 2019, www.cityarts .net/event/angela-davis-ibram-x-kendi.
7. Two of the most influential voices in the development of white Christian theology in America were Jonathan Edwards and George Whitefield. Both, however, had highly problematic histories of complicity with racism. Whitefield, for instance, bought a plantation in North Carolina and became a slave owner as a means to help fund his plans for the ongoing development of his

orphanage. Rick Kennedy ("Did George Whitefield Serve Two Masters?" *Christianity Today*, February 22, 2019, www.christ ianitytoday.com/ct/2019/february-web-only/george-whitefield -peter-choi-evangelist-god-empire.html) and Jared Wilson ("Was George Whitefield a Christian?" For the Church, May 27, 2019, https://ftc.co/resource-library/blog-entries/was-george-whitefield -a-christian) both explore Whitefield's legacy further. Jemar Tisby explores the significance of Jonathan Edwards being a slaveholder in *The Color of Compromise* (Grand Rapids: Zondervan, 2019, pp. 42–48, 51–52) and expands on its meaning in a Q&A with Daniel José Camacho ("On the Brutal, Violent History of Racism in the U.S. Church," *Sojourners*, May 9, 2019, https://sojo.net /articles/brutal-violent-history-racism-us-church).

8. James Baldwin, *I Am Not Your Negro: A Major Motion Picture Directed by Raoul Peck* (New York: Vintage, 2017), 103.

9. Diane Langberg, Twitter post, July 23, 2019, 8:00 a.m., https:// twitter.com/DianeLangberg/status/1153635940549779457.

10. Examples of Jesus healing the blind: Matthew 9:27–34; Mark 8:22–26; John 1:1–12. Other prominent examples of blindness -to-sight are Saul in Acts 9:1–19 and Peter in Acts 10:9–23. Jesus included sight for the blind in Luke 4:18 as one of the signs that the Holy Spirit was on him, and he also mentioned it to John the Baptist as one of the signs of the kingdom in Luke 7:22.

Practice 3: Clearly Define Race

1. Ijeoma Oluo, *So You Want to Talk about Race* (New York: Seal, 2018), 28–29.

2. Oluo, *So You Want to Talk about Race*, 27–28.

3. If you need resources that go more in-depth in their analysis of race, I recommend important books such as Ibram Kendi, *Stamped from the Beginning* (New York: Nation Books, 2016); Nell Irvin Painter, *The History of White People* (New York: Norton, 2010); and Chanequa Walker-Barnes, *I Bring the Voices of My People* (Grand Rapids: Eerdmans, 2019). But when it comes to defining race in white settings, the four words I use to

represent the four interlocking dimensions of race are *construct, narrative, systems,* and *evil.*

4. Sarah Shin, *Beyond Colorblind: Redeeming Our Ethnic Journey* (Downers Grove, IL: IVP Books, 2017), 15.

5. Walter R. Strickland and Dayton Hartman, eds., *For God So Loved the World: A Blueprint for Kingdom Diversity* (Nashville: B&H Academic, 2020), xix–xx.

6. Jemar Tisby, *The Color of Compromise: The Truth about the American Church's Complicity in Racism* (Grand Rapids: Zondervan, 2019), 27.

7. Tiffany Potter, "Writing Indigenous Femininity: Mary Rowlandson's Narrative of Captivity," *Eighteenth-Century Studies* 36, no. 2 (Winter 2003): 153–67, https://muse.jhu.edu/article/38289.

8. If you're interested in studying this concept further, as well as the historical reality of the construction of race, I recommend reading Dr. Chanequa Walker-Barnes's *I Bring the Voices of My People.*

9. Michelle Alexander, *The New Jim Crow: Mass Incarceration in the Age of Colorblindness* (New York: New Press, 2012), 23.

10. Alexander, *The New Jim Crow,* 25.

11. Audrey Smedley, "Origin of the Idea of Race," Anthropology Newsletter, November 1997, www.pbs.org/race/000_About/002_04-background-02-09.htm.

12. Cornel West, *Race Matters,* rev. ed. (Boston: Beacon, 2001), 107–8.

13. "Narrative," www.merriam-webster.com/dictionary/narrative, italics added.

14. Ibram X. Kendi, *How to Be an Antiracist* (New York: One World, 2019), 49, italics added.

15. Kendi uses the term *self-interest* to describe the foundational motivation behind racism (*How to Be an Antiracist,* 230).

16. The term *manifest destiny* will be more closely examined in chapter 6.

17. This phrase was popularized in the song "America the Beautiful," written by Katharine Lee Bates in 1893.

18. Donald L. Fixico, "History Stories: When Native Americans Were Slaughtered in the Name of 'Civilization,'" *History,* March 2,

2018, www.history.com/news/native-americans-genocide
-united-states.

19. For further reading on how this narrative built on the term
savage was developed and deployed to depict Native people, see
David Livingstone Smith, *Less Than Human: Why We Demean,
Enslave, and Exterminate Others* (New York: St. Martin's, 2011).

20. "The Declaration of Independence," Constitution Facts, www
.constitutionfacts.com/us-declaration-of-independence/read-the
-declaration.

21. "Declaration of Independence."

22. The quote in its full context: "The demand for land was
met by invading and conquering larger and larger swaths of
territory. American Indians became a growing impediment to
white European 'progress,' and during this period, the images
of American Indians promoted in books, newspapers, and
magazines became increasingly negative. As sociologists Keith
Kilty and Eric Swank have observed, eliminating 'savages' is
less of a moral problem than eliminating human beings, and
therefore American Indians came to be understood as a lesser
race—uncivilized savages—thus providing a justification for the
extermination of the native peoples" (Alexander, *The New Jim
Crow*, 23).

23. Another example of this narrative is located in article 1, section
2, paragraph 3 of the United States Constitution. Written
during the height of slavery in America, it says this about people
of African descent: "Representatives and direct taxes shall be
apportioned among the several states which may be included
within this union, according to their respective numbers,
which shall be determined by adding to the whole number of
free persons, including those bound to service for a term of
years, and excluding Indians not taxed, three fifths of all other
persons" (Cornell Law School, "U.S. Constitution," www.law
.cornell.edu/constitution/articlei). This notion that black people
were to be represented as three-fifths human was against the
backdrop of white people (which by then was a legal category

that represented citizen rights) being represented as five-fifths human. Some defendants of the Constitution claim it is unfair to use the three-fifths human clause as an example of inferiority because that was just a tactic used to negotiate the tax system. But arguing that point suggests this provision is the only place where we see the historical dichotomy between black life and white life. Another example is the principle referred to as the one-drop rule: any person with even one drop of sub-Saharan African blood was to be considered black. The message sent through this law and others like it was clear: white people were seen as fully human; black people were seen as less than human, and even the smallest of interactions put the purity of whiteness at risk.

24. In her article "Origin of the Idea of Race," Audrey Smedley (www.pbs.org/race/000_About/002_04-background-02-09 .htm) shows us how this story formed:

> Toward the end of the eighteenth century, the image of Africans began to change dramatically. The major catalyst for this transformation was the rise of a powerful antislavery movement that expanded and strengthened during the Revolutionary Era both in Europe and in the United States. As a consequence, proslavery forces found it necessary to develop new arguments for defending the institution. Focusing on physical differences, they turned to the notion of the natural inferiority of Africans and thus their God-given suitability for slavery. Such arguments became more frequent and strident from the end of the eighteenth century on, and the characterizations of Africans became more negative.
>
> From here we see the structuring of the ideological components of "race." The term "race," which had been a classificatory term like "type," or "kind," but with ambiguous meaning, became more widely used in the eighteenth century, and crystallized into a distinct reference for Africans, Indians, and Europeans. By focusing on the physical and status differences between the conquered and enslaved

peoples, and Europeans, the emerging ideology linked the socio-political status and physical traits together and created a new form of social identity . . . The physical features of different groups became markers or symbols of their status on this scale, and thus justified their positions within the social system. Race ideology proclaimed that the social, spiritual, moral, and intellectual inequality of different groups was, like their physical traits, natural, innate, inherited, and unalterable.

25. Joe Feagin, *Racist America: Roots, Current Realities, and Future Reparations* (New York: Routledge, 2001), 6.
26. See Michael O. Emerson and Christian Smith, *Divided by Faith: Evangelical Religion and the Problem of Race in America* (New York: Oxford University Press, 2000).
27. See Ryon J. Cobb, Samuel L. Perry, and Kevin D. Dougherty, "United by Faith? Race/Ethnicity, Congregational Diversity, and Explanations of Racial Inequality," *Sociology of Religion* 76, no. 2 (Summer 2015), https://academic.oup.com/socrel/article/76/2/177/1636873.
28. Sarah Eekhoff Zylstra, "Surprise Change in How Multiethnic Churches Affect Race Views," *Christianity Today*, December 2, 2015, www.christianitytoday.com/ct/2015/december-web-only/surprise-shift-in-how-multiethnic-churches-affect-race-view.html.
29. Oluo, *So You Want to Talk about Race*, 28–29.

Practice 4: Attack the Narrative

1. Johnson Oatman Jr., "Higher Ground" (1898). Public domain.
2. Dr. Martin Luther King Jr., "Letter from a Birmingham Jail [April 16, 1963]," African Studies Center, University of Pennsylvania, www.africa.upenn.edu/Articles_Gen/Letter_Birmingham.html.
3. For more information, visit "Criminal Justice Reform," https://eji.org/criminal-justice-reform; "Racial Justice," https://eji.org/racial-justice; "Public Education," https://eji.org/public-education.

4. Chanequa Walker-Barnes, *I Bring the Voices of My People* (Grand Rapids: Eerdmans, 2019), 48.

5. James McWilliams, "Bryan Stevenson on What Well-Meaning White People Need to Know about Race," *Pacific Standard*, February 6, 2018, https://psmag.com/magazine/bryan-stevenson -ps-interview.

6. See "The Legacy Museum: From Enslavement to Mass Incarceration," Equal Justice Initiative, https://museumandmemorial.eji.org/museum.

7. See "History of Lynchings," NAACP, www.naacp.org/history -of-lynchings.

8. When I use a phrase like this, I'm thinking of both Matthew 28:18 ("All authority in heaven and on earth has been given to me") and Luke 24:27 ("And beginning with Moses and all the Prophets, [Jesus] explained to them what was said in all the Scriptures concerning himself").

9. "The National Memorial for Peace and Justice," https://museum andmemorial.eji.org/memorial.

10. "The National Memorial for Peace and Justice," https://museum andmemorial.eji.org/memorial.

11. See "The Legacy Museum: From Enslavement to Mass Incarceration," https://museumandmemorial.eji.org/museum.

12. James Grossman, "James Baldwin on History," *Perspectives on History*, August 3, 2016, www.historians.org/publications -and-directories/perspectives-on-history/summer-2016/james -baldwin-on-history.

13. See Equal Justice Initiative, "Slavery in America: The Montgomery Slave Trade" (2018), https://eji.org/wp-content/uploads/2019/10 /slavery-in-america-report.pdf.

Practice 5: Duel with the Devil

1. I acknowledge that the way C. S. Lewis uses the word *race* here is different from how I defined it. He is using it in a manner to describe human beings in a universal manner.

2. C. S. Lewis, *The Screwtape Letters* (1942; repr., San Francisco: HarperSanFrancisco, 2001), ix.

3. Though church history says John was thrown by the emperor Domitian into a vat of boiling oil, only to miraculously remain unharmed.

4. I acknowledge that not all commentators agree that the serpent in this passage is the devil. I'm basing this interpretation on Revelation 12:9: "The great dragon was hurled down—that ancient serpent called the devil, or Satan, who leads the whole world astray. He was hurled to the earth, and his angels with him." With that being said, I don't think it's critical to agree on that point to agree on the broader meaning of this point, namely, that evil accomplishes its purposes through deceit and lies.

5. "From George Washington to James Duane, 7 September 1783," *Founders Online*, National Archives, https://founders.archives .gov/documents/Washington/99-01-02-11798.

6. "The Letters of Thomas Jefferson 1743–1826: To Edward Coles, Monticello, August 25, 1814," www.let.rug.nl/usa/presidents /thomas-jefferson/letters-of-thomas-jefferson/jefl232.php.

7. For an in-depth analysis of the history of the one-drop rule, read F. James Davis, *Who Is Black? One Nation's Definition* (University Park: Pennsylvania State University Press, 2001).

8. "Jefferson's *Notes on the State of Virginia*" (1853), www.pbs.org /wgbh/aia/part3/3h490t.html.

9. See Karen Grigsby Bates, "Life at Jefferson's Monticello, As His Slaves Saw It," NPR, March 11, 2012, www.npr.org/2012 /03/11/148305319/life-at-jeffersons-monticello-as-his-slaves -saw-it; see also "Smithsonian Sheds Light on Founding Father's Slaves," NPR, February 20, 2012, https://www.npr.org /2012/02/20/147061449/smithsonian-sheds-light-on-founding -fathers-slaves; Britni Danielle, "Sally Hemings Wasn't Thomas Jefferson's Mistress. She Was His Property," *Washington Post*, July 7, 2017, www.washingtonpost.com/outlook/sally-hemings -wasnt-thomas-jeffersons-mistress-she-was-his-property/2017 /07/06/db5844d4-625d-11e7-8adc-fea80e32bf47_story.html.

10. Gaillard Hunt, ed., *The Writings of James Madison*, vol. 9 (New York: Putnam's, 1910), 134.

11. "Andrew Jackson Presidency: December 3, 1833: Fifth Annual Message to Congress," https://millercenter.org/the -presidency/presidential-speeches/december-3-1833-fifth-annual -message-congress.

12. "Scott v. Sandford: Opinion, Taney," Legal Information Institute, Cornell Law School, www.law.cornell.edu/supreme court/text/60/393.

13. "Dred Scott," Biography, April 2, 2014, www.biography.com /activist/dred-scott.

14. "The Lincoln-Douglas Debates: 4th Debate Part I, Stephen A. Douglas Abraham Lincoln | September 18, 1858," Teaching American History, https://teachingamericanhistory.org/library /document/the-lincoln-douglas-debates-4th-debate-part-i.

15. "A Century of Lawmaking for a New Nation: U.S. Congressional Documents and Debates, 1774–1875," *Congressional Globe* 106 (36th Congress, 1st session, April 12, 1860), 1682; "Jefferson Davis' Reply in the Senate to William Seward H. Seward," The Papers of Jefferson Davis, February 29, 1860, https://jefferson davis.rice.edu/archives/documents/jefferson-davis-reply-senate -william-h-seward.

16. History.com editors, "Jefferson Davis Elected Confederate President," History, November 13, 2009, www.history.com/this -day-in-history/jefferson-davis-elected-confederate-president.

17. Joan E. Cashin, *First Lady of the Confederacy: Varina Davis's Civil War* (Cambridge, MA: Harvard University Press, 2006), 4.

18. Horatio Seymour, *Speech of Hon. Horatio Seymour before the Democratic State Convention* (New York: Van Evrie, Horton, 1862), 8.

19. Quoted in George Sinkler, *The Racial Attitudes of American Presidents: From Abraham Lincoln to Theodore Roosevelt* (New York: Doubleday, 1971), 100.

20. Theodore Roosevelt, *Literary Essays*, vol. 14 of *The Works of Theodore Roosevelt* (New York: Scribner's, 1924), 127.

21. James D. Phelan to William F. McCombs, April 26, 1912, Phelan Papers; quoted in Robert E. Hennings, "James D. Phelan

and the Woodrow Wilson Anti-Oriental Statement of May 3, 1912," *California Historical Society Quarterly* 42, no. 4 (December 1963): 291–300, https://ch.ucpress.edu/content/42/4/291.full .pdf+html.

22. Theodore Bilbo, *Take Your Choice: Separation or Mongrelization* (Poplarville, MS: Dream House, 1947), ii.

23. *Congressional Record*, 75th Congress, Third Session, January 21, 1938, 873, www.govinfo.gov/content/pkg/GPO-CRECB-1938 -pt1-v83/pdf/GPO-CRECB-1938-pt1-v83-17-1.pdf.

24. Quoted in Equal Justice Initiative, "'Segregation Forever': Leaders of White Supremacy," in *Segregation in America* (2018), https://segregationinamerica.eji.org/report/segregation-forever -leaders.html.

25. Quoted in "Should We Adopt President Truman's Civil Rights Program?" University of Chicago *Round Table*, NBC Radio (February 6, 1949), 6–7, www2.mnhs.org/library/findaids /00442/pdfa/00442-00206.pdf.

26. Tom P. Brady, *Black Monday* (Winona, MS: Association of Citizens' Councils, 1955), 12.

27. Brady, *Black Monday*, 11.

28. Quoted in "The Shame of New Orleans," *Ebony* 16, no. 4 (February 1961): 79.

29. "Richard Nixon Presidential Library and Museum Releases Additional 154 Hours of Tapes from Fifth Chronological Tape Release," NixonTapes, http://nixontapes.org/chron53.html; see Charlie Savage, "On Nixon Tapes, Ambivalence over Abortion, Not Watergate," *New York Times*, June 23, 2009, www.nytimes .com/2009/06/24/us/politics/24nixon.html.

30. See Josh Dawsey, "Trump Attacks Protections for Immigrants from 'Shithole' Countries in Oval Office Meeting," *Washington Post*, January 11, 2018, www.msn.com/en-us/news/politics/trump -attacks-protections-for-immigrants-from-%E2%80%98shit hole%E2%80%99-countries-in-oval-office-meeting/ar-AAuzqTo.

31. President Donald Trump, Twitter post, July 14, 2019, 8:27 a.m., https://twitter.com/realdonaldtrump/status/1150381395078000643.

32. President Donald Trump, Twitter post, June 24, 2018, 11:02
a.m., https://twitter.com/realdonaldtrump/status/1010900865
602019329; for the rhetoric of "Hispanic invasion," see Julio
Ricardo Varela, "Trump's Anti-Immigrant 'Invasion' Rhetoric
Was Echoed by the El Paso Shooter for a Reason," NBC News,
www.nbcnews.com/think/opinion/trump-s-anti-immigrant
-invasion-rhetoric-was-echoed-el-paso-ncna1039286. One
analysis shows this same terminology was used in more than
two thousand of President Trump's Facebook ads as well (see
Julia Carrie Wong, "Trump Referred to Immigrant 'Invasion'
in 2,000 Facebook Ads, Analysis Reveals," *Guardian*, August 5,
2019, www.theguardian.com/us-news/2019/aug/05/trump
-internet-facebook-ads-racism-immigrant-invasion).

33. President Donald Trump, Twitter post, July 27, 2019, 7:14 a.m.,
https://twitter.com/realdonaldtrump/status/1155073965880172544.

34. James McWilliams, "Bryan Stevenson on What Well-Meaning
White People Need to Know about Race," *Pacific Standard*,
February 6, 2018, https://psmag.com/magazine/bryan-stevenson
-ps-interview.

Practice 6: Tell the Truth

1. Some examples: "As for everyone who comes to me and hears
my words and puts them into practice, I will show you what
they are like. They are like a man building a house, who dug
down deep and laid the foundation on rock" (Luke 6:47–48).
"For no one can lay any foundation other than the one already
laid, which is Jesus Christ" (1 Corinthians 3:11). "Consequently,
you are no longer foreigners and strangers, but fellow citizens
with God's people and also members of his household, built on
the foundation of the apostles and prophets, with Christ Jesus
himself as the chief cornerstone" (Ephesians 2:19–20).

2. See Michael John Simpson, "Georges Erasmus," *Canadian
Encyclopedia*, January 30, 2008, www.thecanadianencyclopedia
.ca/en/article/georges-erasmus.

3. Quoted in Marlene Brant Castellano, Linda Archibald, and

Mike DeGagné, *From Truth to Reconciliation: Transforming the Legacy of Residential Schools* (Ottawa, Ontario: Aboriginal Healing Foundation, 2008), xiii, www.ahf.ca/downloads/from-truth-to-reconciliation-transforming-the-legacy-of-residential-schools.pdf. The original quote is found in H. Richard Niebuhr, *The Meaning of Revelation* (1941; repr., Louisville, KY: Westminster John Knox, 2006), 61.

4. David W. Swanson, *Rediscipling the White Church: From Cheap Diversity to True Solidarity* (Downers Grove, IL: InterVarsity, 2020), 15.

5. Willie James Jennings, *The Christian Imagination: Theology and the Origins of Race* (New Haven, CT: Yale University Press, 2010), 22–23.

6. "The Slave Bible: Let the Story Be Told," Museum of the Bible, www.museumofthebible.org/exhibits/slave-bible.

7. "'Slave Bible' Removed Passages to Instill Obedience and Uphold Slavery," NBC Nightly News, April 21, 2019, www.nbcnews.com/nightly-news/video/-slave-bible-removed-passages-to-instill-obedience-and-uphold-slavery-1501781059849.

8. See Becky Little, "Why Bibles Given to Slaves Omitted Most of the Old Testament," *History*, December 11, 2018, www.history.com/news/slave-bible-redacted-old-testament.

9. Quoted in Michel Martin, "Slave Bible from the 1800s Omitted Key Passages That Could Incite Rebellion," NPR, December 9, 2018, www.npr.org/2018/12/09/674995075/slave-bible-from-the-1800s-omitted-key-passages-that-could-incite-rebellion.

10. See the BBC's helpful resource titled "The Story of Africa," www.bbc.co.uk/worldservice/africa/features/storyofafrica/index_section8.shtml; *Ebony* magazine also has a helpful article titled "Christianity's African Roots," www.ebony.com/faith_spirituality/christianitys-african-roots-450.

11. Evangelical Press, "Bob Jones University Drops Interracial Dating Ban," *Christianity Today*, March 1, 2000, www.christianitytoday.com/ct/2000/marchweb-only/53.0.html.

12. For a conservative Christian take, read Justin Taylor, "Is

Segregation Scriptural? A Radio Address from Bob Jones on Easter of 1960," Gospel Coalition, July 26, 2016, www.thegospel coalition.org/blogs/evangelical-history/is-segregation-scriptural -a-radio-address-from-bob-jones-on-easter-of-1960. For a secular journalistic take on the impact of this, read Randall Balmer, "The Real Origins of the Religious Right," *Politico*, May 27, 2014, www.politico.com/magazine/story/2014/05/religious -right-real-origins-107133.

13. Personal correspondence with Dr. Dates.
14. John Winthrop, "A Model of Christian Charity" (1630), https:// teachingamericanhistory.org/library/document/a-model-of -christian-charity-2.
15. John Gast, *American Progress* (1872). Public domain in the United States. To view a full-color image of this painting, visit www.pastordanielhill.com/blog/american-progress.
16. Dr. Martin Luther King Jr., "Letter from a Birmingham Jail [April 16, 1963]," African Studies Center, University of Pennsylvania, www.africa.upenn.edu/Articles_Gen/Letter _Birmingham.html.

Practice 7: Choose Your Friends Wisely

1. Chanequa Walker-Barnes, *I Bring the Voices of My People* (Grand Rapids: Eerdmans, 2019), 13.
2. In regard to the book of Luke, commentators often note how strong his emphasis is on Jesus' inclusion of those on the margins of society. And in the book of Acts, Luke repeatedly emphasizes the multicultural dynamics that came with the early church. Examples include the multicultural experience of Pentecost in Acts 2, the dispute between Hebraic and Grecian Jews in Acts 6, the Ethiopian eunuch and Samaritan reception to the gospel in Acts 8, the vision of Peter to include Gentiles in Acts 10, and the emphasis on the multiethnic team that pastored the church in Antioch in Acts 13:1.
3. Both Proverbs 18:21 and James 3:3–6 talk about the power of life and death that our words possess.

4. 2 Timothy 2:15: "Do your best to present yourself to God as one approved, a worker who does not need to be ashamed and who correctly handles the word of truth."

5. See Luke Timothy Johnson, *The Acts of the Apostles* (Collegeville, MN: Liturgical Press, 1992), 141.

6. See "Racism Is Killing Black Americans," Southern Poverty Law Center, July 19, 2019, www.splcenter.org/news/2019/07/19 /weekend-read-racism-killing-black-americans.

7. Risa Lavizzo-Mourey and David Williams, "Being Black Is Bad for Your Health," *U.S. News & World Report*, April 14, 2016, www.usnews.com/opinion/blogs/policy-dose/articles/2016 -04-14/theres-a-huge-health-equity-gap-between-whites-and -minorities.

8. Lavizzo-Mourey and Williams, "Being Black Is Bad for Your Health."

9. Paul Chenoweth, "Wright Edelman Speaks on Children and Poverty," Belmont University, February 5, 2009, news.belmont .edu/wright-edelman-speaks-on-children-and-poverty.

10. Brentin Mock, "The 'Great Migration' Was about Racial Terror, Not Jobs," CityLab, June 24, 2015, www.citylab.com /equity/2015/06/the-great-migration-was-about-racial-terror-not -jobs/396722.

11. "Great Migration," *Encyclopedia of Chicago*, www.encyclopedia .chicagohistory.org/pages/545.html.

Practice 8: Interrogate Power

1. Michael O. Emerson and Christian Smith, *Divided by Faith: Evangelical Religion and the Problem of Race in America* (New York: Oxford University Press, 2000); Curtiss Paul DeYoung, Michael O. Emerson, George Yancey, and Karen Chai Kim, *United by Faith: The Multiracial Congregation as an Answer to the Problem of Race* (New York: Oxford University Press, 2003).

2. Dr. Martin Luther King Jr., "Letter from a Birmingham Jail [April 16, 1963]," African Studies Center, University of

Pennsylvania, www.africa.upenn.edu/Articles_Gen/Letter
_Birmingham.html.

3. See Rodney Stark, *The Rise of Christianity* (Princeton, NJ:
Princeton University Press, 1996), 157–58.

4. Even if this is not what your current leadership complexion
looks like, there are meaningful steps you can begin to take
immediately. There's work you can do now to pave the way.
Regardless of what the complexion is, what are you doing to
actively seek voices not currently being heard?

5. "Dove Awards Full Speech, Kirk Franklin," October 15, 2019,
www.youtube.com/watch?v=jh72qE5C24I.

6. Jack Jenkins, "Kirk Franklin Boycotts Dove Awards for Cutting
His Prayers for Black Victims," *Christianity Today*, October 29,
2019, www.christianitytoday.com/news/2019/october/kirk
-franklin-boycotts-tbn-dove-awards-cut-race-prayers-spe.html.

7. Leonardo Blair, "Kirk Franklin Announces Boycott of TBN,
Gospel Music Association, Dove Awards over Diversity
Concerns," *Christian Post*, October 28, 2019, www.christianpost
.com/news/kirk-franklin-announces-boycott-of-tbn-gospel
-music-association-dove-awards-over-diversity-concerns.html.

8. Blair, "Kirk Franklin Announces Boycott."

9. Here is one very public example. Ekemini Uwan, one of the
cohosts of the highly acclaimed podcast *The Truth's Table*, was
asked to speak about diversity at the Sparrow Conference for
Women. Sparrow Women's mission is to equip women to be
peacemakers, but when Uwan's comments made the white
attendees uncomfortable, many of them began to walk out.
While the Sparrow Women's social media accounts published
photos, excerpts, and highlights from several conference
speakers, no images or quotes from Uwan's comments appeared
on its feeds. A video of the interview of her remarks was
removed from YouTube for copyright violation. Many accused
the conference of trying to erase Uwan's message. For a recap of
the story, see Nicola A. Menzie, "Comments about 'Whiteness'
Prompt Controversy at Sparrow Women Conference," Religion

News Service, April 6, 2019, https://religionnews.com /2019/04/06/comments-about-whiteness-prompt-walkout-at -sparrow-women-conference; see also Deedee Roe, "Captive Audience: A Black Woman's Reflection on the Sparrow Conference," The Witness, April 2, 2019, https://thewitnessbcc .com/captive-audience. Uwan herself addresses the situation (see "The Blood of Jesus Is the Bridge; Not My Back," April 7, 2019, www.sistamatictheology.com/blog/2019/4/7/the-blood-of-jesus -is-the-bridge-not-my-back).

10. "Reverend Dr. James A. Forbes, Jr.," The History Makers, September 21, 2016, www.thehistorymakers.org/biography /reverend-dr-james-forbes-jr.

11. Quoted in DeYoung, Emerson, Yancey, and Kim, *United by Faith*, 82.

12. Korie L. Edwards, *The Elusive Dream: The Power of Race in Interracial Churches* (New York: Oxford University Press, 2008); see the publisher's summary at https://global.oup.com/academic /product/the-elusive-dream-9780195314243.

13. Campbell Robertson, "A Quiet Exodus: Why Black Worshipers Are Leaving White Evangelical Churches," *New York Times*, March 9, 2018, www.nytimes.com/2018/03/09/us/blacks -evangelical-churches.html.

Practice 9: Repent Daily

1. Jill Billante and Chuck Hadad, "Study: White and Black Children Biased toward Lighter Skin," CNN, May 14, 2010, www.cnn.com/2010/US/05/13/doll.study/index.html.

From the Publisher

GREAT BOOKS

ARE EVEN BETTER WHEN THEY'RE SHARED!

Help other readers find this one:

- Post a review at your favorite online bookseller

- Post a picture on a social media account and share why you enjoyed it

- Send a note to a friend who would also love it—or better yet, give them a copy

Thanks for reading!